How to Retire Early and Live Well with Less than a Million Dollars

GILLETTE EDMUNDS

Adams Media Corporation
Avon, Massachusetts

Published by
Adams Media, an F+W Publications Company
57 Littlefield Street, Avon, MA 02322. U.S.A.
www.adamsmedia.com

ISBN: 1-58062-201-1

Printed in Canada

J I H

Edmunds, Gillette.
How to retire early and live well with
less than a million dollars / Gillette Edmunds.
p.   cm.
Includes index.
ISBN 1-58062-201-1
1. Finance, Personal—United States. 2. Retirement income—United
States—Planning. 3. Investments—United States. I. Title.
HG179.E352   1999
332.024'01—dc21   99-28126
CIP

This publication is designed to provide accurate and authoritative information
with regard to the subject matter covered. It is sold with the understanding that
the publisher is not engaged in rendering legal, accounting, or other professional
advice. If legal advice or other expert assistance is required, the services of a competent professional person should be sought.
— From a *Declaration of Principles* jointly adopted by a
Committee of the American Bar Association and
a Committee of Publishers and Associations

This book is available at quantity discounts for bulk purchases.
For information, call 1-800-872-5627.

Table of Contents

PART ONE

Are You Ready to Retire?

PART TWO

Retirement Investing

PART THREE

Investing to Reach
Your Magic Number

Introduction

In 1981 at the age of twenty-nine I began living off investments. At the time, I did not know if I had enough to last five years, ten years, or a lifetime. And I could not find anyone who knew or any books that answered this question. After interviewing more than ten stockbrokers, about ten money managers, and a few trust officers I knew one thing: I would have to figure out for myself if I had enough to live on the rest of my life. No one had a formula to determine if I had enough or a plan to follow to ensure that what I had would last a lifetime. Yet despite their inability to meet my needs, many "professionals" were willing to manage my money for me for a fee and to sell me investment products for a commission. So began my journey living off investments.

From seminars, workshops, books, advice, and experience, I learned how to invest in various markets. I discovered that pension plans and endowment funds had some investment policies that could be helpful to me since they were perpetual funds designed to pay out annual expenses. But there were also significant differences. They were not tax exempt. I paid taxes every quarter. By ignoring tax issues, I could lose half or more of my annual returns to the government. And endowments and pension plans could cut payouts in bad years, although I need to eat every year, in fact, every day of every year. Thus the trading and asset allocation policies of endowments had to be revised to fit the needs of someone living off his assets. I also learned about super wealthy families that used armies of highly paid advisors to manage their assets all over the world for generations. Their investment policies would work for me as long as I could find dirt cheap methods of implementing them. From these sources and from extensive trial and error, I worked out the simple system that is the subject of this book.

Today there are hardly more information sources for someone living off their investments than there were in 1981. Some mutual fund houses have put out brochures and books that discuss these issues and promote their products. Occasional articles in financial journals touch on some aspects of this problem. But this is the first comprehensive book written from the point of view of someone who has lived off his investments rather than from the point of view of a promoter interested in selling a product to a retired person. It is unlikely that many insurance companies, loaded mutual fund houses, or fully commissioned stockbrokers, investment planners, or money managers will agree with the plan set out in this book. But some will. Several chapters in this book show how to find professional help that is appropriate for someone living off their investments.

Today there are an estimated 30 million retired Americans and 15 million with more than $500,000 in assets who are approaching retirement. It is time a book is written from your point of view about preparing for and investing during retirement. Myths about income stocks, municipal bonds, and annuities being the best investments for you circulate today just as they did in 1981. It is time these myths were smashed.

Using the methods described in this book I have outperformed the U.S. stock market fourteen of the last seventeen years, outperformed the non–U.S. stock markets for the last ten years, done far better than the real estate market for the last fourteen years, and have large returns from other, more exotic markets. More important, I have discovered that you do not need to outperform any market to live off your assets. With the proper asset allocation, all you need is to stay even with the markets. This will be sufficient to pay your expenses and to put away something for the future most years. Unfortunately, living off investments requires more than matching the market returns. It also requires a certain emotional and spiritual outlook.

Many who retire with sufficient assets to live off the rest of their lives are unable to enjoy their free time. Some go back to work. Others make wild investments in what I believe are unconscious and successful attempts to lose what they secretly believe they do not deserve. Still others become isolated and miserable. It is a dramatic change of identity to go from work to retirement. Financial fears do not end with retirement. Every year that you withdraw money from your retirement fund and all the markets you are in decline, you will assume the worst and calculate how few years you have left. Surviving these difficult issues is a major topic of this book. Just as I have discovered a method of investing that works during retirement, I have also discovered a method of overcoming these emotional hurdles. The key to both has been to let go of old ideas about investing and try something new.

The word humility appears many times in this book. Getting to humility was a very painful process for me. Following asset allocations designed fifty years ago for those saving for retirement leads to some extreme financial binds. I had to let go of my ideas and of my advisors' ideas, admit that none of us had found the answers, and try the untried. Now I have found the asset allocation, trading, and tax strategies that work for someone living off their assets. Also, focusing on wealth lead me to believe I was somehow different than other people and resulted in unbearable isolation. I had to let go of my ideas about what it meant to have a high net worth and try out other ideas and belief systems. Over time, I found an action plan that gave me some sanity. Hopefully, you the reader of this book will move beyond the ideas presented here, let go of them, and discover new and better investment schemes and ways of living off your assets.

For someone near retirement or just beginning to live off your assets, I recommend that you follow the steps set out in each chapter closely and with as little questioning as possible. This will give you a very good chance to live prosperously and happily off your assets until your experience is greater than mine. Then you will be able to improve on what you have found here.

For the reader who has been retired many years, this book should be a good stimulus to rethink what you have been doing and to consider some new ideas to supplement your own discoveries. For investment professionals, this book offers a client's perspective that your own clients may never articulate. Hopefully, it will challenge some of your ideas that managing money for someone living off their assets is just a matter of allocating between municipal bonds and managed mutual funds. Nothing could be less appropriate. Knowing that, you will be better able to serve your clients' needs.

I hope that all readers will be able to avoid many of the mistakes I made while learning to live off my investments. I have tried to write as objectively as possible. While always recommending low-commission, low-expense, and low-tax strategies, I have not recommended any specific products or investment professionals. My point of view is that of a consumer of financial products and not as a salesperson. There is no best stock, index fund, or REIT for everyone living off their investments. But there is a way to sort through all the mutual funds to pick one that will work for you. Using the step-by-step processes set out in this book, you will be able to pick the best investment products for your needs. No longer will you be sold products that are too expensive.

part one

Are You Ready to Retire?

chapter one

Can
You
Retire
Today?

For anyone wanting to live off his or her investments, the big question is, "Do I have enough to last the rest of my life?" I answer that most middle-class Americans, including me, could live comfortably on the investment returns from $500,000. Of course, the precise answer is a function of your lifestyle and investment return.

If you have $100,000 to invest and no other source of income, you will make it only if you can live very modestly. Indeed, at the level you would on welfare! An average, educated, experienced investor can reasonably expect to make 10% a year for life. This would mean a $10,000 total return per year. Due to inflation, living expenses will go up over time. So some of the $10,000 must be reinvested to cover future increased expenses. Taxes must also be paid from the $10,000 income. A genius could be hired to invest the $100,000, and, with luck, a 20% lifetime return could be achieved. But the genius would have to be paid a genius's wages. And most investment geniuses become average investors over twenty- to fifty-year periods. Few people other than beachcombers can realistically make it on $100,000.

At the other extreme, $1,500,000 is more than adequate for a family of four to live comfortably with only average investment results. Beginning with considerably less money, I and my ex-wife and our two children lived extremely well for eighteen years. Among us, we now have three times as much capital as we began with in 1981.

3

There are five variables that determine whether you have enough to live on for the rest of your life. The five things you need to know are:

- Total expenses per year, including taxes
- Total capital to invest
- Future increases in expenses
- Investment management fees
- Annual total return from investments

The first four of these are reasonably predictable. The fifth, annual total return from investments, will depend on the strategy you adopt and how you are able to execute it and live with it. The higher return strategies also involve higher risk and, for some, an emotional roller coaster.

Begin by figuring out how much cash you will need each year to pay all your expenses, including taxes, money management fees, if any, and reinvestments to cover future expense increases. Then calculate the net amount of investments you have to live on. Divide the expense figure by the net investments to arrive at the annual percentage return you will need from your investment. Easy, right? Now comes the hard part.

Having calculated this target investment return, you must now invest to produce this return every year. For example, if the Thompson family needs $80,000 a year to cover all their expenses, taxes, reinvestments, and money managers, and they have $900,000 in net investments, they will need to average almost 9% a year from their investments. If they follow the suggestions in Part Two, they have a very good chance of living for generations off their investments. The formula for determining what investment return you will need is found on page 13. Each part of the formula will be explained below, beginning with your expenses.

Determine Your Living Expenses and Taxes: Target Living Allowance

You first need to figure your *target living allowance*: the total cash you will need each year from all your investments for living expenses and income taxes. There are several methods of determining your annual living expenses. If your income the past five years has been all salary and you know what you have saved during that period, simply subtract your savings from your take-home pay to arrive at your annual living expenses. I did not have a salary, so I found it very helpful to carry a notebook with me for three months to write down every penny I spent. Then I categorized my expenses and annualized them. For example, gas and electricity were about $300 for the three months. So, to annualize it I multiplied $300 by 4, with the result of $1,200. There were certain expenses that did not come due during those three months, so I also had to account for them. For example, I pay my car insurance every six months and real estate taxes once a year. Neither of these came due during that three-month period.

If neither the take-home pay nor the three-month account method seems appropriate for your situation, develop your own method. For example, if your current lifestyle involves a lot of business travel and expenses that will cease once you start living off your assets, separate out those expenses. Whatever your situation, make the best estimate you can of your annual living expenses and write it down. Do not guess at future expenses or make any assumptions about what will be cheaper or more expensive when you are living off your assets. Estimate your current expenses. The next step is to use the tax multiplier to estimate total expenses, including income taxes.

The Tax Multiplier

If you plan on quitting a salaried job entirely and living solely on investment returns, then your tax rate will drop. Even working part-time, you can expect a much lower tax rate.

Your investment assets will be in two types of accounts: taxable and tax-deferred. Tax-deferred accounts include 401(k) plans, IRAs, Keoghs, SIMPLE accounts, SEP IRAs, and a few others. Pension plans, social security payments, and other benefits that provide a monthly or quarterly check are not treated as investment assets for this purpose. They reduce the income you need from your investments and are discussed under "Living Partially on Investments and Partially on Salary or Pension" later in this chapter. Taxable accounts include all your other investment assets like real estate, ordinary stock accounts, ordinary mutual funds, etc.

Because of the contribution limitations on placing funds in tax-deferred accounts, most of you will have most of your money in taxable accounts. First, I will discuss the tax multiplier for taxable accounts.

Taxable Accounts

One of the many advantages of living on investments is there are no employment taxes. When spending from your taxable accounts, you can choose to have most of your taxable income as capital gains, which is subject to a lower maximum rate. Additionally, you will not spend all your gains every year but will spend some gains and some principal so that your taxable income will be quite low. Let me show you using an example. Helen buys ten different stocks for $50,000 each. They do not pay dividends, but all increase by 10% to $55,000 each. She needs $50,000 to live. She sells one stock for $55,000 and retains nine. She will have a gain of $5,000 ($55,000 minus $50,000) on which to pay taxes even though her total portfolio went up $50,000 in value and she has $55,000 of cash in hand for living expenses. This first year, Helen would probably pay no income taxes!

Over the years, as the value of your taxable investments increases, the amount of capital gains you are sitting on will increase and your tax rate will increase. But your tax rate will always be lower than it was when you were working. Consider this example. Assume before retirement, you had a salary of $50,000 a year. You paid taxes on $50,000 at the full income tax rate, and you paid social security taxes. During retirement, you need $50,000 for expenses. You sell $50,000 of investments that you bought seven years before for $25,000. You pay taxes only on the gains from your investments, $25,000. You pay taxes at a low capital gains rate, and you pay no social security taxes. Your total taxes due will be less than a third of what you used to pay from your salary.

Additionally, living off your assets, you will create only enough income to pay your expenses. You will rarely be in a position where taxable income is as great or greater than your total living expenses, as was the norm when you lived on a salary and saved. For example, someone earning a salary of $100,000 a year, saving

$30,000 and spending $70,000, has to pay taxes on $100,000. A retiree with a total return from his investments of $100,000, spending $70,000 and saving $30,000, need take only $70,000 out of his investments for expenses. He can leave the $30,000 alone. Therefore, he pays taxes only on $70,000, not $100,000.

Including state and local taxes, it is reasonable to assume that anywhere from 10% to 25% of your income will be spent on taxes. (The exception where you have little or no tax cost in your assets will be discussed in Chapter 2.) Use the chart below to estimate your tax rate and to determine your tax rate multiplier. For example, if your records show that your nontax living expenses in the past have averaged $50,000, then your multiplier will be 1.15. You will use the multiplier to determine your living expenses, including taxes, while living off your investments. The multiplier will calculate your typical taxes over the next fifty years, based on tax rates of the past fifty years.

NONTAX LIVING EXPENSES	TAX RATE	MULTIPLIER
$40,000 or less	10%	1.10
$60,000 or less	15%	1.15
$80,000 or less	20%	1.20
$100,000 or less	25%	1.25
Above $100,000	30%	1.30

So a shorthand method of calculating your target living allowance is to add up all your nontax expenses and multiply that by the multiplier. The total will be the amount you need to pay all your living expenses and federal, state, and local government taxes while you are living off your assets. If you need $50,000 for nontax expenses, then you will need $50,000 times 1.15 or $57,500 to maintain the same lifestyle for one year. This estimated figure will be accurate enough for most investors. The amount could be more if you have no basis in your assets or if you choose to live solely on taxable income. I will discuss these and many other differences below and in later chapters. But suffice it to say now, your tax rate will almost certainly be lower than it was before you began living off your assets.

ANNUAL EXPENSES × MULTIPLIER = TARGET LIVING ALLOWANCE

Tax-deferred Accounts

When living off tax-deferred assets, your tax rate will be higher than when living on taxable assets. Withdrawals from these accounts are treated as ordinary income and are taxed at ordinary tax rates. However, your taxes will still be lower than when you were working. Again, there are no social security taxes to pay. And you will be in lower brackets as you will not need enough gross income to fund your savings. Also, by the time you are retired, you may have paid off your mortgage, put the kids through school and other expensive traumas, and sold off the second home you never visit and the boat you never sail. Thus, the withdrawals you need to make from tax-deferred accounts should be much smaller than the amount of income you used to need.

The first tax strategy to follow is to delay withdrawals from your tax-deferred accounts as long as possible. Different accounts have different rules on when you must withdraw funds. But if you can live on your taxable assets for ten years without withdrawing anything from a tax-deferred account, this will save you substantial taxes. In that case, use the tax multiplier chart above to figure your target living allowance.

If you must withdraw half or more of your living expenses from tax-deferred accounts within ten years, then you must increase your tax multiplier. But it is not disastrous. My calculations estimate that you need to add about 5% to each income bracket or about .05 to the multiplier. For example, if you need $50,000 for living expenses, multiply by 1.20 and not 1.15. Thus your target living allowance will be $60,000 and not $57,500.

Now that you have figured out your total living expenses and taxes in retirement, you must calculate the value of the assets you can use to fund your expenses.

Determine Total Capital to Invest

There are many assets you may own that should be excluded from your total investment assets. Include only assets that can be turned into cash without incurring debt or reducing your standard of living. The largest you must exclude is your home equity.

When saving for the future, home equity is often included as an asset. But once you are living off your investments, your home is an expense. If it is too large, it can be sold and the excess added to your investments. In fact, many readers are now in a position to live off their investments because they did just that. Finding their house too big and their life too small, they sold the house and got a triple benefit: more investment income from a larger investment pool, lower housing expenses including lower repairs, utilities, and real estate taxes, and more free time. But once the excessive housing has been sold, the remaining equity in the new house, if you buy one, should not be included in your assets for the purposes of determining whether you have enough to live off.

It is important to distinguish between expenses and assets. Few people would consider their furniture an investment asset. Its value is in its function even though it could be sold for cash. Any asset, which if sold, would reduce your standard of living, should not be considered an investment. Once you are in the home you intend to remain in for the foreseeable future, your equity is like your furniture. Its function is to provide you with a comfortable place to live and not to produce income. Equity does affect your investment formula. A large equity will reduce or eliminate your mortgage payments, and that in turn will decrease your target living allowance.

Pay Off the Mortgage to Eliminate Two Real Worries

Most people living off investments should pay off their mortgage. Living off your assets with a mortgage creates two real worries: will you be able to make your monthly mortgage payment, and will you be able to successfully invest the money that you could use to pay off the mortgage? If you have a $150,000 mortgage with a $1,300 a month payment, you worry about $1,300 each month and about $150,000 of investments that could crash or soar. Paying off the mortgage eliminates both real worries. You will get to have fantasy worries if you like to worry. What if I had invested all that $150,000 in XYZ and it had tripled, and what if my house burns down and I forget to pay the fire insurance? Take fantasy worries to a friend or counselor. To get rid of real concerns, pay off the mortgage.

The psychological benefit of paying off the mortgage, however, does not make your home an investment for the purposes of producing income for living expenses. Home equity simply reduces living expenses. Only if you entered into a reverse mortgage could you justify your equity as an investment you could live off.

If you cannot decide whether to sell a big house, work through the formula in this chapter, based on your current circumstances. Then calculate what your assets and expenses would look like if you sold the house and work through the formula with those figures. This may help you make up your mind.

Other nonliquid assets, such as vacation homes, artworks, and jewels, should not be considered investments unless you clearly own them with the intention of selling them to pay for living expenses in the future. Second homes should be considered an investment only if you rent them out to produce a positive cash flow. As long as they cost you more out of pocket than they bring in, they are an expense no matter how much equity you have in them. Do not include the equity in a second home in your total of investments. If a second home is sold, then the net cash received or the amount reinvested in commercial real estate should be added to your total investments.

Total Investment Assets

Total investment assets is calculated as a net figure. Subtract any mortgages on commercial real estate from the appraised value. If you have borrowed against a stock or bond account, then you must subtract any borrowings from your accounts to arrive at the net figure. If you have borrowed against any other investments, subtract the debt from the value of the investment to arrive at a net figure. (Note that unsecured personal debts such as credit card debt or lines of credit are treated as expenses when payments come due and are not netted against any assets.)

After you have excluded noninvestments and subtracted mortgages, add up everything else you have. Include the current value of all stocks, bonds, real estate, mutual funds, gold, money market accounts, and other assets you might own. Include the value of assets in retirement plans and IRAs, but do not include anything you expect to inherit from Mom and Dad. For assets that are not easily sold, like real estate or a small business, make the best estimate possible of the net value. (Make a few phone calls or take an accountant to lunch, but do not spend money now on an expensive appraisal. You are just trying to get an estimate of whether you can quit your job and live on your investments.) Now, add up everything you've got to arrive at your total investment assets.

Divide your target living allowance by your total investment assets and multiply by 100 to figure the percentage return you need to meet your current living expenses. For example, if your target living allowance is $75,000 and you have $1,100,000 in net investments, you need just under 7% a year to meet your current living expenses.

Estimate Future Spending Increases: Personal Inflation

Unfortunately, for most of you, your living expenses will go up over the next ten to fifty years, so you need to reinvest some of your investment returns every year to produce increasingly greater investment returns. Actually, considering the alternatives, like death or an insured permanent stay in a rest home, it is fortunate that you will be having increased living expenses.

So you need to estimate the inflation in your expenses in future years. Note that for now you are not concerned with increases in the consumer price index or any other governmental or economist's measure of inflation. Overall consumer price inflation affects everyone, so it will affect you. But each individual's expenses differ from those measured by the broad gauges of inflation.

For most individuals living off assets, expenses rise much more slowly than they do for the general population. For most of you, large spending requirements will go down over the years as mortgages are paid off, children earn their own incomes, and so on. If you have full health insurance, your out-of-pocket medical expenses will not be substantially higher in the future than they are now. Other spending requirements, like food, transportation, entertainment, and apparel, will increase due to inflation.

If you have yet to hit sixty years old, some or all of your future expense increase may be offset by benefits you will receive in the future when social security or other defined benefit retirement plans kick in. Or, let's say you get married and have someone splitting expenses with you. For reasons such as these, you must decide for yourself what your personal inflation rate is likely to be.

I think overall inflation will average 3% in the future but, due to personal circumstances, I expect my spending needs will increase only 2%. So I use a 2% inflation adjustment. If your inflation forecast over the long term is higher or you have reason to believe your individual spending will increase or you have no prospect of any additional social security or other retirement benefits, you'll need to use a higher inflation adjustment.

Many major institutions, such as universities, use 4% as their inflation adjustment because of their expansion plans. If you own one home and plan on buying another or have other large spending plans, use the 4% adjustment. If you do not own your own home, then your rent will go up over the years. Or you will need to save to put a down payment on a home. For renters I recommend using a 3% inflation adjustment. If you have a mortgage or own your house free and clear and intend to remain there for the foreseeable future, you may get away with using a 2% inflation adjustment. Once you have estimated your personal inflation adjustment, you can determine what type of return you will need from your investments to live off them for the rest of your life.

Since most of you are do-it-yourself investors and do not anticipate using professional help, I will first demonstrate the formula assuming you have no investment management expenses.

Determine Your Necessary Annual Return: Target Investment Return

Here is the formula for determining your *target investment return*. The target investment return is the total return you need to make each year to live off your assets the rest of your life.

(TARGET LIVING ALLOWANCE / TOTAL INVESTMENT ASSETS × 100)
+ INFLATION ADJUSTMENT = TARGET INVESTMENT RETURN

Insert the figures you have calculated in the formula and determine your target investment return as in these two examples.

Joe: $600,000 and $62,000 a Year in Expenses

Assume Joe needs $4,500 a month to live on without taxes. That is $54,000 annually, close to $60,000. Using the 15% total tax rate, Joe multiplies $54,000 by 1.15 to get $62,100 total living expense. Joe has $600,000 to invest. He has lived in the same condo for twelve years and intends to stay there for the foreseeable future, eventually paying off the mortgage. His two children are in college, and, though he currently helps both with expenses, that will end after three more years. He figures his personal inflation rate at 2%. If he divides his $62,100 needed by the $600,000 to invest, multiplies by 100, and adds 2%, he finds he needs to average 12% per year to live the rest of his life on his investments. This is a possible but difficult task.

Susan: $1,200,000 and $5,000 a Month

Susan needs $5,000 a month to live and support her two children. She has $1,500,000 in total assets, $300,000 of which is a mortgage-free home. So she has $1,200,000 in total investment assets. (Note the importance of netting out any assets that will not produce liquid gains or income because such assets may enhance lifestyle but will not help pay the utility bills.) Susan will need $60,000 per year before taxes and $69,000 or so after taxes. Divide that by $1,200,000, add 2%, and she needs to average 7.75 % per year to live on for the rest of her life. In fact, she could expect an increasingly improving lifestyle the longer she lives, without taking excessive investment risk, since almost anyone should be able to produce a 7.75% return.

What Is a Possible Target Investment Return?

If your target investment return using the formula is 8% or lower, you will have no difficulty living the rest of your life on your investments. If your target investment return is between 8% and

12%, then you have a good chance of living off your investments the rest of your life. If your required return is higher than 12%, you're unlikely to make it. This is the high-risk, emotional roller coaster area. I have done better than 12% for the last eighteen years, but there were some very bad months and years. If you require a return of 12% per year or higher, do not give up your job. You will not make it. Refer to Chapter 3 on how to increase the odds in your favor. Be creative. Spend some time cozying up to an ailing wealthy relative. After all, your brothers and sisters are already sending the old bird Happy Arbor Day cards. Why should you be left out of the will? There may be ways to increase your assets or decrease your spending, but there are no reliable ways to increase thirty-plus-year investment returns above 12% a year.

What If You Do Have Money Management Expenses?

A final factor to consider when determining if you have enough to live off is money management expenses. This in an area where you do not necessarily get what you pay for. If you turn all your investments over to a money manager or a stockbroker, your living expenses will be higher and your investment results may be lower than if you had invested yourself. The trick is to pick areas where you can do well investing yourself, then hire and supervise the best managers you can find to manage your other assets. In later chapters, I will discuss active (do-it-yourself) versus passive (hire someone) management of specific assets and how to pick money managers. For now, though, it is important to adjust your living expenses for the management fees and loads you can expect to pay if you choose a passive management approach.

Reasonable management expenses and transaction costs typically average about 1.5% per year of the value of the assets under management. If you intend to have all your money under management, multiply your total investments by 1.5% and add this figure to your annual income needs. Then figure your target investment return. If Joe and Susan, from the previous examples, choose total passive management, Joe would be paying out $9,000 a year and need to make 13.5% per year and Susan would be paying out

$18,000 and need to make 9.5% per year. Few managers can achieve Joe's target of 13.1% over the long term. Even Susan may need to worry as many managers produce returns below 9.5% per year. Most people would be better off managing at least a portion of their assets themselves and saving the fees.

Professional Fees Can Save Huge Sums in the Beginning

Many people in a position to live off their investments began businesses or professions with few or no assets and worked their way to the top. Along the way, they hired the best accountants, lawyers, salespeople, employees, and assistance they could find. Yet, when it comes to managing their money, they assume that the only way is to do it themselves. Some, who had only dabbled in real estate or the stock market along the way, suddenly invest huge sums in developing new buildings or buying high-tech stocks without first getting an opinion from a seasoned professional real estate developer or stock investor. A few such speculations work out, but most are disasters.

In their business or profession, these investors would never have put this much money at risk without consulting many people and doing extensive planning. Yet these investment mistakes are not usually made in an attempt to save the cost of professional investment advice.

Stories that circulate at parties and in locker rooms suggest that anyone can make a killing by investing. Someone's cousin is always said to have bought Microsoft at $1 and now be worth millions. You never hear about all the investment disasters for a very simple reason: no one wants to brag about his or her mistakes. A popular myth is the belief that investing skill is something that you are born with and not a profession you learn. Anyone who has had success in business or other areas of life is all too prone to believe that he has the gift.

Admit to yourself when you do not know what you are doing, get advice, pay the fee, and then make the investment. After you have some experience working with a pro, decide whether you can do it yourself. Reading and studying this book is a good first step.

Living Partially on Investments and Partially on Salary or Pension

The principles in this book can also be applied if you are living partially off your investments and partially off part-time work such as consulting. The same is true if you are currently living off social security or a defined benefit pension plan.

In this situation, figure out what portion of your living expenses will be covered by your take-home pay or pension and what part will be met by investment income. Use the part you want covered by your investment income as your annual expenses. Having two sources of income will increase your tax rate. If less than half of your living expenses will come from your take-home pay or pension, add .05 to your tax multiplier. If more than half of your living expenses will come from your take-home pay or pension, add .10 to your tax multiplier.

Gene and Mickey: Part-time Work Plus Investments and Pension

For example, Gene and Mickey need $70,000 a year to live on before taxes. They are both retired, although Gene works part-time with take home-pay of $20,000. Mickey gets $20,000 a year from his pension plan. They have $350,000 in investment assets. To figure their target investment return, subtract $40,000 from $70,000 to arrive at the amount before tax they will need from their investments. Multiply $30,000 by 1.10 +.10 to get the total needed after tax, which works out to $36,000. Divide this by $350,000 and add 2% to get a target investment return of 12%. This might seem like a difficult return to achieve. However, if Gene's work is secure and Mickey's pension is inflation-adjusted and not likely to disappear, they may be comfortable with high-risk, high-return investments.

chapter two

If You Retire Today, Beware!

Even though the formula says you can retire, beware. There are still traps to consider. It would be a lot easier financially if you had $10 million. But you don't. You are reading this book. And even with $10 million, some of the emotional traps can scare you badly. Here are some dilemmas to consider.

Flaws in the Formula

This simple method of determining how much you will need has several flaws and one overriding strength. Among the flaws: the method for determining annual income needs is simplistic. To address this flaw, you could spend more time estimating anticipated future expenses and savings. You could spend a lot of time going over prior years' checks and credit card statements to get better average figures. You could use Quicken to keep track of all expenses and categorize them for several years before you make any estimates.

Another flaw is that the method of estimating taxes is very simple. You might, therefore, sit down with an accountant and project your likely tax picture for the next five years of living off your investments. These are all good ideas, and I would not discourage anyone from doing them.

Yet you can't get away from it, investing involves estimating. Nothing worth investing in is certain. You will not know in advance how any market will do over the next year or years. You will not know whether your individual stocks or real estate properties or oil and gas partnership will pay off this year, next year, or ever. All you can do is make estimates, play the percentages, go with things that have worked for you or other people in the past, and watch. Over time, there are clear patterns.

Living with uncertainty will be the norm. This is sometimes referred to as living in the question. You will have to learn to be comfortable with not knowing the answer to questions such as:

- What will the stock market do?
- What will tenants do?
- What will the Federal Reserve do?
- What should I do: buy, sell, hold, change asset allocations?
- How long will I live?
- Will my money last?
- Could the U.S. government default on those bonds?

Everything in the world of investing is in flux. Values change every day. This has sent more than one person back to a salaried job. More often, it causes people to invest in much less lucrative "safe" things like CDs and money market funds. People who cannot handle uncertainty or cannot learn how to handle it will not be comfortable with this lifestyle.

You could spend $1,000 working out an elaborate financial plan and the next day the bond market could crash and all your plans will be wrecked. You have always lived in an uncertain economic world but perhaps did not notice it. While it seemed your paycheck was secure, was it really? Maybe when it stopped coming you bought this book to see if you could make it without going out to look for another job. That is the same type of uncertainty you will be subject to in the future, only now it is out in the open and must be faced head on.

It is important to begin estimating rather than calculating. An estimate gives you the freedom to change the figures to meet changed circumstances. I tend to get locked in with exact calculations and experience a lot of disappointment when my numbers do not come out. But with estimates I can see if the concept or trend the estimate represented is still valid rather than whether my calculation was right or wrong.

Let's go back to the example of Joe. I have said that Joe needs $4,500 a month to live. But if he had used his exact average of the last five years of $4,627.12 and his accountant's estimate of future taxes of $1,078.95 per month and he only had $593,542 to invest, then Joe would need a return of 13.54% per year to live. That would throw Joe into a panic because he would need a return of greater than 12%, which is very difficult to obtain. Yet the reality is most markets fluctuate .50% a day. So the extra 1.54% that has panicked Joe is achievable in just three turnaround days a year. It is also possible that his $593,542 has gone up enough since he last added it up, so now he only requires a return of around 12.00%. Still, the basic assessment remains valid. Joe is still at the point on the spectrum where living off his assets the rest of his life is not a sure thing.

I don't reject using a fee-based financial planner and accountant to help you. In fact, I recommend it. But do realize that their seemingly exact numbers are in fact inexact estimates of unknown future values. Their numbers are middle points in a range of possible results. Joe's need for 13.54% should best be seen as a need for between 11% and 15%, a difficult target to hit. If Joe is to give up his job, he will need to pay close attention to his investments and keep his stress under control. Calculating to the hundredths of a percent will not reduce Joe's stress when markets can drop 20% in a day.

Emotional Issues

Let's talk about some of the emotional tools you will need to live on your money the rest of your life. Every year that I add $100,000 to my investments I have a sense of financial security. Every year my total investments decline because of low returns and normal spending, I get afraid. My fear of financial insecurity gets high. I do not have actual financial insecurity. In those years, I have a fear of financial insecurity. These fears have sent many people back to 9-to-5 jobs. Others just drop into a deep depression. A few even commit suicide. The day before I wrote this paragraph, I was told another story of a man who sold his business for a huge sum, had a normal setback with his investments, became severely depressed, and killed himself. Conquering these fears will be a big part of living off your investments. The fear can grow from "I don't have enough money," to "I am not enough," to panic attacks and anxiety attacks, to suicide in extreme cases.

Most of you won't experience this kind of extreme fear, but pay attention to the fears you do have as you read this book and think about shifting from a savings mode to a spending savings mode. You will have to develop a strong faith in this way of living to avoid acting on fears. When you worked for a salary, you did not spend all your time worrying about being fired or the company going bankrupt. If you had, you would have been very ineffective at your job. When living off investments, it is not helpful to spend all your time worrying about market crashes and ending up on the street. If you do, you will not be effective at picking out the right real estate or foreign stock fund. Your results will suffer.

Fear is an inevitable part of every lifestyle, but you have a choice of how you act under the influence of fear. You can panic and take losses, or you can spend more time researching and improving your portfolio. For now, remember that you will be increasing your total investment assets most years. This is why you calculated the personal inflation adjustment. The adjustment determines how much you do not spend of your investment returns each year. Over the long term, your total investment assets will increase faster than your spending.

Diets Lead to Binges

Don't cut back on your lifestyle in order to live off your investments. There is a saying that for every diet there is an equal and opposite binge. This is because the forced diet causes a sense of deprivation that can be remedied only with overindulgence. True, you might be able to cut back somewhat on your spending because you will have more free time. Some of this time you can use to cook meals instead of eating out, or to drive on your vacations instead of flying. But maybe you just do not like to cook and a few weeks of cooking and feeling like a martyr will just lead you to eating every meal in restaurants for the next few months to compensate. Or you may find driving long distances is so tiring that you stop off at expensive hotels along the way to rest and end up spending more than if you flew. Pay attention to the effect any cutting back is having on your feelings about your new life and yourself and those around you.

Make changes slowly and feel free to go back to the old spending patterns in the areas where you are feeling deprived. You will be better off finding other ways to save. Do not sell the house and move into something smaller right away. Don't get rid of the vacation cottage. The real estate commissions are gone forever if you decide to buy a new one. Go slow. When estimating your annual expenses, do not plan on making big changes that will save money and do not cut back at all on your fun money. There is no point in giving up the day job if it means not skiing or going to Hawaii or the theater or shopping. You do not want to feel deprived and miserable. In fact, I don't know of any people who have successfully made the transition to living off investments who did it by severely reducing their lifestyle.

Investment Return Is More Important Than Reducing Spending

Concentrating on your investment returns will have a bigger impact on your financial well-being than concentrating on your spending. More people have gotten themselves in trouble from poor investments than from excessive spending. The Hunt brothers went from billionaires to bankruptcy following insane investment strategies, not from excessive consumption habits. Over the years, learning about your material needs and instincts will be important, but understanding and applying investment principles will be the key. I have one friend who started with $2,000,000 in a trust account. He lived on less than $3,000 a month for ten years and yet had only $1,000,000 left. It turned out the trust department managing his investments knew nothing of basic investment principles. He naively believed that as long as he lived modestly he was doing his part. When he came to realize that he would be out of money in ten more years, he broke the trust, hired professional money managers, began spending freely, and now has more than doubled his net worth.

It is much easier and much more common for people to lose large amounts of money investing than spending. Focus on your investing and your spending will generally take care of itself. If your investment returns are at or above your target investment return and yet the value of your portfolio is declining, that's the time to consider whether you are a spendaholic. If you even suspect you qualify, get professional help and join a support group.

Life Expectancy

The formula I have presented assumes you wish to hold onto your capital the rest of your life. But some of you plan on spending your last penny as you are lowered into the grave. You have figured out that if you spend capital every year you can live on a lower annual return. The problem is that you may outlive your life expectancy. Then in your elder years, when you are least able to work and when social security may no longer exist, you would have nothing left. It is best to err on the side of financial security. A man who has reached the age of sixty-five can expect to live another fifteen years. But half of sixty-five-year-olds will live more than fifteen years, and half will live less. To be on the safe side, a sixty-five-year-old should plan on living thirty years. Investing for thirty years requires substantially the same asset allocation as investing for one hundred years. But living for thirty years requires less capital than living for one hundred years.

Once you have reached age sixty-five, it is reasonable to take a look at spending some of your capital as well as giving some away or leaving certain amounts to heirs. If you plan on spending it all, then decide upon your likely life expectancy and double that figure. Doubling it will give you the margin of error to live twice your life expectancy. Divide your total investment assets by this number. This will tell you how much you can spend the first year from your investments without getting any return. Subtract this figure from your target living allowance and from your total investment assets to calculate your target investment return.

Sarah: Age Sixty-nine, $600,000, Spends $45,000 a Year

For example, Sarah at age sixty-nine has a life expectancy of fifteen years. She has $600,000 to invest and has a target living allowance of $45,000 a year. She has no heirs and no favorite charity. She wants to spend it all. If she wanted to retain all her principal for heirs, she would need a target investment return of 9.5%. Instead, divide her $600,000 by thirty years, twice her life expectancy. This figure, $20,000, is the amount of capital she can spend the first year of the thirty years. By subtracting the $20,000 from her total investment assets and from her target living allowance, you find she needs a target investment return of only 6.5%. This is, however, only a rough estimate. To get a better estimate, she could consult a fee-based financial planner.

Use a Fee-Based Not an Insurance Financial Planner

There are several formulas that you could use to get an exact figure on how much more or less you need to make on your money to reach your estate planning goals. The more complex your wishes, the more complex the formula. If you want to give some to charity now, some to children now, and some at death, the investment return formulas are strained. If many factors are involved, sit down with a fee-based financial planner and an estate-planning attorney to look at the alternatives. A fee-based financial planner charges by the hour and does not sell commission products. If the person you are dealing with appears to be working for you for free, then he is interested only in selling you a high-commission product. Do not use a commission-based financial planner or anyone even remotely connected with the insurance industry for your estate planning. You do not need to pay out huge amounts in commissions for products that do not serve your needs to solve what is essentially a mathematical problem.

Once the mathematical problems are solved and you can see on paper exactly how much principal you will spend, how much you will give away, and how much you will leave in your estate, the emotional problems may become acute. Living off less principal each year is similar to living through a market decline or crash each year. Pay particular attention to the suggestions in the epilogue on dealing with these issues. If spending is not an issue for you, taxes may be.

The Tax Basis of Your Assets

Another factor that affects your ability to live off your assets is the tax basis of those assets. Tax basis is essentially the cost of the assets at the time of purchase, not their present value. For example, if you bought 100 shares of IBM for $50 each and they are now worth $150 each, your tax basis is $5,000 but their present value is $15,000. If you had bought your IBM for $175 a share, your tax basis would be $17,500, even though their present value is still $15,000. If the tax basis of your assets is near their current value or higher, this is a considerable tax advantage. But if you have substantial gains, this can affect your flexibility. Over a period of years, it will somewhat increase the return you need to achieve. In the IBM example, if you bought at $50 and needed to sell all 100 shares, you would pay taxes on the $10,000 gain. If you bought at $175 and had to sell, you could claim a tax loss of $2,500.

If you are holding stock entirely from one company in which you have very little or no tax basis, plan to sell at least 80% of that stock over the next ten years to set up a diversified portfolio. The future returns from a single-stock portfolio are not predictable. The long-term returns from a diversified portfolio are reasonably predictable. Selling 80% of your single-stock portfolio will take 80% of the risk out of your portfolio, but it will also create substantial capital gains. In this situation, use a tax multiplier of 1.25 for living expenses of $50,000 or so and 1.50 for living expenses of $75,000 or more.

Mary and Todd: $2,300,000, Tax Basis Zero

For example, assume Mary and Todd, with two children in college, need $8,000 per month to live. They have $2,300,000 in stock from the company he has worked for since it was founded twenty years ago. He received the stock when the company began, and it had essentially no value at that time. Using the 1.5 multiplier, they will need $96,000 for expenses but $144,000 including taxes to live on the rest of their lives. Adding 2% for spending increases, they need a return of 8% to live comfortably the rest of their lives. This should be easily achievable, and when the children finish college, graduate school, home down payments, and divorce expenses, Mary and Todd will be able to thrive on an even smaller return unless they have very large money management expenses.

Money management expenses of 1.5% could increase their target investment return to 9.5%. However, they should gradually turn their stock over to a money manager as they liquidate it. This way, only a portion of their assets will be subject to fees of 1.5% or higher. If they did this, it would be many years before they were paying 1.5% on 80% of their investments. They should never pay any fees on the 20% of company stock they hold for the long term.

Take Time to Plan

If you have worked through the formula and determined that you have enough to live off, take your time in implementing your plan. Read the rest of this book carefully to determine how to proceed. Read a few other books. Talk to a fee-based investment planner. But leave your investments alone for a few months or even a year or two. Unless you own a lot of commodities or options or other derivatives, or you own only one security, your best bet for now is to educate yourself until you know what you are doing in at least some areas. If you do own a lot of derivatives, talk to a fee-based investment advisor soon to determine whether to hold them or to sell and go into a money market fund until you are ready to implement your long-term plan. If you own only one security, begin following my suggestions for diversification while you develop your plan. Generally, you will want to sell up to 20% of your stock soon and develop your plan for the other 80% over a period of years.

The initial moves you make can have a long-term effect on your results. It is better to sit in a money market fund for two years than to jump into high-commission, high-expense, poorly thought-out investments. One of the most expensive thoughts you can have is, "If I don't buy it now, I will never get another chance."

If you do not have enough to live on now, the next chapter will tell you how much more you need to save.

chapter three

How Much More Do You Need?

Okay, you are not retiring yet. There are two things to do. Work on your attitude toward your present circumstances and determine when you can retire. Attitude adjustment is beyond the scope of this book. It is the more difficult and yet more important task. With a good attitude you will enjoy your work, work hard, make a lot of money, and retire sooner and prosperously. With a bad attitude, you may get fired, bounce around from job to job, and never retire. With a bad attitude, retirement is depressing. Attitude adjustment requires help from other people and from spiritual sources. To determine when you can retire, if you are able to work for it, just follow the instructions in this and the following chapters.

How Long Until You Retire?

How much more do you need? A lot? Not necessarily. Retirement may be just around the corner. Again I will take you step-by-step through some simple calculations to estimate how much more you need and how long till you retire. Be patient. You are just estimating. This is not a math test; exact answers are not the goal. You are just trying to get a general idea of when you can cut your commute time to exactly zero minutes and zero seconds.

In Chapter 1, you calculated your total investments, target living allowance, and personal inflation rate. When you applied the formula, your target investment return was well above 12%. By rearranging the formula, you can determine exactly how much you need to retire today. The new formula is:

TOTAL INVESTMENTS = TARGET LIVING ALLOWANCE /
(TARGET INVESTMENT RETURN / 100 − INFLATION/ 100)

Total investments in this formula is the amount you would need today. Subtract the amount of your current investments to determine how much more you need to retire.

The target investment return is your projected return on your investments between now and retirement, and during retirement. The higher the return, the less you have to save and the sooner you will retire. It is important to use realistic numbers. Eight percent is realistic; 10% can be accomplished with some effort; 12% requires effort and luck. Higher than 12% is not realistic. Let's look at three examples.

Hillary, age sixty-eight, has been a legal secretary for many years. After her divorce, she had no savings. However, her elderly parents just passed away, leaving her with $200,000. She is in excellent health but ready to retire from the law firm where she now works. Her current target living allowance is $3,000 a month. Between a small pension from the law firm and social security she anticipates benefits of about $2,000 a month. Thus adjusting her target living allowance, she would need $1,000 a month ($12,000 a year) plus an inflation adjustment to live forever off her total investments. She anticipates about 3% inflation as her rent could be raised or her health could deteriorate in the future, leaving her with some uninsured medical expenses. Knowing nothing of investing, she does not anticipate an investment return greater than 8% a year.

Applying the formula, Hillary calculates the total investments she needs to retire as $12,000 divided by (.08 minus .03), or $240,000. She is $40,000 away from permanent retirement.

Fred and Ginger, ages forty-eight and forty-three, with two high-school-age children, have $400,000 in investments and

$250,000 in equity in a $400,000 house. Their gross income for the past ten years has been $7,000 a month, from which they have saved $2,000 a month. Their oldest starts college this year and their youngest in three years. Both are excellent students and could need help through graduate school after college. Fred and Ginger estimate the present value of their target living allowance for at least the next ten years to be $7,000 a month or $84,000 per year. They do not anticipate any additional savings until after the children have finished their education, and even then they may need help with down payments and other large expenses. Fred and Ginger have done better than 12% on their investments for the past fifteen years but they do not anticipate doing so well in the future. They do believe that 10% a year is possible. Since they anticipate covering their children's future education and other needs out of their $7,000 a month, they are comfortable with a personal inflation rate of 2%. Applying the formula, they determine that they would need $1,050,000 today to retire or an additional $650,000. However, because they have substantial equity in their house and large expenses that at some point will disappear, they may need less than $650,000 additional to retire. This will be discussed below.

Mike and Doris of Beverly Hills have $1,200,000 in stock options, three homes, and adult children, but they cannot retire at their current target living allowance of $20,000 a month or $240,000 a year. Their expenses have always risen as fast or faster than their income. Mike believes his contacts in the financial services industry will turn him on to investments returning at least 12% a year, but Doris says, based on his past tips, negative 12% a year is more likely. For the sake of argument, I will assume they can get 12% a year on their investments with an inflation adjustment of 4%. Applying the formula, they need $3,000,000 to retire today.

Now, make your own calculation of how much more you need to retire today. With this figure in mind, consider some strategies to get from where you are today to long-term retirement. The simplest strategy is to save more.

Better Utilization of Existing Income

Most of you already have substantial savings. But saving enough to meet your magic number requires you to take additional action.

The first step is not to spend the savings you have already accumulated. This will allow your savings to grow while you live on your current income. For many of you, this is all that is required. If you get 10% a year on your investments after taxes, they will double in value in seven years. If you continue to get 10% for another seven years, your investments will double again. Thus if you started with $400,000 in investments, in fourteen years you could easily have $1,600,000 for retirement. Depending on your personal inflation rate and other factors, this may be more than enough to live well the rest of your life. But if you spend a substantial portion of your savings every year, they will increase in value either slowly or not at all. Again, if you spend $20,000 a year of your $400,000, it could take you fifteen years to get to $800,000 and more than thirty years to accumulate $1,600,000. If you spend $40,000 or more a year, your position will get worse every year. It is very important not to spend what you have already accumulated.

Not spending sounds easy, but for many of you, it is the most difficult step. Many of you came into your money suddenly. Inheritance, exercise of stock options, sale of a business, insurance settlement, and many more events can change your financial life quickly. If you have not developed the habit of putting money away every month, your only experience with money is making it and spending it. You have no habit of saving. Saving requires two things: not spending what you have already accumulated and adding to your nest egg on a regular basis.

Saving money is not easy. The pressures to buy come from everywhere. You spend for basic necessities and for luxury. You also spend for fun, ego, status, to feel better, and countless other reasons. There are few messages in your society suggesting that you should save. And those messages are usually messages of fear. "Save so you do not end up on the street." "Save so you can pay for that impending heart attack, cancer, car wreck, earthquake, hurricane, stray bullet disaster." Yet for most people, fear is a very weak motivator to save.

Most people spend out of fear, spend to try to make themselves feel better. New clothes, a vacation, a sports car, chocolate, vintage wine. People save out of love. They have a genuine interest in taking care of themselves and their families. Increasing your fear level will not increase your savings. It will increase your spending. Learning to love yourself, your life, and the people in your life will lead you to save.

There are numerous books, workshops, support groups, and therapies available to teach you how to save. If you find yourself unable to hold on to your nest egg or to add to it on a regular basis, get help. Many people have a problem with this, including me. I have joined several groups over the years and gotten counseling. It has worked for me, and it can work for you too.

Tax Breaks for Saving

If you can hold on to your savings or even save more, then invest your savings to bring about your retirement as soon as possible. This requires two things: taking advantage of all the tax breaks available to savers and investing in the best portfolio you can. Designing your portfolio and selecting individual properties and securities are the subjects of Part Three. Here I simply want to encourage you to look for tax breaks wherever you can find them.

The first place to look is at work. Get all the information you can on your company's retirement plans. If they are 401(k), 403(b), Keogh, or SIMPLE plans, find out:

- How much can you invest?
- Does your employer match any of your contribution?
- What are the choices to invest in?
- Is there any service available to help you make your selections?

If you have a pension plan, find out the rules for vesting, early retirement, lump sum distributions, etc.

Once you have all the information that is available to you from work or employment, look into IRAs, SEP IRAs, Roth IRAs, or your own Keogh. Stay away from insurance company products like tax-deferred annuities unless that is the only thing for which you are eligible.

Generally, you first want to put as much into your tax-deferred savings plans as possible. Then continue to save outside any tax plan. At the end of this chapter, you will consider the question of how much to save and project your retirement date, based on your savings rate.

Saving in a tax-deferred plan will shorten the wait till your retirement. Tax-deductible contributions allow you to save more because there is no tax due on the income you contribute to the account. For example, if you earn $10,000 and normally pay taxes of $2,000 on those earnings, you have $8,000 left to invest for retirement. If you earn $10,000 and contribute the whole $10,000 to a tax-deferred plan, you will have $10,000 to invest for retirement since you pay no taxes on income contributed to a tax-deferred plan. Also, employer matches double the amount you contribute. Contributions to pension plans by your employer are not taxed to you either. And realized gains on your investments in the accounts are not taxed.

But once you retire there are tax disadvantages to living off assets in tax-deferred accounts. The disadvantage is that the tax deferment is over and you have to pay taxes on everything you take out of the account. Your deduction for the cost of the assets has been used up, and any gains are taxed at ordinary income rates. For example, assume you contributed $10,000 to a 401(k) plan, purchased an S&P 500 index fund, and it doubled in value between the time of contribution and your retirement. If you sell the fund in retirement and withdraw the $20,000 for living expenses, you will pay taxes on the whole $20,000 at that time. If instead you had purchased $10,000 of the same fund while working, held it until retirement, and then sold it, you would pay taxes only on your gain, $20,000 minus $10,000 or $10,000. Plus, the taxes would be at a lower capital gains rate, not at a full ordinary income tax rate. So it is useful when living off your assets to have money that is not in tax-deferred accounts. Once you have reached the maximum contribution level for your plan, keep saving, if possible. Assets in taxable accounts are an excellent holding during retirement.

Two Methods to Increase Savings

There are two techniques to add to existing savings. One is increasing income while keeping spending relatively stable.

In Chapter 1 you figured out your monthly and yearly expenses. If you can keep your expenses the same over many years while you get raises, move into higher-paying jobs, and receive bonuses, inheritances, insurance settlements, or other windfalls, you can invest the excess and retire sooner. But this is not easy. When your income goes up, you feel entitled to spend more. "Marlene bought a new car when she got a raise. I think I'll buy a new house because now I'm a vice president. All the vice presidents live in the better neighborhoods." And, in fact, you are entitled to spend more. But if your goal is early retirement, spend more on your retirement savings. Unfortunately, people never show off how much they have in their retirement accounts. It is the office secret. There is no prestige in saving. This is where the love comes in. If you have enough love in your life, enough connection now to the people, places, and things already in your life, you do not need to spend more. You have enough. You can save any increased income for your family's future.

The other technique to add to existing savings is decreasing spending while keeping income stable. In Chapter 2, I discussed the concept that for every diet there is an equal and opposite binge. But there are some tricks that can be utilized.

One trick is to keep the money from touching your hands. For example, taking retirement plan contributions out of your paycheck or checking account automatically leaves you with less disposable income. This is particularly helpful with IRA and other retirement accounts that are not sponsored by your employer.

Another powerful trick to increase savings is to refinance your mortgage at the lowest available rate and shorten the term to ten years. Then have the payment automatically deducted from your checking account to keep the money out of your hands. This decreases your disposable income because it increases your monthly payment. It puts you ten years away from living without a mortgage. I highly recommend paying off your mortgage before retirement.

None of these spending restraint systems works if you simply supplement your disposable income with credit card purchases. If you are under the illusion that you are spending less yet your credit card balances go up dramatically, it is time for serious action. Pay off and cancel all your credit cards. Eliminating the credit cards forces you to find creative ways to spend less or make more. And, yes, you can rent cars, buy airline tickets, and charge over the phone without credit cards. Check cards are acceptable everywhere.

In addition to using your current income better, you might also be able to retire sooner by better utilization of your existing assets.

Better Utilization of Existing Assets

Home equity is often the most underutilized asset. In Chapter 1, I said home equity is not an asset you can live on, so it should not be included in your total investments in determining by the formula whether you can retire today. I also suggested calculating your target investment return with your current home equity and with smaller home equity and more investments. However, home equity has drawbacks in addition to not producing any income you can live on.

Too Much Home

Home equity lacks diversity. In Chapter 4 and Chapter 10, I will discuss diversification in great detail. But in the context of home equity, the problem is simply that a very large portion of your net worth may be tied up in your home equity. If this equity disappears or just fails to grow, your future retirement may be delayed. Many homeowners in Southern California in the late 1980s thought they were millionaires. Houses they had purchased for $500,000 in the early 1980s had appraised values of as much as $1,500,000. Had they cashed out in 1989 and invested the $1,000,000 profit in a diversified portfolio, they could have retired. But few sold then. By 1993, these same houses were selling for $750,000. Most of the profit was gone. A diversified portfolio, as explained in Chapters 4 and 10, will gradually increase in value with few negative years.

There are many factors to consider to determine if you should downsize your house now. The major questions are:

- How much equity do you have?
- What is your current mortgage payment?
- What are your current home maintenance expenses, including taxes, utilities, insurance, lawn care, house cleaning, etc.?
- What will be the net after taxes if you sell?
- How much new home will you need?
- What will be your new mortgage payment?
- What will be your new maintenance expenses?
- What kind of return could you expect on your equity if you did not sell?
- What kind of return could you expect on a diversified portfolio?

Probably the toughest question is, how much new home do you need? If your children are still living with you, you probably cannot tolerate a smaller home. If you do a lot of entertaining, a cheaper neighborhood or one farther away from your friends or clubs might not work. However, you might be ready for an easy-to-maintain condo or a place on the outskirts of town combined with some telecommuting. If you have job flexibility, moving from California or New York to Arizona, New Mexico, Florida, Oregon, or Colorado can dramatically reduce your housing expenses. This may not only speed up your retirement, it may start it.

After you have determined all the factors listed above, recalculate the formula with new figures for total investments and target living allowance to see if you can now retire or if the amount you need to save has been reduced substantially.

Let's go back to the example of Fred and Ginger. They have $250,000 of equity in a $400,000 home. Of their $7,000 a month target living allowance, $2,800 is for mortgage payments and home maintenance. Ginger has found a three-bedroom condo in a new development south of town that sells for $225,000. With one child leaving for college next year and the other soon thereafter, Ginger would like to minimize the house cleaning and eliminate the lawn care. Plus there is a swimming pool, spa, exercise room, and much greater energy efficiency than their old home. They would have no mortgage, and could reduce the rest of their home maintenance to $800 a month and add $25,000 to their savings. Applying the formula and using $5,000 a month as their new target living allowance and $425,000 as their new current investments, they now need $750,000 to retire, which is $325,000 more than they currently have. Plus they now have $2,000 a month to add to their retirement savings. They are much closer to retirement than they were when they needed an additional $650,000 and had no excess income to save each month.

However, Fred and Ginger are not entirely comfortable with $225,000 of their net worth in one condo. While it will meet their housing needs, it may not be a good investment. As an alternative, they could consider making a down payment of $50,000 on the condo and taking out a mortgage of $175,000. This way they could add $200,000 to their retirement savings immediately and diversify that $200,000 among many assets. This would make their mortgage and home maintenance expenses $2,100 a month. Their target living allowance would now be $6,300 a month. Applying the formula, they would now need $945,000 in total investments, which is $345,000 more than they currently have. They could save $700 a month and would have only $50,000 or less than 8% of their total net worth of $650,000 tied up in their house. Should the condo fail to appreciate or even decline in value, their future would not be jeopardized.

There is a very strong demographic argument for downsizing your home sooner rather than later. The generation that retired in the 1980s and 1990s did so in large part by downsizing. Homes that they had owned since the 1950s had huge appreciation because there was a large baby boom generation that needed more housing and was willing to pay above listing prices for homes. When the current baby boomers retire en mass, there will be no huge generation to sell their homes to. Space will not be nearly as in demand, so appreciation cannot be expected to match that of the past. It is likely that if you downsize now and reinvest your excess into a retirement portfolio, as described in Chapter 10, you will be better off.

You may have other assets besides your home that are not contributing to your retirement savings.

Too Much Stuff

Take a look at your assets and ask two questions:

1. Will these assets appreciate in value between now and my retirement?
2. Will there be a market for these assets when I am ready to retire?

If you own your own business, that is the first asset to look at. What are the prospects for this business over the next few years? Which is better: sell it now and stay on as a consultant, or build it up a few more years and then sell it? Look at the tax consequences as well as the return you could get from investing the proceeds. Talk to a financial planner about this.

Many personal businesses have very little tax basis. When you sell them for cash, all the proceeds will be capital gains. So you can figure that 20% of the proceeds or more will go to taxes. But this would be true both if you sell now and if you sell five years from now.

The advantage of selling now and working as a consultant to cover your living expense is you will get years of portfolio gains between now and your retirement. However, if the prospects for the business appear to be better than the 10% return you could expect from a portfolio and there will be a good market for the business in the future, it may make more sense to sell just before retirement.

There is also the possibility of having the business taken over by another larger company and receiving stock for your company. This defers the taxes until you sell the new stock, but it can create the problem of lack of diversity in a portfolio. Many Silicon Valley entrepreneurs have sold their companies for stock only to watch the buyer become obsolete and their new stock become worthless.

If you own stock options or any other non-common securities, take a look at exercising them now rather than later. Options and other derivatives have a way of losing all their value quickly. Look at the tax consequences of a sale, the prospects of future gains versus a return of 10% on a portfolio, and so forth. Liquidity is particularly a concern with non-common securities. If there is little market for them when you are ready to retire, you will have to sell at whatever price a buyer is willing to pay, which may not be much. If you think the prospects are good but you are not sure, it might be best to sell some now, and sell other pieces each year as you approach retirement to be certain you realize some value from your securities.

Take a look at your cars, jewels, second homes, boats, airplanes, artwork, and any other large assets. Some of this stuff is not only not appreciating, it is costing you money. If you have a loan against it or have maintenance expenses, consider selling and investing both the proceeds and the excess income for your retirement. Cars always depreciate. By getting rid of a BMW and switching to a Toyota, you could add thousands to your retirement savings. The capital you raise and the amount cut from your current expenses, if properly invested, could allow you to retire a year or two sooner.

The question is: would you rather have this stuff now or retire years sooner? Let's look at second homes. Do you really use the second home that much and will it really appreciate in value? Many second homes in the country never appreciate and require continuous maintenance. Real estate is a supply and demand business (see Chapter 7). There is a nearly endless supply of land and homes in the country, but demand varies with the economy and demographics. It is much more difficult to make money with a second home than it is with commercial real estate or most other standard investments. If there is a decent market for your second home right now, consider selling and investing the proceeds in a retirement portfolio.

Almost everything you can own you can rent cheaper. You can rent a vacation home for a month rather than own one for a year. You can rent jewels for an evening. You can rent artwork, boats, airplanes, and everything else you might already own. It is worth spending some time calculating how much you can raise by selling your stuff, renting when you need, and saving the proceeds and the maintenance expenses.

It is also worthwhile to spend some time talking to a tax accountant to be sure you are paying the government the lowest legal amount of taxes possible so you can save as much as possible for retirement.

Tax Planning Is Not the Key

Tax planning is a very large subject. I will explain throughout this book how to save taxes during your retirement. But it would take several volumes to explain how to save taxes during your preretirement years. The best advice I can give in this space is to get help. You will save much more in taxes than it will cost you to talk to a tax accountant. Most of you pay at least one third of your income to various tax authorities. If you can save just a fraction of that, you can get to retirement sooner.

But tax planning is not the key to retirement saving. Saving and good investing is the key. If you save nothing or very little, it does not matter that you get a tax deduction. If you save in a tax-deferred account and lose all your money in bad investments, you will not make it. I have never used a single tax-deferred account, yet I have lived off my investments for eighteen years. Good investment results were the key.

The main thing is to take a look at every aspect of your life to see if it affects your tax situation. I have already discussed retirement plans. Throughout the rest of this book, I will discuss how to keep taxes low on your taxable retirement accounts. However, there are other taxes to consider.

States and cities have different tax rates. Income taxes can be high, low, or nonexistent. Sales taxes differ by location. Real estate taxes are much higher in some states than others. Moving across borders can free up a lot of money for your retirement. If you have to move for the business anyway, be sure to check into the tax differences between various communities you could live in. Nevada, for example, has no income tax. California has among the highest in the United States. A commute across the border every day can save you a lot of money.

Incorporated businesses have different taxes than sole proprietorships and partnerships. Incorporating and creating deductions where there were formerly none can speed up your retirement. Health benefits can be converted from taxable income to deductions. The amount you can place in a retirement fund each year might be higher.

If you expect to inherit some money, it is worthwhile to check on the tax planning your relatives have done. If their estate is structured right, you may be able to get a lot more when they die. Insurance trusts, marital trusts, annual gifts, and other devices can legally save hundreds of thousands of dollars. For any estate larger than $600,000, it is well worthwhile to talk to a tax attorney about tax-saving estate planning. These attorneys are expensive, but they can save you much more than their fees. Ask about using a living trust to save on probate fees while you are there. This can also save thousands of dollars that you could use to live on. While you are at it, look into the planning of your own estate so your heirs do not have to pay estate taxes.

Once you have found all the ways to save on taxes, are using your assets to your greatest benefit, and are saving as much as you can from your income, you can project the date of your retirement.

Your Projected Retirement Date

Let's start with the example of Fred and Ginger. They have decided to buy the condo outright. They have been very comfortable saving $2,000 a month. They are not worried about the condo losing value. They think it is well located in an up-and-coming neighborhood and has a better chance of appreciating than their old house. This leaves them with $425,000 in investments. At current values, they would need $750,000 in investments to let go of both jobs and get the kids through school. They anticipate their current target living allowance of $60,000 a year will increase about 2% a year. (Note: they earn $7,000 a month but save $2,000, so they will need only $5,000 a month in retirement.) Because their target living allowance will increase, by the time Fred and Ginger retire, they will need more than $750,000.

Most of the increase in their investments will come from appreciation of their existing $425,000. If it increases in value 10% the first year, that will be an improvement in their investments of

$42,500. If they then save $24,000, their investments after the first year will be worth $491,500. If this then increases in value 10% and they add another $24,000 to their savings, they will have $564,650. At this rate, by the end of year 5, Fred and Ginger will have $831,000. If these increases occur either in a tax-deferred retirement account or by following the tax planning suggestions in the following chapters, the increasing value of their portfolio will not increase their tax bill.

If their target living allowance increases every year by 2%, they will need $66,000 by the end of year 5 to get by. Applying the formula, it is clear that they can retire at the end of year 5. Their target living allowance for year 6 is $66,000, which divided by .08 is $825,000; if all goes according to plan, they will have investments worth $831,000.

Investment Returns Determine When You Retire

However, there is one major problem in this analysis. Mathematically it is correct. But the certainty of achieving a 10% a year return on investments over a five-year period is very low. This will be discussed in detail in the following chapter. Returns on investments vary widely from year to year. Over periods of decades, they show definite patterns. Five years, however, is too short a time to predict investment returns. It is best to say that there is a significant possibility that Fred and Ginger will be able to retire five years from now. However, if the markets all suffer losses over the next decade, or Fred and Ginger follow a poor investment strategy, they may not be able to retire for ten or more years.

The volatility of investment returns is the most important factor in determining when you can retire and how well you will be able to live once you have retired. That is why the rest of this book is devoted to the topic of getting the best possible return from your investments. *You must do well with your investments if you are to live well in retirement.* In Fred and Ginger's case, they have nothing else to live on. It makes no sense for them to consider social security a factor during their retirement. Neither will be eligible five years from now, and fifteen years from now social security will probably pay less than 10% of their expenses.

Hillary, however, is eligible for social security right now. It will be a major factor in her retirement. At present, she needs to generate $12,000 a year from her investments. She expects her expenses to rise 3% a year. Thus, next year she will need $12,360 from her investments, the year after $12,730, at the end of year 3, $13,100, and at the end of year 4, $13,500. (This assumes her pension and social security benefits will also increase in value 3% a year so that she does not have to draw on her inheritance for more than one third of her living expenses.) She expects her investments to increase in value by 8% a year. By the end of year 3, she should have about $250,000 and by the end of year 4, $275,000. She should be able to retire at the end of year 4 as $13,500 divided by .05 is $270,000 and Hillary will have about $275,000.

Hillary's retirement date is more certain than Fred and Ginger's. The investments she will need to make 8% a year are much less volatile than those Fred and Ginger will use to achieve 10% a year. Still there is a range of possible retirement dates for Hillary, somewhere between three and six years from now.

It is not possible to predict with any degree of accuracy when Mike and Doris of Beverly Hills will be able to retire. They own $1,200,000 in stock options. They assume they can make 12% year on their investments and their expenses of $240,000 a year will grow by 4% a year. Mathematically, it appears they could retire at the end of year 13. Then their expenses would be about $400,000 a year and their assets about $5,200,000. Their target living allowance of $400,000 divided by .08 is $5,000,000. But stock options are among the most volatile of investments and not subject to predictability of returns even over a period as long as thirteen years. In fact, this Beverly Hills couple is in a very precarious financial position. If Mike's agency were to lose a major client and collapse, his stock options would become worthless, he would have no job, three mortgages, and $240,000 a year in expenses. He should immediately sell his stock options if there is a market for them, pay his capital gains taxes, and invest the remaining $960,000 in a diversified portfolio. Doris and he should also take the steps discussed above to better utilize their assets and income. Selling two houses would eliminate two mortgages and free up more retirement capital. They may be in a position to retire immediately. If they take no action, they are only a short run of bad luck away from bankruptcy.

Now Estimate Your Retirement Date

From the three examples above, you probably have a good idea how to estimate your retirement date. In Chapter 1, you calculated your current target living allowance and your total investments. Here is how to estimate the date of your retirement.

1. Adjust the Chapter 1 figures for expense savings and asset additions you have discovered in this chapter.
2. Take your new target living allowance and increase it by your inflation adjustment for a period of ten years, one year at a time.
3. For each year, use the formula to calculate the total investments needed to produce that target living allowance.
4. Increase your total investments by your expected annual returns plus expected additions for a period of ten years, one year at a time.
5. Compare the results from step 3 to the results in step 4. The year when the results in step 3 are lower than the results in step 4 is the year you may retire.

You can make the calculations either with a calculator that measures compound interest or by hand.

If you do not find a match after ten years of calculations, concentrate on increasing your savings, reducing your expenses, and improving your investment returns. Life changes. It is not realistic to estimate retirement dates beyond ten years.

I have seen many people within ten years of retirement go on spending sprees that eliminated all their savings. Even more common are people who follow insane investment strategies. I have seen potential retirement portfolios disappear without even the fleeting gratification of a spending spree. In the long run, investment results will determine whether you can retire and the quality of your financial life during retirement. The next eight chapters are devoted to this topic.

If Your Retirement Is Less Than Ten years Away

If your retirement date is less than ten years away, do not take excessive risk in your investments. Pay close attention to the suggestions in Part Two, Retirement Investing. You may want to begin now investing as if you are already retired so you do not have to make any large portfolio shifts on retirement. These large shifts can cost you in taxes and commissions. This will be fully discussed in Chapter 10.

If your retirement date is more than ten years away, you have time to pursue a prudent, aggressive growth strategy. This strategy will be set out in Part Three, Investing to Reach Your Magic Number. However, do not skip Part Two. The principles set out in these chapters are the basics for the strategies set out in Part Three.

part two

Retirement
Investing

chapter four

Designing Your Retirement Portfolio

In this chapter you will learn how to set up your portfolio to achieve your target investment return. If you need more that 12% per year, there are certain investments to use. If you need 6% and want only 6%, then other investments will suffice. If you need 8% but want to shoot for 11%, then your portfolio will have a different design than at 8%.

Designing your portfolio is an ongoing, long-term process. You will adjust your portfolio over a period of years just as you change the pictures on your walls or the rugs on your floor. Achieving your target investment return is also a long-term goal that should be judged as an average of the results of many years. This average return may in fact never happen in one given year. If you are shooting for a 9% return, you may be up 15% one year, down 4% the next, up 7% the next, up 18% the next, and so on. When you look back, you realize that over time your returns are doing between 8% and 10% a year.

Target investment returns are just targets. They give you a focus. As everything in the world of investing is in flux, there are no guarantees you can hit them. It is certain that you can invest in things that, if they perform in the future as they have in the past, will produce returns over ten-year periods similar to your targets. You do have control over what you invest in. You do not have control over how those investments perform. Based on ten-year holding periods, it is likely those investments will perform in the future as they have in the past.

How to Achieve Your Target Investment Return

To achieve your target investment return over your lifetime, you must allocate your assets between three to five noncorrelated asset classes and maintain that allocation through both bull and bear markets.

Choice of Asset Classes Is the Most Important Decision

The asset classes discussed in this book include U.S. large- and small-company stocks, real estate, bonds, oil and gas, foreign and emerging market stocks, and more. The asset classes you invest in are the most important determinant of your investment returns. In later chapters, I will discuss different *forms* of investing in each asset class. For example, you can buy U.S. large-company stock in at least three different forms: through purchasing mutual funds, using a money manager, or buying individual stocks yourself. In the long term, decisions on the form of investment will have much less effect on your results than the decision on what asset classes you invest in. If you invest primarily in money market funds, CDs, and short-term bond funds, using in every case the best managers around, over a thirty-year period you will still significantly underperform those who invest only in U.S. stocks, using a mediocre manager, perhaps themselves. The form of investment does matter, and there are managers who consistently outperform the market averages. But even Peter Lynch and Warren Buffett together could not manage a money market fund that would outperform the average stock fund.

The Best-Selling Asset Allocation versus the Best Asset Allocation

You already have an asset allocation, and chances are someone sold it to you. Every money manager, financial advisor, insurance salesperson, Wall Street firm, financial journal, and other investment group sells asset allocations. Most do not even realize this. They are selling what sells. The best-selling asset allocation in the

United States is something like 40% to 50% U.S. stocks, 40% to 50% bonds, and 0% to 20% cash. This allocation includes no commercial real estate, no foreign stocks or emerging market stocks, no oil and gas, no gold, no venture capital, and so on. This is the allocation taught in business school, financial planning school, insurance school, and so on. It was advocated in *The Intelligent Investor*, which is the bible of several generations of investors.

In 1996 the typical investor actually had 40% in U.S. stocks, 30% in bonds, 30% in cash, 0% in commercial real estate, 0% in foreign stocks. This speaks well for the sales power of the financial services industry and creates an opportunity for you to invest in stocks of many financial service companies, but it is not an allocation you will be interested in yourself. This is a bad allocation for those saving for retirement. It is a terrible allocation for people living off their investments.

This formula was developed for people saving for retirement in a zero-inflation era when international investing and real estate ownership were only for the exotic or super-rich. Today, international investing and real estate investing are relatively simple and have many advantages over other assets for those of you living off your investments. The problem with the old allocation is that it contains all U.S. financial assets that have been on the same cycle since the end of deflation and the onset of steady inflation in the late 1930s. To achieve a steady return you can live off, you need to diversify away from this cycle and invest in foreign stocks and non-financial assets such as real estate.

The vast majority of products out in the market are U.S. stocks, bonds, and money market funds. These products are heavily promoted and sold everywhere. That does not make them appropriate for you. The miracle on 34th Street was not that Kris Kringle was Santa Claus. The miracle was that Macy's sent a customer to Gimbals. The miracle on Wall Street will be when a stockbroker turns down a retired person's money and suggests he buy a small apartment house instead of stocks.

Before you hire an advisor or buy a product, you must first figure out what asset allocation works best for you, considering all available asset classes. Then find the advisors who understand the products you need and choose which individual products to buy.

Though this sounds like common sense, it is not common practice. *Most investors are sold their asset allocation by their advisors or the product salespeople rather than establishing their allocation first and then finding the appropriate products and advisors.*

Determine Your Current Asset Allocation

Begin by determining your current asset allocation. In Chapter 1, you calculated your net investments. Determine your current asset allocation by calculating what percentage of your net investments is made up of each asset class. The chart on page 51 lists the major asset classes. As best as possible, determine which of your assets fit into which classes. Do not at this point consider what form you are using to invest or the tax status of your investment account. Consider this example.

Ernie and Claire

Ernie and Claire have $900,000 in assets: $200,000 is in money market funds, $300,000 is in stock mutual funds in a 401(k) plan, and $400,000 is in stock of her employer, a small company. They have 22% in money markets, 44% in U.S. small-company stock, and 33% in mutual funds. It is unimportant at this time that some of their assets are in a 401(k) plan and other assets are held in personal accounts or that some assets are managed by mutual fund managers. They do need to know, however, what type of stock is held by their mutual funds.

After calling all the mutual fund 800 numbers, Ernie and Claire determine that their mutual funds are $60,000 U.S. small-company stocks, $60,000 foreign-company stocks, $60,000 treasury bills, and $120,000 U.S. large-company stocks. Their final asset allocation would be as follows:

ASSET CLASS	ALLOCATION
U.S. small-company stock	51%
Money market funds	22%
U.S. large-company stock	13%
Foreign-company stock	7%
Treasury bills	7%

Ernie and Claire might note whether they chose this asset allocation or whether it was sold to them by her employer, their investment advisor, a financial magazine, or their mutual fund managers. In fact, they may have not been aware that their mutual funds owned any foreign stocks or treasury bills.

After you have determined your current asset allocation, determine the asset allocation needed to achieve your target investment return. Begin by looking at the returns available from different asset classes.

List of Returns for Periods Longer Than Ten Years

Below is a list of average annual returns that can be expected over periods longer than ten years from the major liquid asset classes:

ASSET CLASS	EXPECTED LIFETIME RETURN
Emerging market stocks	14%
U.S. small-company stocks	12%
U.S. large-company stocks	10%
Foreign-company stocks	10%
U.S. real estate	10%
U.S. oil and gas	8%
Corporate bonds	7%
Foreign bonds	7%
Treasury bonds	6%
Municipal bonds	5%
Money markets and CDs	4%
Treasury bills	3%
Gold	3%

There have been hundreds of studies over the years of returns from different asset classes. Different studies have shown different results depending on the length of the studies, the beginning and end of the time period studied, and the methodology used. For example, studies of U.S. stock returns that include the crash and depression years 1929 to 1932 when stocks declined by 90% show lower returns than studies that start after the Depression. The returns shown above are typical of the longest studies available for the particular asset class. These long studies are most appropriate for your purposes because you are lifetime investors. Long studies show the results from many different economic environments, including booms and busts, inflations and deflations, recessions and wars, eras of great technological innovation and free world trade, and eras of technological stagnation and closed trade. As you are likely to face many different economic environments over your lifetime, these long-term studies reflect the most likely returns you will get from the specified asset classes.

Studies of the last fifteen years are particularly suspect for your purposes. The last fifteen years were a period of dramatically declining inflation and interest rates that resulted in huge stock and bond returns that are unlikely to continue. Now that inflation is low, it can only stay the same, go slightly lower, turn into deflation, or increase. All of these scenarios are likely to produce investment returns different from those of the last fifteen years.

There are no choices that produce returns over 14% for the long term. I do not recommend using options or derivatives of any kind, and I recommend leverage in real estate only under the conditions that will be discussed in the chapter on that topic. I will describe in later chapters ways to get the best possible returns from each asset class, which could lead to long-term returns a few percentage points higher than those listed above. But these suggestions may also lead to less consistent or more volatile returns. For the purposes of setting up your portfolio, it is better to use the returns listed above. Over the years, as you learn more and understand more, you will see ways to enhance your returns.

Pick Three to Five Noncorrelated Asset Classes

Over the next thirty years, some asset classes will do better than their long-term record, some will do worse, and some will perform as expected. Unfortunately, there is no way to know which asset class will fall into which performance category. It is necessary to invest in at least three asset classes to ensure that you have a good chance to get average returns over the next thirty years.

From the list above, pick three to five asset classes that will comprise your portfolio and give you your target investment return.

Each asset class will be discussed in detail in the following chapters. For now, just pick asset classes that you may be comfortable owning and that are likely to be on different cycles. Be aware that the asset classes with the highest returns also have the highest volatility. Although emerging market stocks and U.S. small-company stocks can go up 50% in a year, they can also drop 50%. Treasury bills never go down, but they rarely return more than 7% and then only for a year or two.

It is important to know that most high-return, volatile investments are on different cycles. If you own two volatile investments on different cycles, the total volatility of the two is smaller than the volatility of either. For example, U.S. small-company stocks and emerging market stocks are on different cycles, so a portfolio containing half of one and half of the other would be much less volatile than a portfolio all of one or the other.

In general, U.S. small-company stocks and large-company stocks have similar cycles. Foreign stocks have different cycles than U.S. stocks. Emerging market stocks have different cycles than U.S. stocks and other foreign stocks. Real estate and oil and gas have similar cycles, though real estate is more local market–driven. Both have different cycles than stocks. The oil cycle is somewhat different from the natural gas cycle. The oil cycle is based on world economic conditions; the natural gas cycle is based on U.S. and Canadian economic conditions.

Bonds and stocks of the same country are generally on the same cycle. High inflation hurts both, and declining inflation helps both. A rising currency helps both, and a declining currency hurts both. The rise of the dollar in the late 1990s drew foreign investors into both U.S. stocks and bonds. The collapse of the Korean currency scared foreign investors out of both Korean bonds and stocks. There are exceptions during periods of deflation. As a rule, when bonds pay the highest coupon rate and seem a much better investment than stocks of the same country, it is tempting to shift heavily into them. Unfortunately, this is usually the time when the stock market is about to turn and far outperform the bond market. While the cycles of the same country's stocks and bonds are usually the same, stocks will drop further on the down cycle and rise further on the up cycle, resulting in higher returns for stocks over ten-year periods.

Relative to other investments, money markets, CDs, and treasury bills have minor cycles generally correlated with the bond market, but at times of Federal Reserve tightening, they can go up in yield while bonds' total returns can be negative.

Recent Cycles of Asset Classes

The main reason to own three to five different asset classes is to avoid overcommitment to a declining asset class when you are regularly withdrawing money from that asset class for living expenses. The double decimation effect of a bear market and withdrawals on a one- or two-asset class portfolio will send you back to work. From 1972 until 1982, U.S. stocks and bonds did poorly but real estate and oil and gas did well. If you had all your money in U.S. stocks and bonds during this period and had a target investment return of 10% a year, you would have been bankrupt before Jimmy Carter was defeated. If you had all your money in real estate and oil and gas, you may well have doubled or tripled your net worth, even after withdrawing your living expenses and taxes.

In August of 1982, U.S. stocks and bonds started a long upward move that continues in 1999, though the general public did not catch on until after the 1987 correction. Commercial real estate began a downward move in the mid-1980s that ended in the early 1990s. In the late 1990s, commercial real estate is doing quite well. Oil and gas declined sharply in the first half of the 1980s and remained subdued through 1994. My opinion is that a major shift began in 1999 to the upside that the general public will not catch on to until 2009, though it will last for at least another decade. If you have been invested entirely in U.S. stocks since 1982, you have doubled or tripled your net worth. If you have been invested entirely in real estate, you may not have a net worth.

Emerging markets began an up cycle in the late 1970s which could well last twenty-five more years but will eventually end as the world's economies begin to equalize. Other foreign stocks peaked relative to the U.S. in 1989 and should have returns similar to U.S. stocks with cycles two or three years apart.

Since you are interested in a steady, perpetual return on your investments, it would be insane to put everything in U.S. stocks and bonds. Though no one can predict when the next ten-year period of underperformance for U.S. stocks and bonds will begin, there will be one, and you will need to eat and play during those ten years just like during any other ten years.

A Big Pension Fund Misses the Point, but Not Harvard and Yale

Recently an eastern state fired more than twenty-five investment management companies for underperforming investments on its $13 billion public employee pension fund. For the previous ten years, the fund had averaged 10% versus the Standard and Poor's 500 stock index, which averaged 15%. The state made the decision to put 56% of its assets directly into the S&P 500 stocks and to put most of the rest in other U.S. stocks and bonds. The rationale was to try to catch up with the S&P 500. The state seems to have failed to notice that the S&P 500 has far outperformed its own historical average of 10% a year and is unlikely to continue to do so. By staying focused on only one asset class, it failed to see the potential in real estate, foreign stocks, emerging market stocks, oil and gas, and many other assets. This trap of looking at only one asset class will likely lead to ten future years of returns below the 10% the state was unhappy with for the past ten years.

Contrast this with the experience of the Harvard and Yale endowment funds. Since 1990 Harvard has had about half its endowment in U.S. stocks and bonds. The typical endowment fund has about 80% in U.S. stocks and bonds. Seeking a high but steady target investment return, in any given year Harvard has between 5% and 15% of its assets in real estate, between 5% and 15% in foreign stocks, between 5% and 15% in emerging market stocks, and between 5% and 15% in private equities. It has up to 5% in commodities, foreign bonds, and junk bonds. This has produced the second highest returns of any U.S. endowment fund since 1990 and, even if the U.S. stock and bond markets underperform in the future, Harvard can expect to meet its target investment return. Yale has even fewer U.S. stocks and bonds than Harvard. It has large positions in real estate, hedge funds, foreign stocks, venture capital, and buyout funds. Yet Yale also has one of the highest returns of all endowment funds and should continue to hit its target investment return even if the U.S. markets crash or simply revert to their mean returns.

Examples of Individuals Allocating Their Assets

I will discuss the prospects for stocks and other assets over the next ten years much more fully in the next chapters. Each chapter will fully discuss the cycles of the different asset classes to enable you to pick noncorrelated asset classes. For now, pick three to five asset classes that appear noncorrelated, based on what you have read so far, and determine what percentage of your assets you need in each class to achieve your target investment return. Use the examples below as a model.

Joe: 12%

Let's start with the toughest example first. Joe, from Chapter 1, needs to earn 12% on his money. He could put everything in emerging market stocks. Thus 100% of his portfolio could be expected to return 14% very long term, an extra 2% a year. But he might be frightened out of his mind or severely depressed, or have some other extreme feelings if the first year his portfolio dropped 50% from $600,000 to $300,000. If he had one quarter of his money in emerging market stocks returning 14%, one half in U.S. small-company stocks returning 12%, and one quarter in real estate returning 10%, he would likely hit his target of 12% over a twenty-year period. The target return is arrived at as follows:

% IN ASSET CLASS	× EXPECTED RETURN FROM CLASS	= TARGET RETURN
25% Emerging markets	× 14%	3.5%
50% U.S. small co.	× 12%	6.0%
25% Real estate	× 10%	2.5%
Total		12%

It would be very unlikely that Joe would ever see his total portfolio down 50% in one year, as all of these markets are on different cycles. Since all the markets he is in are volatile, it would be possible, but unlikely, to see his whole portfolio decline to $400,000 or increase to $900,000 in a single year. For investors in this situation, take a close look at the epilogue on surviving the emotional ups and downs of investing.

Susan: 8%

Susan needs to make 8% on her $1,200,000. She has many options. She could put 70% in U.S. corporate bonds returning 7% and 30% in U.S. large-company stocks returning 10% and achieve her result. This would be a typical solution. However, the U.S. bond market did exceedingly well from 1982 to 1998. Should the trend reverse for ten years, as it did from the early 1970s to the early 1980s, Susan will be unhappy with her returns and may even end up bankrupt. By adding foreign stocks, real estate, and money markets to her mix, she could achieve a steadier return. For example, 20% foreign stock, 20% U.S. large-company stocks, 20% U.S. real estate, 30% corporate bonds, and 10% money market funds would give her a much steadier, predictable return over the long haul. Since U.S. stocks and corporate bond returns are highly correlated, she could substitute emerging market stocks for corporate bonds or U.S. stocks and get both a steadier total return and a higher return. This would also give her less interest income and more capital gains so her tax rate would go down as well. This mix, however, would require her to regularly sell holdings for living expenses, whereas the traditional 70% bonds, 30% stock mix may require her to sell stock only once or twice a year.

Investments Are Not Gambles

Notice that all the expected lifetime returns from all the asset classes listed on page 51 are positive. Over periods longer than ten years, investing is not gambling. In gambling, the house always takes a cut. Over ten-year periods, you will lose in gambling at least as much as the house's cut.

In investing, you are the house. You are putting up the money to build the corporate headquarters, to finance the government roads, to dig the oil wells. The returns I have discussed represent the cut you can expect each year from the projects you are financing with your money. Speculative projects, like those in far-off emerging markets where governments can be overthrown and companies nationalized, require and get a bigger cut. Safe projects, like the financing of financially sound General Electric's day-to-day operations over 30- to 90-day periods, give you only a small cut. Thus money market funds that finance these day-to-day operations pay very little. Yet over ten-year periods, all these investments pay off.

How to Turn Long-term Investments into Short-term Investments: Leverage

Time and the economy turn a $100,000 investment into a $300,000 investment. Along the way, your $100,000 may become $50,000 or $500,000. If you borrow $90,000 to make your $100,000 investment, the lender will become nervous the minute your investment value drops below $90,000. The lender may force you to pay back the loan and leave you with no investment and a $10,000 loss. If you could wait for a recovery, you could end up with a $300,000 investment. Leverage turns long-term investments into short-term speculations and worse.

Leverage means you invest borrowed money as well as your own money. By allowing you to invest more, leverage increases your returns and your losses. These strategies have high commissions, financing fees, interest payments, and other loan costs. In this book I am focusing on very long-term investing. Anything that gets more expensive to own the longer you own it is not useful for living off your assets or saving for retirement. Two Nobel Prize winners forgot this and ran Long-term Capital Management into huge losses. But they have their Nobel Prizes to live on; you do not. Do not borrow money in retirement. There is a limited exception for real estate. That is the only exception. If you borrow money to invest, study short-term investing, not this book. This book is about the asset classes that have the best long-term records. It is about how to achieve long-term positive returns.

How to Turn Positive Returns Negative: Derivatives

A sure method to turn investing into gambling is to buy options and other derivatives. As derivatives have limited duration, time is against you. The costs eat up your returns as the limited duration of these instruments requires you to buy, pay costs, get out, buy again, pay costs, get out, buy again, and on and on. Even if you always pick the right derivatives, you can lose money paying all the fees in and out.

Factors That Will Prevent You from Achieving Your Expected Return

From the previous section, you may have gotten the idea that if you own U.S. large-company stocks in any form and for any time period you will get the return listed on page 51, 10% a year. This is not true. That 10% is the average return. Many investors do much better than the average. More than half do worse. The mean return is about 9%. This is also true for the other asset classes listed. More than 50% of investors get less than 10% from real estate, less than 14% from emerging market stocks, less than 7% from bonds, and so on. It is my belief that most investors break even or lose money their first few years. Some give up and put everything in CDs or savings accounts. Those who learn and persist a few more years get the average returns listed above. Experts, who work at it for years, consistently get above-average returns.

The current stock mutual fund mania provides an excellent example. A fund began with around $100 million in assets. In the first year the fund was up 70% and ended the year with assets of around $200 million from this return and new accounts. The fund got a lot of publicity and by February of the second year attracted $800 million in new accounts. The second year the fund lost 10%. More than $600 million of the second year accounts left the fund in the first months of the third year, locking in their losses. The third year the fund was up 20%. Over three years, this fund returned better than 25% per year. Yet more accounts lost money in this fund than made money.

One purpose of this book is to show you how to get the average returns from the beginning. It is not necessary to be the first investor in a hot new mutual fund to get an average return. It is necessary to stay with good investments in bad years. In the example above, $800 million in accounts invested in the down year. The owners of $600 million made the mistake of pulling out at a loss. They tried to time the market, getting in at the right time and out at the right time. They lost. The owners of $200 million that invested in the second year and stayed for the third year did fine. They did not try to time the market.

As you will be living off your money, you cannot afford several avoidable down years. The suggestions below and throughout this book are designed to get you an average return immediately. Once you are comfortable with these suggestions, others hereafter could help you achieve above-average returns.

Do Not Time Markets

The biggest mistake novice and expert investors make is to try to time markets. Do not market-time. Once you have set up your asset allocation, stick with it. Stay fully invested in your three to five noncorrelated asset classes at all times.

Over the next thirty years, we will have rising interest rates and declining interest rates, a rising dollar and a falling dollar, rising inflation and falling inflation, rising GNP and falling GNP, oversupply of real estate and undersupply of real estate, collapsing foreign economies and booming foreign economies, and more. This is a certainty. What is uncertain, what is not predictable, is when. If you are in three to five noncorrelated asset classes the whole thirty years, you will both survive and thrive.

If you think U.S. large stocks are about to crash, do not sell all your U.S. large stocks and put the proceeds into cash or real estate. No one has ever consistently predicted short-term market results. Never. And you will not either. The odds are your crash prediction will be wrong. Play the percentages, go against your own prediction, and do *not* sell. You are setting up a lifetime portfolio designed precisely to survive short-term market crashes yet produce excellent long-term results.

Raising Cash Feeds the Ego and Depletes the Portfolio

If you raise cash or periodically change your asset mix, you will increase your taxes and expenses and decrease your long-term results. I have done it, it does not work. Every day I was in cash I increased the percentage of my portfolio getting 3% and decreased the percentage getting 10% or better. I also did some stupid, impulsive things with some of that cash. When I am not fully invested, I get ideas for investments that will substantially outperform everything I already own. These ideas feed my ego and have lost me a lot of money.

This is an issue of humility. Every time I think I am smarter than the market I have to go through a painful process of defeat and ego deflation. But when I realize I am just part of the market, I get excellent results. I can choose patient investing in foreign stocks and real estate and do well, or I can choose to predict stock market peaks or stock market bottoms, shifting in and out of cash accordingly, and get increasingly desperate. My ego will be deflated either by defeat or by choice.

It is a lot easier now to choose to cooperate with the markets, ride with their flows, and let go of the belief that I can outsmart them. However, like most of us, you may need to learn this the hard way. Just keep in mind that you do have a choice. No matter how much humiliation you have suffered, you can still get off the market-timer system and become a part of the market.

Do these examples of bad market timing seem unlikely to happen to you? In fact, they are the norm. Dalbar, Inc. has studied the performance of individual investors since 1984. From 1984 till 1995, the U.S. stock market increased 491% yet individual investors averaged only 113%. Why? Individuals traded in and out of the market. The same is true for investors in real estate, foreign stocks, oil and gas, and so on. Market timing is an infallible system for turning good investments into bad investments.

Stay Patient with Stagnant Assets

Often the hardest situation is watching assets stagnate. This can lead to a great urge to do something. I have watched many a stock trade up and down for years at approximately what I paid for it. I have to remember that the company is doing everything right. The stock price can stay flat for four years paying no dividend, but if the market finally understands the company and the stock price doubles the fifth year, I have made 14% a year. I have had this happen with big stocks like Johnson and Johnson and little stocks like Smith International. If I had sold in the first four years, I would have missed all the profits.

International stock funds have always had two- or three-year periods of flat to negative returns, followed by huge up years and then flat to negative years, followed by huge up years. If I get clever in those three-year lulls, I miss the huge years.

I own a building that has not gone up in value for ten years. With that building I forget that I have net operating income of more than 12% every year and no mortgage. So what if the appraised value stays the same every year? The cash I deposit every month is more than my target rate of return on this asset. If I sold, I would have to pay taxes because the property has been depreciated and I would have to pay real estate commissions and other expenses.

For me, lack of patience stems from my desire to be somebody. Essentially, I have a hard-to-break belief that if I do not do something, I am not a worthwhile person. Achievement is supposed to be a result of continuous action toward a set goal. *Often investing success is the result of continuous inaction.* The difficulty is that when I am doing nothing about my stock portfolio but watching the prices and reading reports, I have a lot of free time and I will have to listen to the inner voice that says I am lazy and no good at investing or anything else. Yet my results will be better than if I buy and sell all the time, running up expenses and turning a well-chosen portfolio into a series of quickly chosen and discarded investment ideas.

What has worked for me has been to learn to talk gently to myself and to spend time doing positive things for other people. First, I focus on the investments that have worked out after slow years. I congratulate myself for buying them and sticking with them. Then I check to see if it is reasonable to assume my current slow assets will also work out over time, and, if so, I congratulate myself for buying them and having the patience to hold on to them. Then I get involved in helping other people with problems much greater than my own and the need to "do something, not just sit there" disappears for the time being.

"Only Spend Income and Not Principal"— a Prison Sentence

While market timing is probably the biggest obstacle to achieving returns available from a given asset class, there are other ways to underachieve. Following bad advice often given by well-meaning but uninformed investment advisors is another. One of the worst common pieces of poor advice is "only spend income and not principal."

The returns listed on page 51 are "total returns" that include both any cash payments from the asset and increases in value of the asset. For example, U.S. large-company stocks historically pay out cash dividends of 4% a year and rise in value 6% a year, for a total return of 10% a year. The cash payment is considered the income from the asset. There is a notion that has been around for hundreds of years that will reduce your long-term results by as much as 60% if you believe it. This is the concept that you should "only spend income and not principal." This is a prison sentence. It is a legal concept that has to do with restrictions on the trustees and beneficiaries of trust accounts. It has nothing to do with investing for the best total return. The concept made sense before World War II when deflation was as common as inflation. In that era, all that was necessary to live off your assets was to keep principal intact as rolling deflations and inflations kept prices steady for hundreds of years. Since World War II and the end of the gold standard and the dominance of Keynesian economics, we have had continuous inflation. In this environment, living solely off "income" will lead to a lower living standard year after year.

Unfortunately, many investment advisors to this day apply the phrase "only spend income and not principal" in setting up investment plans for their clients. The results can be disastrous. Consider Tina.

Tina

Tina needs a 9% target return on her $1,000,000 of investments. Applying the phrase "only spend income and not principal," Tina needs $90,000 of "income." Many financial planners would tell her it could not be done. She would have to cut her expenses or go back to work part time. The best the planner could do would be to put her entirely in U.S. corporate bonds paying 7% and ask her to figure out a way to make up the $20,000. This would leave her completely undiversified. If bond rates dropped below 7% for an extended period of time, forcing Tina to reinvest any redeemed bonds, Tina would need to make up more than the $20,000. Yet by living off principal and income from a portfolio of three to five noncorrelated asset classes, Tina would not have to make up any deficit and would be well diversified.

The return from assets such as stock or real estate is both from the increase in value of the stock or building and from the income component such as dividends and net operating income. It would be easy to assemble a portfolio from the asset classes listed above that would both outperform the all-corporate-bond portfolio and be much more diversified.

Over long time periods, far more money is made from increases in asset values than from income. Bill Gates and Warren Buffett became the country's richest men not from income but from appreciation in the stock price of Microsoft and Berkshire Hathaway. In fact, neither stock pays a dividend, and both Bill Gates and Warren Buffett make moderate salaries compared to the bosses of similar-sized businesses. This is true in all areas of investing. Despite what you may have learned from playing Monopoly, the big fortunes from real estate come from appreciation and not from rent.

Living Off "Principal" Simplifies Inflation Reinvestment and Saves Taxes

Rather than being a negative, living off increases in asset value, so-called "principal," simplifies the process of reinvesting made necessary by inflation. In Chapter 1, I suggested that everyone should save 2% to 4% of his net worth each year to compensate for inflation. In practice, this can be done two ways. If you are living primarily off so-called "income," then you will need to actually add cash to various asset classes each year. For example, say you have $100,000 invested in a mortgage-free building, your target investment return is 10%, you get $10,000 a year in net rent from the building with no expectation that the building will increase in value, and your expected inflation rate is 3%. Each year you must write a check for $3,000 to your chosen asset to compensate for future inflation. If your allocation requires the $3,000 to go to real estate, then you will either have to start an account to get together a down payment on another building, or buy shares of a REIT, or come up with another idea for reinvestment.

On the other hand, if you are living off primarily "principal," then reinvesting to compensate for inflation simply means not taking out as much principal. For example, if you have $100,000 in a small-stock fund that pays no dividends, your target investment return is 10%, your inflation rate 3%, and it increases in value $10,000, you simply withdraw $7,000 for expenses and taxes. The $3,000 you did not withdraw continues to be invested for you. Failing to reinvest over a period of years can reduce your returns significantly. Not having to think about it is a real advantage.

If the money you are reinvesting is paid out to you, it is likely to be a taxable event. Dividends received on stocks or stock funds are taxable. Therefore, you will have to pay taxes on those dividends and be able to reinvest only what's left. Leaving money in an asset that appreciates in value is not a taxable event. If a stock that pays no dividends goes up in value and you sell some shares to live off and leave the rest, there is no tax taken out of the portion you leave. Over a lifetime of investing, avoiding taxes on your reinvestments can dramatically increase your returns.

Living Off "Principal" Is the Ultimate Tax Shelter

The greatest advantage to spending principal is that there are no taxes to be paid. If you own ten stocks and nine go up in value and one stays even, which should you sell for living expenses? The one that stayed even can be sold without incurring any taxes. The proceeds from the sale of the others would all have to be reduced by taxes before you would have any spending money.

In fact, it is important to look for opportunities to spend principal rather than income. If two mutual funds could be expected to return 10% a year, one all from dividends and the other all from appreciation, which should you buy? The second. In the first there is no opportunity to spend principal. The full 10% will be taxed every year. To get 10% to spend from the second fund you will have to sell shares. Up to 90% of the proceeds will be a non-taxable return of principal to you and the rest a capital gain. In real estate, even rent paid to you without selling a property is sometimes treated for tax purposes as a return of your principal. Here you can live off income and get the tax advantages of living off principal.

Less Than Three Asset Classes Is Hazardous

Market timing and failing to spend principal are two examples of failing to fully exploit given asset classes. Overcommitting to one or two asset classes will also prevent you from achieving a return you can live on. Since appreciation in any asset class is unpredictable on a short-term basis, to live off appreciation you must have multiple asset classes. But income from any asset class can also be cut. So to live off income, you must also have multiple asset classes.

Appreciation is half or more of the long-term return from all classes of stock and real estate. But over short time periods, one to three years, appreciation is not predictable. I cannot buy a building today and know that it will be worth more two years from now than what I paid for it. However, it is very likely to be worth substantially more ten years from now. Despite the experience of the last fifteen years, in the last hundred years many times U.S. stock prices have been lower three years after purchase. Yet it is extremely rare that stock prices will be lower ten years after purchase. Because short-term appreciation is not predictable, it is absolutely necessary for anyone living off appreciation to have multiple asset classes. This increases the likelihood that every year you will have some appreciation.

Income is more predictable than appreciation, though not entirely. Rents get delinquent, tenants go bankrupt. Bonds default, dividends get cut. To help ensure that income continues year in and year out, it is also wise to have multiple asset classes. The old formula, solely U.S. stocks, bonds, and cash, was not invented by someone living off assets since 1950.

How to Classify Pension Plans as Asset Classes

There are many different types of retirement plans. Some, like 401(k)s and IRAs, allow the owner to determine the makeup of the assets in the plan. Others, like defined benefit pension plans and social security, give the beneficiary no choice as to the makeup of the plan and the timing and method of payment. Living off your assets, you need to integrate tax-deferred plans into your asset allocation and take advantage of any tax benefits available.

Plans that provide annual payout but do not allow the investor to control the asset base can be classified either as fixed income or growth income. In some plans the annual payment is adjusted for inflation or other factors every year. This I call growth income. In Chapter 1, I suggested subtracting the annual payment from such a pension from your annual expenses to arrive at your target living allowance. This gives you a clear picture of what to aim for as your target investment return. However, it does not suggest how to solve the problem of owning assets on different cycles. Assuming the payer is a government or large corporation and that there is little risk of default on this obligation, a defined benefit pension plan is on its own cycle. Only a thirty-year or longer treasury bond or AAA corporate bond if held to maturity could be said to be on a similar cycle. Both will be good in deflationary eras. The advantage of a pension, though, is that it is often increased with inflation. An inflation index–linked treasury bond, if long enough in maturity, is perhaps the closest asset. So for diversification purposes, buying bonds would not be a good idea. Most other assets are on different cycles and could be bought.

Another advantage of the growth income plans is that there is no need to reinvest a part of each payment as payments rise each year to match inflation. But if the pension payments are fully taxed, then the other assets in the portfolio should have some tax advantages. For example, assets that have substantial appreciation that is not taxed until sold would be good. Leveraged real estate or index mutual funds might work. If the plan is a fixed annuity with no growth in payments, then some portion of each payment should be reinvested. To keep a steady asset allocation, a long-term bond fund could be used to deposit reinvestments.

The Psychological Damage of One Asset Class

Owning only one asset class causes even greater risks than simply years of no appreciation and no income. I had a friend who had about $3.5 million of equity in real estate in one city and no other assets. He had been incredibly correct about this market for many years, having started investing with only a small amount of savings. He retired and lived primarily off this real estate. When the local real estate market crashed, he lost several properties and his equity was reduced to something over $1 million. He saw no way out and killed himself. After a few years, that market recovered. Being dead, he did not.

This is an extreme example. In the epilogue, I will discuss surviving crashes psychologically. But in terms of setting up a portfolio, this is an example of being solely in one asset class and what can happen. If he had divided his $3.5 million among three to five asset classes, he never would have experienced such a severe decline. Had he phased his $3.5 million in real estate into five asset classes over a period of years, he likely would have sold some real estate at low post-crash prices and some at good pre-crash or post-crash prices. There is never a better time to start diversifying than now.

Keep It Simple

Just as it can be dangerous to have too few asset classes, it can also be a problem to have too many. In setting up your portfolio, keep it simple. Another mistake I have made over the years is to own too many asset classes and too many assets within each class. This has not enhanced my returns and has added considerably to my time requirements and has reduced my learning speed. You can learn more by watching three or four investments very closely over the years than you can by watching fifty rather loosely. The only advantage of owning fifty is your overall portfolio will be less volatile. But sufficient consistency can be achieved with far fewer assets.

You should be able to write down, from memory, everything you own, what you paid for it, its approximate current value, and the reason you own it on a single side of a single sheet of letter-sized paper. If you are in a hotel room in Paris and the U.S. stock market crashes, you should be able in fifteen minutes to figure out what to do next and then go on to your trip to the Louvre knowing you have done everything that needs to be done.

There is never a need to buy exotic or complex investments. I have discussed the problems with commodities, puts, calls, and other options and derivatives. The investment sellers of the world have great imaginations and are coming up with new investments every day. Simple investments are cut into pieces and each piece sold separately. For example, stocks may be cut into the capital gain or loss portion and the dividend portion and each portion sold separately. Mutual funds can hold an infinite combination of asset classes and derivatives with or without leverage and hedging. Mortgages can be sold as rights to receive the principle payments, the interest payments, or the interest payments above or below certain amounts where the interest rate is adjustable. These investments do not serve your needs.

You want a direct interest in assets with a long history of performance because you intend to own your assets for a long time and need to base your expected return on the past returns from many different economic cycles. No one knows how these spontaneously birthed investments will perform over time.

You want to buy your investments for the lowest possible sales charge. All these new, complex investments have high sales charges even though many of these charges are hidden on first examination.

You want investments that are liquid, meaning they can be bought and sold easily without having to take a big cut in price. Many of these exotics are difficult or even impossible to sell.

You want investments on which current information is readily available. If you bought Iranian oil interests or Peruvian gold shares or a mutual fund shorting Singapore, hedging yen, and loaded with biotech IPOs, you would have difficulty knowing when to sell to use the proceeds for your living expenses. As you have expenses every day, you need information access every day.

The investments suggested in this book range from very simple and very liquid to moderately complex and moderately illiquid. In deciding what to buy, keep in mind how much time you want to spend on investing and whether you can afford to own any assets that are moderately illiquid. There will be no exceedingly complex investments discussed or recommended or any illiquid investments recommended. All the assets discussed have long histories of performance and can be bought and sold with moderate to no sales charges.

Gotta Have It Investing

Some of you will have practiced the "gotta have it" method of asset allocation. These are the people who bought every hot idea that came along over ten or twenty years and still own them all. These investors bought sector funds, real estate limited partnerships, individual high-tech and biotech stocks, gold, asset allocation funds, small-cap emerging market funds, options and futures funds, zero coupon bonds, 100-year corporate bonds, condos, vacation properties, time-shares, and things named after animals.

If you are in this crowd, first try to classify what you have by the categories listed on page 51 and come up with a current liquid value.

Some things like asset allocation mutual funds fit in several categories. Look at their current holdings and allocate a percentage to each category. For example, Fund X has a current value of $10,000 and is 60% U.S. large-company stock, 20% treasuries, and 20% cash. So put $6,000 under U.S. large-company stocks and $2,000 each in treasuries and money markets. Some assets will not fit the categories. List these under the heading "*To Be Liquidated*."

After you have sorted out what you have, finish reading this book and then figure out what you want. Look at what you paid for each asset and determine whether there will be a lot of taxes owed if you sell it. First get rid of the assets that you think will perform the worst and that have the lowest tax consequences and reinvest in something with a solid future. Save your best assets with the highest tax consequences. With all the rest, sell those off you want to get rid of over a period of years to minimize the tax bite. Build up your new allocation as you sell off your junk. If you see some screaming bargains right away, get second and third opinions before you buy. Acknowledge that you are new at rational investing, have made many compulsive buys in the past, and need to be cautious.

How Come I Own Real Estate and All My Friends Own Only Stock?

Having a portfolio in three to five different asset classes is ideal for living off your investments but often entails unforeseen social and psychological problems. It is easy to read the headlines in the paper about how well the U.S. stock market is doing and to regret having only 30% in U.S. stocks. Then the U.S. market declines and you think why did I have so much in U.S. stocks? Or your real estate has just been appraised at twice what you paid for it five years ago, but there are no headlines anywhere and very few people to talk to about it.

These feelings of being out of sync with the rest of the investment world and out of sync with the world in general are real. Very few people have portfolios of three to five noncorrelated asset classes. The point is: do not go back to all U.S. stocks, bonds, and cash just because everybody else invests that way. Over the long haul, you will not be able to live off that asset allocation. Find a way to stick with your new allocation until your experience shows you that it is working over the long term.

How to Maintain Your Asset Allocation over the Years

As markets fluctuate, your asset allocation will change. As you spend assets, your allocation will change. Gifts, inheritances, marriages, and divorces will change your asset allocation. Every year you need to check to see if you are saving enough of your returns to meet your long-term requirements.

Check Your Inflation Target Every Year

The most important measure of your results is the amount your investment portfolio increases or decreases every year. What you need to know is whether you are keeping up with your inflation target. For example, if you started 1995 with a net investment portfolio of $600,000 and at the end of the year your investment portfolio was $630,000, then you increased your portfolio by $30,000 or 5%. If your inflation target was 3%, then you exceeded it. This very simple measure is all you need to know. Many financial planners will confuse you. They suggest you calculate your total return on your investments by subtracting cash from each asset as it is spent and adding back cash to each asset as it is reinvested and making various assumptions about how your investments would have performed had you not used money for living expenses and so on. All of that is way too complicated for your purposes. All you need to know is if you are keeping up with your inflation target.

Spending As It Affects the Asset Allocation

Spending can cause you to miss your inflation target if you spend from the wrong assets. When owning many different investments, some of which pay monthly or quarterly income, but most of which do not, it is sometimes difficult to decide which assets to sell for living expenses and when to sell those assets. This is an area I have made several mistakes in.

At one time I thought it prudent to live off my investments that were doing best. The mistake was they continued to do best for many years and I continually cut into my future growth. Then I thought it best to live off my least productive investments. Unfortunately, when these investments suddenly turned up dramatically, I had again cut into my future growth. All the while my average investments never got spent.

I had to again realize I couldn't predict when each class of investments would do best. The prudent thing is to live off your investments in the same proportions that you invest in them. If you have 20% in oil and gas then you should get 20% of your living expenses from oil and gas. And if the income portion of the total return from your oil and gas is greater than 20% of your living expenses, you should reinvest that excess money. Sometimes it is difficult to keep your asset allocation intact.

With some of my assets, like buildings, it was impossible to get enough cash out of them to pay their share of my living expenses.

They were leveraged and had gone up substantially in value, but they had only modest positive cash flow. In this case, at the time I sold a building I played catch-up and did not reinvest in another building. Rather, I obtained an entire year of living expenses (including taxes) off the sale of one building and reinvested only the excess. If I never sold any real estate, I would at times be over-invested in real estate when it was not performing well. It is more important to keep my basic asset allocation intact rather than to try to avoid all taxes by always fully reinvesting all my real estate proceeds.

Asset Allocation within Tax-deferred Plans

Plans that allow the beneficiary to determine their makeup can be funded in whatever way best fits the beneficiary's asset allocation and tax situation. The simplest system is to determine what target investment return you need and what asset allocation would most likely provide that return. Then determine which assets are likely to produce the most taxable gains and fund the retirement plan with those assets.

For example, assume Ron and Nancy have $600,000 in taxable accounts and $200,000 in treasury bonds in a 401(k). Their asset allocation calls for $250,000 in small-company U.S. stocks, $250,000 in real estate, and $300,000 in foreign stocks. They want to spend most of their investment time managing two small apartment buildings; that is, their $250,000 equity in real estate. They have found two small-stock funds that they like and two foreign stock funds. One small-stock fund is a value fund with about 25% annual turnover, and the other is an aggressive growth fund with 100% annual turnover. As will be discussed in later chapters, funds with high turnover require you to pay high taxes. To reduce taxes, they sell the treasury bonds and buy $125,000 worth of the aggressive fund in the 401(k). In the 401(k), any tax liability for the turnover is extinguished. One of the foreign funds has 40% annual turnover and the other is an index fund with no turnover. The remaining $75,000 in the 401(k) will be invested in the foreign fund with 40% annual turnover. They would have to hold the remaining $50,000 of the foreign fund in a taxable account.

Some asset allocations will not allow the investor living off his assets to take full advantage of the tax benefits available in a defined contribution plan. For example, assume Ben and Jerry have $500,000 in corporate bonds and $500,000 in a 401(k) invested half in an emerging market stock fund with low turnover and half in an S&P 500 index fund. From a tax standpoint, they would be better off with the $500,000 in corporate bonds in the 401(k) as all the interest from the corporate bonds is taxable. But Ben and Jerry are not yet fifty-nine and a half years old. They need all the interest plus some principal from the corporate bonds to live off. If the bonds were in the 401(k), they could not take the interest and principal without either substantial penalties or being forced to take periodic payments. If they sold the corporate bonds to change their asset allocation, they would have a large capital gains tax as they bought them when interest rates were much higher.

How Much Time Do You Want to Spend Investing?

When making an asset allocation decision, consider what effect it will have on your future time constraints. Some asset classes are easier to manage than others. The more asset classes you have, the more time will be required. If you plan on investing full-time, get into five asset classes and manage all the assets yourself. But if you wish to spend as little time as possible investing, still use three non-correlated asset classes. Read through the rest of this book to find the best way to have each class managed by someone else.

This does not mean you will hire one person to manage all your assets for you. It is rare that the same person who will manage your real estate will also be competent to manage your foreign stocks. Also, some assets, such as treasury securities and other fixed incomes, are easy to manage. You may wish to handle these yourself even though you want to minimize the amount of time you spend on investing. The following chapters have extensive information on how to hire managers for different asset classes and how to manage assets yourself. Whatever your choice on management, if you wish to live the rest of your life off your assets, you must spend some time every week on your investments.

Start with One Hundred Hours for Every 10% of Assets

Many people fear that they spend either too much time on their investments or not enough. The first year or two of setting up your portfolio, keep track of your hours. Twenty hours a week is about right at the beginning. If you are spending significantly less time, you are probably missing important feedback. For every 10% of your assets, it should take about one hundred hours or five twenty-hour weeks to decide what to invest in and to execute that decision. This time will include taking classes, reading books, interviewing money and property managers, and many other activities described through-out this book. Fifty weeks or a year of this and you will be set up for life. After the first year or two, ten hours a week is plenty unless you love it and want to do more.

But do not spend less than ten hours a week. I have seen more money lost from people hiding from their investment decisions than from any active mistakes. You will buy things that go down. You will hire managers who are incompetent. The markets will crash. The key is to spend time analyzing what happened, get advice, do research, talk it over with family and friends, make decisions, and move on. Large losses ignored can turn into bankruptcy. Large gains ignored can disappear. A steady ten hours a week is the best course.

Most people worry about money. People with $10 million can worry just as much as people with half a million or people with nothing. Having money does not reduce the fear of financial insecurity. It reduces actual financial insecurity but not necessarily the fear. It has been my experience that active involvement with my investments reduces my worry. Learning about investing and taking an active role in your own investing are extremely important.

chapter five

U.S. Stocks–
Large
and Small

Until recently, most U.S. stocks were considered too risky for retirees. The standard investments for retirees were municipal bonds, U.S. government bonds, and supposedly safe high-dividend-paying utilities stocks. Now you hear of people retiring on 100% U.S. stock portfolios. Let's begin with the fundamental question.

Are U.S. Stocks Appropriate for a Retired Investor?

Yes. U.S. stocks can be relied on for positive investment returns over thirty-year periods, and they are on different cycles than other major investment classes.

Stocks Advance Because the Business Grows

Stocks represent ownership in businesses. Stock prices go up because value is being created every time a nail is hammered into a board. Each fax that crosses the wires adds valuable knowledge to the economy. Well, not most of the faxes I get, but the faxes you get. At any rate, as the owners and workers build up businesses, the value of the businesses rises. Long term, it is a near certainty that stock prices will rise. There is a school of thought that stocks return 10% to 12% and bonds return only 7% because stocks are riskier. Risk has nothing to do with it.

Large businesses that grow 10% a year go up in value 10% a year, and that is why the stock price goes up 10%. Stocks over long periods of time do exactly as well as the businesses they represent. Over short time periods, ten years or less, stock prices can get out of sync with their true values. Investors desperate to increase their retirement savings can bid large stock prices higher than their true values. But eventually, the prices reflect values. Bonds pay whatever rate is negotiated between the lender and the borrower. Over the years the agreed rate has averaged 7%, so bonds on average pay 7%.

U.S. stocks are also good investments because they are on different cycles than other investments. When stocks have down years, they do not pull everything else down with them. Thus they function well with certain other assets in a diversified portfolio. But their returns are correlated with some asset classes and not with others. You need to own U.S. stocks in a portfolio containing asset classes that are not correlated.

Asset Classes That Are Not Correlated with U.S. Stocks

It is said that small stocks and large stocks are on different cycles. But the truth is small stocks and large stocks of the same country are on similar cycles, though the magnitudes of swing are bigger with smaller stocks. As the economy approaches a recession, generally both small- and large-stock prices decline, but small stocks decline more. As the economy begins to recover, both small- and large-stock prices increase, but small-stock prices increase more. You will get much better diversification by owning real estate, international stocks, oil and gas, and large stocks than by owning large and small stocks. Real estate cycles are local in nature. For example, when the United States economy was booming and all stocks were doing well from 1982 to 1987, Texas real estate was in a severe bear market. When the U.S. was entering recession in 1990 and the stock market was down, the Texas real estate market was moving up. As the U.S. stock market did well, particularly small stocks, from 1991 to 1993, California real estate suffered. As I write this book in 1999, California real estate is hot and U.S. stocks may be ready to drop.

The point is, when you are looking to diversify to produce a steady long-term return, owning both small U.S. stocks and large U.S. stocks will have little effect compared to owning one class of U.S. stocks and owning real estate, oil and gas, foreign stocks, emerging market stocks, or money markets. U.S. bonds are not a good diversifier for U.S. stocks.

Bonds and Stocks of the Same Country Are Usually on the Same Cycle

Investing in both U.S. stocks and bonds will not produce a steady return. When inflation goes up in the U.S., both stocks and bonds will do poorly. When inflation goes down, both stocks and bonds will do well. You, however, need to eat both in years of high inflation and years of low inflation. The best-selling asset allocation exists because the sellers of the allocation, stockbrokers and mutual fund houses, have these products to sell, not because it produces a steady return. Only in times of deflation will stock returns and some bond returns go in opposite directions. This will be explained in Chapter 8, Fixed Income Investments. But ninety out of the last one hundred years stocks and bonds in the U.S. were on the same cycle.

How Much Should You Put into U.S. Stocks?

Okay, U.S. stocks are a good investment for a retiree. But how much should you invest in U.S. stocks?

Everybody Is in Stocks Today

In 1999 as I am writing this book, most investors I know have major portions of their assets in U.S. stocks. In 1980, when I started investing, everybody was in real estate—a string of single-family houses, apartments turned into condos, duplexes, tax shelters. Every professional wanted to buy his or her office and rent out the extra space. Now every professional is looking to get the first month rent-free. Oil and gas were big and gold was even bigger. Most investors today do not know what an oil and gas partnership looks like, but they know which software company will be the next Microsoft. In

1980 no one had ever heard of the Magellan fund. Now it's hard to find anyone who hasn't owned it at one time or another.

In the late 1970s and early 1980s, real estate tax shelter sales were growing rapidly. The implied promise was $3,000 invested would result in $10,000 in tax savings and real estate appreciation in three years. Investors were shown the records of tax shelters that started in the 1970s and how well they had done. More real estate tax shelters were sold in 1982–1984 than in all the previous decades of sales combined. The real estate markets were flooded with capital from individual investors, pension plans, foreign investors, savings and loans, banks, and others. In 1985 Congress began legislating the end of tax shelters, and the real estate markets collapsed over the next few years from overbuilding, excessive leverage, and fraudulent practices. Few who invested $3,000 in the boom years broke even. Most got $1,000 in tax savings and lost the rest.

Today stock mutual funds are sold on the implied promise that all those who invest now will do as well as those who came before them. Most expect that $3,000 in a mutual fund today will be worth $10,000 three years from now. Sales in the last five years have been greater than those in all the previous decades of sales combined. The stock market is flooded with capital from individual investors, pension plans, foreign investors, endowment funds, trust funds, insurance companies, and more. The tax shelters of the new millennium are 401(k) plans. Regardless of the returns on 401(k) stock funds, you are guaranteed to save on your tax bill.

I suggest you do not get overcommitted to U.S. stocks. I have full confidence that over a lifetime they will average 10% a year for large companies and 12% for small. But the next ten years may be on the short end of the average.

Investment Fads: Do Not Overcommit to Stocks

It is possible for all investment classes to rise at the same time as the economy grows. Business can grow and as it grows become self-financing and borrow less but agree to pay higher rents on the buildings it rents, as no new buildings are being built. Thus stock prices, bond prices, and real estate values all go up at the same time. But what usually happens is that investors pour everything into one asset class and ignore the others till the first is overpriced and the second underpriced, even though underlying values in the second may have risen as much as the underlying values in the first.

In the 1970s and early 1980s, institutional investors and individuals poured huge sums into the commercial real estate market, driving prices way above values. At the same time, they abandoned their supposed one decision, nifty fifty stocks. Today institutions and individuals are pouring huge sums into U.S. stocks and ignoring commercial real estate. This process may continue for many years.

In general, as the baby boom generation ages they will spend less and invest more, creating the possibility that some or all investments will be bid way up in price over the next twenty years. By some measures, stock prices are at all-time highs already. The price of stocks to the value of assets owned by corporations has never been higher. Yet no great deal of selling is taking place as baby boomers keep adding to accounts rather than withdrawing. The Japanese stock market bubble of the 1980s had a similar buy and hold underpinning. There corporations bought and kept buying, supposedly never to sell as the purchases were to strengthen corporate relationships rather than speculate in stocks. The theory is that boomers will keep buying until 2015 or so and then liquidate to live off these investments.

Even if boomers continue to save for twenty years, I would not bet my money that U.S. stocks would be the best place to be that whole twenty years. For one thing, it is easy right now to make 10% or better in real estate and foreign stocks. If it becomes harder to get good returns in U.S. stocks, a shift to other assets can occur quickly. Baby boomers are uneducated, undisciplined lenders of their capital. They are less educated and less disciplined than the lenders who fueled the real estate boom and bust of the 1970s and 1980s. Money market funds or foreign stock funds can be bought over the phone or the Internet, and real estate deals can be closed in a month. There is no reason to believe that U.S. stocks are a better retirement savings investment than real estate or foreign stocks. A big shift could occur quickly.

This is not to imply that large U.S. stocks will do poorly over the next thirty years. They should average 10%; but there will be periods when they will return less and when they will return more.

And it feels like a period when they will return less is coming up. From 1965 to 1975 total returns on U.S. stocks were about 4%. I am not predicting that will happen again. For most people living off their assets, U.S. stocks should be a component of their portfolios. Just do not overcommit.

If you have three asset classes, do not put over one third in U.S. stocks. If you invest in both U.S. large and small companies, your total commitment to both should not exceed one third of your portfolio.

Should You Invest in Small Stocks or Large Stocks?

Assuming you do invest in U.S. stocks, should you invest in large- or small-company stocks?

Differences Between Large and Small Stocks

There are several differences between large and small stocks. To determine the size of a stock, you take its current price and multiply by the number of shares outstanding. The total is the stock's market capitalization, or its cap. If the total is $1 billion or less, then you have a small-cap stock. Everything above that you can call a large-cap stock. Many people these days also talk about medium-sized stocks as well as large and small stocks and define anything between $1 billion and $3 billion as a medium-cap stock. In this book I will deal only with small and large cap as there are no long-term studies of medium-cap stocks to rely on.

Take the example of Albertson's Grocery Store. The price at the start of 1999 was about $65 a share and there were 250 million shares outstanding. The total market capitalization was $16.25 billion, so this is a large stock. Thirteen years ago when I bought it, there were 32 million shares outstanding and the price was around $25 a share, so the market cap was about $800 million. This has gone from a small stock to a large stock.

Performance of Small Stocks versus Large Stocks

In general, small stocks return better than large stocks, but their price swings are much greater. Whereas I expected

Albertson's to do 12% or better thirteen years ago, I now expect it to do 10% or better. Thirteen years ago Albertson's was a Rocky Mountain chain of grocery stores. It had the intent to move into many more states and cities. Like most small caps, there was huge growth potential, at least 12% earnings growth per year. In fact, it surpassed 12% a year by a large margin. But today, like most large caps, it does not have room to grow so briskly. Today Albertson's is the second largest grocery store chain in the country and operates in almost every state. There are a few more states and cities to move into but many fewer than thirteen years ago, and many already have competitive grocery chains. So 10% a year would be healthy growth in these conditions.

While small stocks can be expected to do better than large stocks, they are also more erratic. They have bigger downs as well as bigger ups. Albertson's has more than five times as many stores as it had thirteen years ago, and almost all of the old stores have been enlarged. It is in many more cities. This diversity should provide a steadier return. Business has been slow in California but very good in the Southwest and Midwest. When Albertson's was in only a few Rocky Mountain states, business was either good everywhere it did business or bad everywhere it did business, and the stock price was subject to larger swings. Also few institutions add small stocks to their portfolios and then sit on them for generations, as they would do with Coca-Cola or General Electric or Microsoft. Small stocks come in and out of fashion to fill in the gaps of the big portfolios, causing wild price swings. Rarely do they become core holdings. Big institutions need to buy blocks of 100,000 or more shares. Some small companies do not have that many shares outstanding.

As a group, small stocks outperform large stocks only a few months of each decade. If you are not in small stocks for those few months but in large stocks or cash, you will get none of the advantages of owning small stocks. For this reason, it is very important to stay fully invested at all times in your small-stock allocation. While market timing is never a good idea, because small stocks tend to run up quickly and for only a few months, market timing with small stocks is a huge mistake.

How to Get the Return You Are Looking For

So here is the question: what is the best way for someone living off his or her assets to get 10% a year from large U.S. stocks and 12% from small U.S. stocks?

An Index Fund

The direct approach to getting the market return is to buy the market. While it is impractical to buy all the large stocks or small stocks in the market, index funds that represent those two segments of the market are available. An index fund is a stock mutual fund that owns all the stocks in a popular stock index. For example, the Standard and Poor's 500 index contains 500 large stocks. An index fund would own those 500 stocks in the same proportions as the S&P 500 index. If the index ever dropped a stock and replaced it, the fund would sell that stock and replace it as well. Small-stock index funds operate slightly differently. Because there are as many as 10,000 small stocks, small-stock indexes buy a statistically significant sample of small stocks.

Most of your U.S. large-company stock money should be in an index fund. Index funds are the surest method to achieving a return you can live off the rest of your life. Index funds do better than 80% of all large-company stock mutual funds over the long term. They do better than 80% of all stock money managers, better than 80% of all stock pension funds, and better than 80% of the stock recommendations of all stock gurus writing newsletters. This has been true in the 1970s, the 1980s, and the 1990s. It is true in up markets, down markets, and flat markets. In 1996, for example, only 17% of managed mutual funds beat the S&P 500 index funds. The odds of doing better than an index fund are 1 in 5. You may want to play against the odds with a small portion of your U.S. large-stock money. But most of your large-cap money should be in index funds.

Index funds have other advantages for someone living off his or her assets. For one, you can target large stocks or small stocks with great accuracy by buying an index that contains only such stocks. Many other mutual funds that call themselves small- or large-cap funds often contain both. This precise selection of stocks will give you a better chance to achieve the long-term return and volatility with which you are comfortable. Mixed mutual funds may produce either higher or lower returns and volatility.

In taxable accounts, there is a significant tax advantage to owning an index fund. Each time a mutual fund manager sells stock at a gain, the shareholders of the mutual fund must pay taxes on that gain whether or not cash is distributed to them. There are only two reasons for an index fund to sell shares. The first reason is that the index may change, forcing the manager to sell the stocks that are no longer in the index. Since indexes rarely change, stocks are rarely sold for this reason. The second reason an index manager sells shares is to pay the owners of the fund who liquidate their shares. Since most index fund owners are long-term investors, this rarely creates a problem for the non-selling owners. Only in years of great redemptions like 1987 and 1990 are these sales a problem. A general mutual fund manager has many reasons to sell stocks and often does, creating capital gains on which you, the owner, are taxed even though you do not get cash out of the fund. And if there are great redemptions as in 1987 or 1990, a general mutual fund will do more selling than an index fund. Only an owner of individual stocks can avoid being taxed on sales made by others.

When choosing between two otherwise equal index funds, generally the newer fund with the least embedded gains is the better pick. If an index fund has been going up 10% a year for ten years it is likely that it will have large unrealized gains, also known as embedded gains. If a crash forced the manager to sell stock to cover large redemptions, the nonselling shareholders, that is, you, would get slapped with some big tax liabilities. A new index fund without any embedded gains would not cause any gains for the nonselling shareholder and may even distribute some losses to them.

Since taxes on capital gains are currently 20%, avoiding these taxes can make the difference between having enough return to live on and not. If a managed mutual fund is up 12% one year and because of 100% turnover that gain is all taxable, then after taxes you will have less than 10% to live on. If an index fund is up 12% a year and there is no turnover so none of the gain is taxable, you have 12%. Over a period of many years, these taxes can erode your capital and affect your lifestyle.

Another advantage of an index fund is that anybody can run one. There is no expensive stock research to do, no high-priced manager to pay. So you will lose very little of your return to expenses. It is important, however, to look at the expense ratio of an index fund. Rates for individuals can be as low as .2% a year and as high as .5%. Over many years, this can make a difference. If you invest enough to qualify as an institutional investor, you may pay as little as .1% a year. These rates are substantially lower than the 1.5% we talked about in Chapter 1 for managed money.

Another advantage to an index fund is that you can get monthly or quarterly checks sent to you in the amount you designate. If you have $250,000 in an S&P 500 fund and you need $1,500 a month from it as part of your living expenses and taxes, most funds will just send the check out. You do not need to call every month or worry about how the market is doing. The amount you are re-investing as your inflation hedge simply stays put. The only calculation you need to make is how much to take out monthly and how much to reinvest. Once you have figured that out, there is nothing to think about until your expenses have gone up. Then you increase the amount of your monthly check.

In general it is very easy to deal with index funds. Most have 800 numbers and long office hours. It is easy to phase your money into them and to take it all out if you have decided to change your asset allocation.

Finally, there are many no-load index funds to choose from. Since your strategy here is to get a market return with the smallest possible costs, avoiding loads, 12b-1 fees, and all other fees is very important.

Drawbacks of an Index Fund

There are some drawbacks to this strategy. If the market goes haywire, there is no one to hold your hand. This is true with all mutual funds, load and no load. If you have hired a money manager, he or she will sit down with you and talk about the big picture. A money manager can look at your whole financial situation and put things in perspective. If you bought a loaded mutual fund, the salesperson will most likely take the market drop as an opportunity to sell you another loaded, high-commission product. If you call the 800 number of a no-load mutual fund, they will give you the prepared rap that came down from headquarters, which may have nothing to do with your particular situation.

Another negative of an index fund is there is no chance ever to outperform the market. All you are going to get is 10% or 12%. This is a disadvantage only if you need more or want more. If those returns are fine with you long term, then stick with them. Remember that over the long term, stock index funds outperform 80% of managed stock mutual funds, money managers, stock gurus, and pension plans in bull markets, bear markets, new age markets, and cavemen markets. That is because the other methods charge large management or advisor fees, trade actively and run up commissions, and usually hold some treasury bills and other cash that pays only 3% a year over the long haul. The fees and commissions come off the top, and the cash brings the average return down. Learning to live with the smallest possible amount of cash will enhance your total portfolio return over the long haul.

Advantages of Managed Funds and Money Managers

One advantage of a managed mutual fund or a money manager is that it is possible to invest in such a way as to smooth out the swings in the stock market. Years when the market is down 15%, you will be down only 5%. But when the market is up 20%, you will be up only 10%. Your long-term return will be lower than with an index fund. With an index fund, there is no chance to smooth out the swings. The questions are, do you really need this and how much are you willing to pay for it? If you have five asset classes already and they are not highly correlated, your total portfolio will not have huge price swings to begin with. Is this worth costs of 1.5% a year or more?

Index Funds Are Boring

The index fund is also the most boring thing to do. If you want to really get involved with the stock market, this is not the way. Index funds own so many stocks that it is not worthwhile to pay much attention to any of them. With a concentrated managed mutual fund or a money manager, there may be one stock that is 20% of the portfolio or a few stocks that are 50%. It can be fun to read the annual reports and go to the shareholders meetings of these companies. You can tell stories at parties about your fabulous returns. Owning index funds, you know you have done better than 80% of the people at the party, but no one wants to hear how you were up .5% one week, down .25% the next week. However, if you are planning on spending substantial time on your real estate portfolio or working at your job or volunteering at the shelter, index funds are an ideal choice for your stock portfolio. They require no time, not even quarterly meetings with a money manager or phone calls to an 800 number.

Biggest Risks in Index Funds

The biggest risk in a large-company index fund is that the index stocks have been overbought and are not representative of the whole market. Very few indexes are large enough to contain all the stocks in their asset class, large or small. Yet right now indexing is very popular, so there is a greater demand for stocks in the popular indexes than there is for stocks not in the indexes. The index stocks are currently selling at higher valuations than the nonindex stocks. At the start of 1999, the S&P 500 was by my calculation about 20% more expensive than other large-company stocks.

However, there are ways to hedge against this. The simplest is to buy the nonstandard index funds. The typical large-cap index fund contains the 500 stocks of the S&P 500. Probably 90% of large-cap index funds are based on the S&P 500. But there are several large-cap index funds that contain 1,000 stocks. These should hold up better if the potential sell-off were to take place.

The biggest problem for small-stock index funds is finding the right index. Some small-stock indexes represent stocks with market caps under $150 million. Others represent stocks with market caps between $500 million and $1.5 billion. Others attempt to represent every stock not in the S&P 500. For people living off their assets, the best small-stock index is one representing stocks with market caps between $500 million and $1.5 billion.

These index funds are likely to outperform mutual funds, money managers, and individuals buying stocks of this size. Since indexing is new for small-cap stocks, it cannot be said with certainty that small-cap index funds will outperform all other methods of owning small-cap stocks 80% of the time. But index funds that have market caps around $1 billion appear to be doing just that. As more and more mutual funds pour more and more time and money into investing in small-cap stocks, the small-cap market becomes more efficient and the index funds' advantage of very low costs, very low turnover, and no cash should lead them to beat the alternatives 80% of the time.

How Much Are You Willing to Risk for 4% a Year?

Some elite mutual funds, money managers, and stock gurus have managed to outperform index funds by 3% to 4% a year long term. Incompetent mutual funds, money managers, and stock gurus have lost up to 100% long term. If you knew which would be the winners and which would be the losers in the future, then you would all go for the winners and avoid the losers. Unfortunately, past performance does not guarantee future returns.

Mutual funds change managers and strategies, money managers retire or change firms, gurus get hot and cold. A mutual fund that has outperformed index funds for ten years only has a 50% chance of outperforming for the next ten years if the manager stays the same. There is only a 20% chance if the manager has changed.

Most investors living off their assets should keep most of their stock money in index funds. If you are willing to risk a 100% loss for an extra 3% to 4% a year, play with only a small percentage of your stock money.

Managed Mutual Funds

A few managed mutual funds can, if carefully picked, and with some luck, outperform index funds. These are appropriate only for aggressive investors wishing to speed up their retirement date. They are discussed in Part Three. A retired investor should stick to index funds, money managers, or individual stocks.

Using a Money Manager

I have mentioned some of the advantages of using money managers. You get personal service, you have a chance to outperform the market, and you may be able to smooth out some of the swings in the market. Another advantage is that it is easy to arrange for you to receive your living expenses on whatever basis you want.

When living off your investments, instead of having taxes withdrawn from your paycheck, you must make quarterly payments to the IRS. A money manager could be instructed to send you your regular check two out of every three months and a larger check one of every three months. Or if you have other large expenses due, like children's tuition, they can be instructed in advance to have the funds available by the needed dates. They can also be instructed to minimize your tax liabilities by selling only loss or small gain assets and by engaging in little or no portfolio turnover. Index funds and mutual funds cannot provide this degree of living expense and tax reduction service.

Who Is Not a Money Manager

Before I discuss how to find a money manager and share some of my experience with them, I want to talk about who is not a money manager. A money manager does not charge commissions on the trades he or she makes or receive a commission for buying mutual funds or for any other reasons. Money managers do not receive commissions. A money manager is paid a fee based on the assets under management. The typical fee is 1.5 % of amounts under $1,000,000 and 1% on amounts over $1,000,000 per year. Money managers have the prudent policy of requiring fees to be paid in advance. This is prudent for them as they are sure to be paid even if they lose all your money. With some money managers, the percentage to be charged may be negotiated.

A money manager has no association of any kind with any insurance company. A money manager does not take a percentage of the profits he or she makes on assets under management. Those are hedge fund managers. (See Chapter 9 for more on hedge fund managers.)

A money manager is not a broker but uses a broker to trade stocks. You will need to hire both a money manager and a broker. Many brokers will offer to manage your assets for you and save you the 1.5 % fee. *You cannot afford this offer.* A broker can and usually will run up commissions well above 1.5% in a matter of months, sometimes days. Hiring a broker to manage your stock portfolio is like hiring the clerk in the hardware store to build your house to save architect's fees. You are not going to get a long-term house or a long-term portfolio.

Usually a money manager has a graduate degree or two in business, economics, or some other money-related subject. This kind of person watches PBS and goes to the opera. A money manager is called a money manager and not a financial consultant, an account executive, an investment representative, a trust officer, a financial planner, or any other title.

How to Pick and Manage a Money Manager

- You find a real money manager by asking a stockbroker for a referral or asking a friend for a referral. They are not listed in the yellow pages. Beware that most brokerage houses have their own money management departments that have decent results but typically charge 3%. This includes commissions, but it is too expensive. Usually a broker will be happy to refer you to a real money manager because he or she wants your trades. Discount brokers have lists of money managers in your area.
- Call five different brokerage houses, and they will each give you a broker who will refer you to a different money manager. Remember that just because a broker referred you to the money manager you choose, you are not legally obligated to use that broker. You can choose the broker you are happiest with as well as the money manager you will use. If you are not happy with any of the brokers, your money manager may suggest someone.
- Most money managers have minimum amounts they will manage, often $250,000 or more. If you cannot find a money

manager who will manage the amount you want to put into U.S. stocks, then use a no-load index fund. Do not use a 3% fee brokerage house money manager.

- Interview five money managers.
- There are many things you need to find out. Many money managers handle large stocks, small stocks, bonds, cash, and foreign stocks yet only have expertise in large stocks. It will be tempting to use one money manager to handle all your assets for lower fees, but this can be costly in the long run. Find out where your manager's expertise is and where it is not. Use other money managers or other methods to handle your other asset classes. Bonds in particular are easy to handle in a long-term portfolio, so it would a waste to pay even 1% to manage them. I will discuss better alternatives in the chapter on fixed income investing.
- Get a copy of the money manager's long-term record. This sounds simple, but it is actually quite complicated. Money managers have many different types of clients: pension funds, endowment funds, wealthy retirees, wealthy young people, business people. Every client sets certain guidelines with the money manager. Pension funds may want only large stock with high dividends. A businessperson may want only small stocks with no dividends. The long-term record you need to see is of a client with needs closest to yours. Also, be sure the record you see was audited and that the record is typical. I was shown an outstanding client account that turned out to have been hyped by a series of initial public offerings allocated to it year after year to produce an actual but not typical account to show potential clients. As there were not enough shares of the initial offerings to go around, the firm always gave them to this one star portfolio.
- Ask what their biggest mistakes were in the bear markets and what have they done differently since. Every money manager makes mistakes. Look for someone who admits his mistakes and has learned from mistakes. A manager who cannot admit to mistakes is still making them.

- Many money management firms experience tremendous turnover. Hot managers start mutual funds or get hired by other firms or clients. Make sure the manager you are using is the one who has produced the record you are happy with. Often small firms with one or two lead managers stay together for decades whereas the large firms have constantly shifting personnel.

- It is also important that you can work with your money manager. You have to be able to talk frankly about your financial situation with this person, and he or she needs to be able to talk frankly with you about the realities of investing.

- The big firms with poor service do not have better investment results. In fact, it is more likely that the opposite is true. Big firms tend to buy big stocks that average 10% a year, and small firms often pay attention to small local companies that average 12% a year. Nor do big firms in New York have better information than small firms in Billings. Everybody has the same information sources plugged into their computers. The difference is how they use that information. One in ten investors is gifted in Billings, just as one in ten is gifted in New York. But they probably have more time for you in Billings. Also, big firms tend to invest by committee decision whereas small firms may have only one investor. If there is one genius on the committee, her genius will not be understood by the others, and you will get an average portfolio, not a brilliant one. At a small firm, the genius's brilliance will come through. The downside is that the incompetent's mistakes show up at a small firm as well. But this will be apparent in the audited record of the firm's typical client.

- Money management firms within brokerage houses are not a good bet because of the large fees they charge. Money management firms attached to mutual fund houses can also be problematic. Most managers at mutual fund houses handling private accounts are looking to get their own mutual fund and are not handling your money on a long-term basis. They are sometimes willing to take risks to get short-term results that will impress the firm management enough to land them their own mutual fund. These may not be the risks you, the client, are willing to take.

- Any decent small money manager can do good-quality research. Warren Buffett by himself has done better-quality research than armies of highly paid analysts. Since you do not need more than twenty stocks to outperform the market, quantities of research are not any use to individual investors.

- The most important factor in your long-term return will be your instructions to your money manager as to the asset class you want her to invest in. If you have asked for small stocks and you see the cash level in the account at 15%, then you are in two asset classes, one of which provides a very low return. You need to instruct your money manager to invest that money or place it in another account so you can invest it. A large amount of cash over time will severely hurt your results. Similarly, if you are looking for stability and large stocks, you want to see company names you are familiar with and dividends above 3%. If you have never heard of half the companies in the portfolio and few pay any dividend, then you are going to see a volatile return.

- Watch closely what your money manager does. Educate yourself and decide if you want to stick with it. I had a situation where my money manager switched from buying high-dividend large stocks to small- or no-dividend growth stocks. He had changed his investment philosophy. After talking with him and reading some investment books and going to a few seminars, I decided he was right and I stuck with him.

- It is useful to compare your results over the years to the results of an appropriate index fund and ask if you would not be better off with the index fund. Do not compare your results to the index but to the fund. You cannot buy the index, only the index fund. Are your results really less volatile or better than the index fund? If your results are not as good, put a dollar figure on that amount of deficit and ask if the personal service of a money manager has been worth that dollar figure. Be sure you have subtracted your money management fees from your results.

- Only you can decide this one. If the deficit has been large, you may want to find another money manager, phase into an index fund, or manage your stocks yourself. If the deficit is large but you cannot stand the idea of going it alone, realize you do not have to go it alone. There are fee-based financial planners whom you can pay on an hourly rate to help you. There are investment clubs, seminars, workshops, books, and other money managers. There is a lot of help out there.
- If your money manager's results are poor, try to find out why. In the typical case, the money manager consistently underperforms the relevant index fund by 1% or 2% a year. Maybe they are ahead 3% one year and behind 5% the next. What is going on? The money manager has bought fifty stocks for you to ensure diversification. Unfortunately, she has also bought a big enough sample of the universe of large or small stocks available to mimic the relevant index fund. Generally 20 stocks out of an index with 500 stocks is a sufficient sample to reproduce the result of the index. If you subtract out her fees of 1.5 % and high commissions for buying small amounts of many stocks, you realize your manager has provided you with a very expensive index fund. With this type of money management, your long-term return from large stocks will be 8% and from small stocks, 10%. The question then becomes, can you meet your spending needs with those returns? It will do no good to hope the results will get better. Your money manager comes from the diversification school or the efficient market school, whose practices over the long haul always lead to a market return less fees, commissions, and expenses. About 80% of money managers fall into this category.

How Money Managers Can Outperform the Market

To have a real chance of making up for fees, commissions, and expenses and then do better than the market, in other words, to outperform an index fund, your manager must not replicate a statistically significant portion of an index. There are three common ways to do this.

There are managers who buy stocks in ten or fewer companies that they have thoroughly researched and followed for many years. A portfolio like this can far outperform an index. But it can also far underperform an index. Here you have to carefully look at a manager's long-term record to see if she got through 1972–1974 all right and if she survived 1987. What companies did she invest in then, and how do they compare with the companies she is invested in now? With this type of manager, you are placing your faith in companies and not in the stock market, which represents the whole economy. If you need better than 12% to live on, then this is the type of manager who could conceivably help you. It may concern you that you are not diversified enough. But remember that this is only one of your asset classes.

Another technique of outperforming an index fund is to make large bets in certain industries. A manager might buy you fifty stocks, but ten will be high-tech companies, ten oil companies, and ten financial companies, with the rest scattered around. If those three industries do well, you will outperform. The manager will shift the emphasis from time to time to different industries. But again there is the risk that those industries will do poorly and you will underperform. Here you are betting on your manager's ability to predict industry and economic trends as well as to analyze individual companies. You again need to carefully look at the record. What industries did he emphasize in the past, and where is the emphasis today? Given your understanding of the economy, does the current emphasis make sense? Note that good investors are always anticipating trends. The current emphasis should be on industries that may or may not be doing well now but that will logically be doing well in the future and for a long period of time.

The third way to outperform is to concentrate on specific stock characteristics without much regard for the industry. For example, some managers will buy only "value" stocks with low price-to-book ratios and low price-to-earnings ratios, regardless of whether the company is high-tech, retail, or banking. This system has an added benefit of producing steadier returns than the overall market. Other managers buy only "growth" stocks that have rapidly increasing earnings, regardless of the industry. This system tends to have more volatile returns than the overall market. Other managers buy stocks based on their price charts.

These systems have been shown in academic studies to outperform over the long haul. The problem is some managers will fail to follow their own disciplines and begin raising cash or market timing just when their stocks are about to do well. Or they will buy so many stocks in the name of diversification that they end up with stocks that do not really meet their criteria; the results will look like those of an expensive index fund. Even where the manager follows the discipline, your portfolio of stocks may underperform for many years until its time comes and it dramatically outperforms, making up for those tough years. Here it is important that you understand what the manager is doing. It might be useful to ask for a copy of some of the academic studies the manager's system is based on to bolster your faith in the tough years. By switching managers at the wrong time, you might cost yourself a lot of money.

If, however, you want total control of your stock portfolio, buy individual stocks yourself.

Buying Individual Stocks

You may already own individual stocks. The question is whether to hold them and manage them yourself or to sell them and invest in an index fund or turn them over to a money manager. Here are some guidelines on what to do. I do not have space in this book to make more than a few suggestions.

- Manage your own stocks only if you enjoy it. Do not do it to save money. No-load index funds are the cheapest alternative. You will spend more money on brokerage commissions, research, newsletters, magazines, newspapers, seminars, workshops, books, Value Line, etc. than the fees you will spend on an index fund. And it is not likely that you will outperform an index fund. Be sure when you figure out your annual return to subtract all your expenses to get the true result.

- Put as much money as you can in an index fund and only manage yourself as little as possible. Since only 9% of U.S.

stock money is in index funds, I realize this advice will not be followed. I know for myself the attraction of outperforming the market is greater than the fear of underperforming. I also have less than one third of my assets in U.S. stocks.

- If you own twenty stocks in roughly equal proportions in twenty different industries, you will get a return very close to that of an index fund. This is a good starting strategy. This is the humility portfolio. This one decision will have a greater effect on your return than any other. You admit you are an amateur, but you still want to get at least a market return in small-cap and large-cap stocks. Most investors have done worse, many of them professionals earning high salaries and managing multiple millions of dollars.

- The twenty stocks you buy should each look like a good candidate to return 10% to 12% a year. Buy stocks that have been publicly traded at least ten years and that have made steady profits for those ten years.

- Phase into the humility portfolio from what you have now. Sell down the stocks in which you have more than 5%. Buy more of the ones in which you have less than 5%. Add a few big-cap, steady growers like Albertson's, Bank America, Bell Atlantic, Berkshire Hathaway, Carnival Corp., Citigroup, Coca-Cola, Disney, Exxon, GE, General Mills, Gillette, Intel, Johnson and Johnson, Microsoft, Newell, Pepsi, Sara Lee, Time Warner, Walgreen's, and Wal-Mart until you have roughly twenty stocks in equal proportions in twenty different industries. Only add steady growers with P/Es below the market P/E and below their average P/E of the last five years.

- Buying large, steady growers like GE and J&J is like buying excellent mutual funds. These companies are as large as large mutual funds and have as many businesses as smaller mutual funds but are better run than both large and small mutual funds. Yet you do not have to pay a mutual fund manager as well as the corporate managers to own the company. There is no extra layer of management fees and expenses as there is when you own these stocks inside mutual funds. Commissions on buying them through a discount broker are minimal. They will be easy to unload when you have found your own stocks.

- Once you have a humility portfolio assembled, then do the work to improve on it.
- Do nothing most of the time. Among professional investors, four out of five of their trades are mistakes. The fewer trades you make, the fewer mistakes you will make. Follow the do nothing rule: the less you do, the more you will make. Since you will periodically need to sell for living expenses, you are already at a disadvantage. You cannot do absolutely nothing. Try to make no more than one trade a year other than those to provide cash for living expenses.
- Avoid cyclicals, companies that are up dramatically with the economy and then down dramatically with the recessions. Steel companies, autos, and airlines are typical examples.
- Buy long-term growth companies. The best growth in the next few decades is likely to come from services, entertainment, software, computers, the Internet, health care, communications, retirement, and education. In the United States, little population growth is expected. The need for new cars, new housing, new roads, and other new infrastructure should be small. Stick with growing industries.
- Avoid stocks with heavy debt payments. Steady growers with good margins can handle long-term debt up to about 50% of capital. But you do not want to see debt levels above that. You would be better off with much less or no debt. No debt gives a company many advantages over its rivals in recessions and other times of financial stress. Low-margin businesses particularly require companies to have low debt levels.
- Never buy stocks with P/Es above 25. P/E is the price per share of a stock divided by the annual earnings per share of the stock. For example, a stock selling for $15 that earned $1 per share in 1995 had a 1995 P/E of 15. The earnings in the fraction are sometimes actual earnings, sometimes projected earnings, and sometimes a combination. It is best to rely on historical earnings when measuring P/Es. Buying and holding high P/E stocks long term is a sure way to lose money.

Over time, both the P/E and the growth rates decline and the stock prices tumble. These are appropriate only for very active investors who either like paying taxes or are trading in a tax-deferred account.

- Know the managers' record. Make sure long-term managers are still with the company and are continuing to run the company as they have in the past. Just as you want experienced money managers, you need to see experienced company managers protecting and enhancing your investment.

- There is no need to know the managers personally. You do not need to take them to lunch at their favorite restaurant. It is their record, all public information, that counts. If the record shows they are good at making acquisitions and there is one pending, then rely on the record and not what analysts assume will happen. If the record shows they have never made a major acquisition and there is one pending, do not buy the stock or, if you already own it, sell. Any major change in management strategy from a successful long-term record is a reason not to own a stock. But do not believe the headlines. Articles about reengineering, restructuring, spin-offs, and so on are often more dramatic than the minor cost cutting that is really taking place.

- Do not overanalyze a company. Many money managers and mutual fund managers know too much about a company. You are not going to run this business. You can rely on the employees of this business to figure out who the competition is and to decide what strategy to pursue. You can rely on the employees of this company to understand its markets and the economy and to make whatever adjustments are necessary. You are looking to buy stock in companies that are much better run than you would run them and have a much better understanding of their own strengths and weaknesses than you do.

- Look for companies with dominant market shares or strong niches with a long history of growth and profitability, companies like Carnival Cruise Lines, State Street Bank, or Service Corp. International. It does not matter how Carnival got to dominate the cruise business or who the competition is now.

The question is do they have the employees, the culture, and the financial ability to continue to grow? Are they, not you, on top of the market and the competition? Worrying about too many details of the business leads to buying and selling stocks frequently. This runs up taxes and commissions and eliminates any chance to outperform the market.

- Alter the humility portfolio to outperform the market. Do some research. Read academic studies. Talk to managers, employees, and customers of different companies. Compare the financial characteristics of different stocks. Join an investment club. Follow an investment newsletter or the Value Line system. Study dividend stocks, growth stocks, cyclical stocks, and value stocks for their volatility characteristics. Use your education, training, connections, and experience in any industry or trade to find the companies with the best prospects in those industries.

- When you think you have found one good, cheap stock with a lot of potential, double up on it. Put 10% of your stock money in that stock, and leave 5% in the other 18 stocks. See if your theory is working. If you find another stock, go slow. Give it a year. If it catches fire and shoots up beyond your buy range, let it go. The knowledge you have gained, that your theory works, is more valuable than what you could have gotten from one stock. Use your knowledge to buy another stock or wait for the price to come back to you. Stocks that have had spectacular runs tend to falter after about a year. It is not unusual to see a 30% drop in a very good company because it had one slow quarter.

- If your theories are working, over a period of ten years, pare your list down to eight to ten stocks. This number will give you a chance to outperform the index fund and will not take up all your time. Remember, you have other asset classes and you have a life. It may worry you that you have $100,000 in each stock. If your theories are good, that is a benefit, not a liability. Also, this is only one asset class. You have money in bonds or international funds or real estate too. Your entire portfolio is highly diversified. But do not go below eight stocks. All your bets will not come in no matter how good you are. Some diversification is necessary to ensure some of your stocks come through and to keep you in the market over the long haul. Even a genius like Warren Buffett owns more than eight stocks and businesses.

- If your theories are not working, go back to the humility portfolio or the index fund. You are developing discipline. Discipline is faith in action. Play with stocks until you find what works for you and then demonstrate your faith in what you have found by sticking to it year after year.

- Every year, compare your results to what you would have gotten with the index fund. Remember to subtract your expenses. You will want to keep track of them because many of them are tax deductible. Do not bother to keep track of your results every month or every quarter. Those time periods are too short to judge your results. You are trying to develop a long-term theory to live off the rest of your life.

Living Off the Humility Portfolio—Selling to Meet Expenses

Every time you have to sell stock to meet your expenses, you get to evaluate all your companies and your portfolio strategy. If you own twenty stocks and need 5% of your money for spending, you will have an opportunity to either sell parts of several stocks or eliminate entirely one or two stocks. This is a time to think about adding new names to your portfolio. If you are serious about getting down to eight to ten really good selections, then you should not add a new name unless you get rid of two or three. I am convinced that this discipline forced on me by the need to raise spending money has annually improved my stock selection.

Many mutual fund managers and money managers have constantly increasing pools of money coming their way. As a result, they add new names to their list year after year and get more and more mediocre returns year after year. Because they are not forced to prune their portfolio, they keep both their best stocks and their worst stocks and they add both excellent selections and poor selections. As both the stock list and the employee list increase, the manager loses touch with quality. A genius like Peter Lynch could handle a huge list and huge staff, but most managers cannot.

No matter what form you use to invest in U.S. stocks, they should comprise less than one third of your portfolio. In the 1990s the U.S. market was the best of the world's major markets. In the 1980s the Japanese and Asian tiger markets were the best in the world. What will be the best stock market over the next three decades? There is no way to know. But chances are good it won't be the U.S. market. Foreign stocks and emerging market stocks may be a good alternative choice for up to one third of your portfolio.

chapter six

Foreign
Stocks and
Emerging Market
Stocks

Foreign stocks and emerging market stocks have never been considered appropriate for a retired investor. There are several reasons
for this. Few investment advisors have ever lived off their assets.
They do not realize from actual experience how non–U.S. stocks
can provide needed returns in a year when all the other asset classes
decline. Retired investors must pay their bills every year, not just
years when the U.S. markets do well. Also, until recently, commission-based advisors did not sell any non–U.S. products. And, until
recently, there was little understanding of non–U.S. market trends
and few no-load products available.

Before we fully consider whether non–U.S. stocks are appropriate for the retired investor, let's define the two major classes of
non–U.S. stocks.

Definition of Foreign Stocks and Emerging
Market Stocks

For the purposes of this book, I am defining foreign stocks as publicly traded stocks of companies headquartered in developed countries other than the United States. The developed countries are
Australia, Austria, Belgium, Canada, Denmark, Finland, France,
Germany, Italy, Japan, Luxembourg, Netherlands, Norway, Spain,

Sweden, Switzerland, and the United Kingdom. Emerging market stocks are the publicly traded stocks of all other countries with freely functioning stock markets. This includes places that are relatively developed like Hong Kong or Taiwan and countries emerging from communism like Poland and the Czech Republic. It includes China, India, and the rest of Asia, all of South America, Central America, and Africa (provided the country has a stock market) as well as economic laggards on the edge of Europe and the United States like Greece, Turkey, Portugal, and Mexico. Many of these countries used to be called "third world," but to promote sales of mutual funds that invest in these countries, fund promoters began calling these "emerging" markets. After the Mexican market collapse at the end of 1994 brought down many of these markets, I started calling these "submerging" markets.

The developed countries generally have highly liquid stock markets and many multinational companies that do significant business in the United States. Companies like Nestlé, Shell, Toyota, Canal, Sony, and Canon are household names in the United States. The emerging markets tend to do less business with the United States and more with regional trading partners. They have fewer multinational companies. Their stock markets tend to be dominated by huge local businesses and conglomerates, often banks, telephone companies, real estate and finance companies, and commodity producers. Over eighty emerging countries have stock markets, but some of them are rarely used.

Currently emerging market stocks are less than 15% of the total world stock capitalization. Ten years ago they were less than 10%. Emerging markets are growing rapidly and in the next twenty-five years will equal or surpass the capitalization of the developed markets.

Just as small-company U.S. stocks become large-company U.S. stocks, emerging markets can become developed markets. Japan had no economy following World War II, and thirty years later was a leading economy of the world. Today, Japan is seeking to become an emerging market again. As much as one fourth of its economy needs to be restructured. This would triple the unemployment rate, but lead to strong long-term growth. To prevent this, the Japanese are willing to put their entire economy at risk. South Korea has developed a major stock market, but the crash of its currency and economy in 1997–98 has proven it is not yet a true developed market.

Are Non–U.S. Stocks Appropriate for a Retired Investor?

Non–U.S. stocks are appropriate for a retired investor because they can be relied on for positive long-term returns and because their returns are not correlated with the returns on U.S. assets. Returns on foreign stocks have been particularly good over the last thirty years. European stock markets have had annual returns of 15% versus annual returns of 14% for the U.S. stock markets. Japan has been the laggard with returns of 9%. Still, Japan had solid, positive returns. Emerging markets have had even higher annual returns over the last thirty years. What kind of returns could a retired investor expect from non–U.S. stocks over the next thirty years?

Expected Returns versus Historical Returns
In Chapter 2, I wrote that foreign stocks will return 10% a year and emerging market stocks will return 14% a year. These are the returns in U.S. dollars. The actual returns over the past fifty years have been higher. The actual returns for foreign stocks, including Europe and Japan, have been 14% a year and for emerging market stocks closer to 18% a year. But it is unlikely that these returns will materialize over the next fifty years.

Many countries in the foreign category were emerging from the devastation of World War II and from extremely regulated monarchial economies. Japan, Germany, and France fifty years ago were less developed than Poland, Turkey, or Indonesia are today. Now that these countries are fully developed, it is unlikely that they can grow as quickly as they have in the last fifty years.

In recent years, foreign stocks, except Japan, have done about as well as U.S. stocks. Given that foreign economies on average are about as developed as the U.S. economy, it is likely that foreign stocks will return about the same. There will be large differences between countries as there always have been and opportunities to profit from these differences. But for your purposes it would be foolish to believe that for the rest of your life you will get 14% a year from Japan, Germany, and France. The figure of 10% is one you can rely on based on both prior U.S. returns and likely returns in developed countries.

An argument can be made that foreign stocks will do better than U.S. large-company stocks over the next ten years. European and Japanese companies are just beginning the process of restructuring, downsizing, computerizing, and creating shareholder value that U.S. companies have been in for more than ten years. While this process may result in better stock market returns in Europe and Japan over the next decade, there is no reason to believe these markets will return 14% over the long term.

Emerging market stocks can be relied on to return 14% a year. They have considerable room to develop, and, if they follow rational policies, there is no reason to believe they will not do as well as Japan, Germany, and France over the past fifty years. As a country emerges from a command economy or a state or elite economy, a severe recession or a depression is usually experienced. But this downturn can then be followed by decades of growth in excess of 5% a year. This was the experience of Japan, Germany, Korea, and Taiwan. It is currently happening in China, New Zealand, Chile, Malaysia, and Thailand. It may yet be the experience of Russia, the Czech Republic, Argentina, Mexico, Poland, and Brazil.

Paul Krugman, a professor of economics at MIT, has compared the growth of Asian economies in the last twenty years to the growth of the Russian economy under communism. Essentially, he argues that the growth is based on putting more people to work and adding more capital investment. Once the additions of labor and capital stop, the growth will stop unless productivity improves. He states that Asians have shown no clear signs of productivity improvement. For your purposes, this does not matter. There are many underdeveloped countries to invest in. If one stagnates, you can shift to another. Over your lifetime, you very well may see African countries added to the list of those putting people to work and adding more capital investment. As long as such countries exist, you can expect to get 14% a year from investing in a diversified group. If these countries can figure out how to improve their productivity, then your grandchildren will also get 14% a year from investing there.

How Will Your Return Be Affected by the Dollar?

The returns you can expect are measured in U.S. dollars. The exchange rate against other currencies has already been factored into the returns of the last fifty years. Factoring in exchange rates over the next fifty years should be either neutral or beneficial to your returns.

There are three things you need to know about the dollar.

1. If the dollar goes up against foreign currencies, the value of your foreign stocks and emerging market stocks goes down.
2. If the dollar goes down, the value of your foreign stocks and emerging market stocks goes up.
3. Over the course of your lifetime, the value of the dollar will gradually go down.

The dollar has been declining against foreign currencies for decades. Many readers can remember when European travel was cheap. College students went to Europe for bargains as they go to Mexico today. Now European travel is as expensive as American travel. It used to be that European roads were bad and toilets worse and hotels run down. Do you remember the cardboard toilet paper? But the food was cheap and wonderful. Now there are autobahns and first class hotels and ridiculously expensive restaurants. The bathrooms still need a little work.

As a country develops relative to the United States, its currency appreciates relative to the dollar. The process has many ups and downs, but the long-term trend is inevitable. Many developed country currencies are already at or near parity with the dollar, as are their economies at parity with our economy. Emerging market currencies have a long way to go, as do their economies. But someday Mexico will have an economy as strong as ours and the peso will move up against the dollar as a result. College students will have to go to Africa for the bargains.

The United States is also the world's biggest debtor, and we have the lowest savings rate among developed and developing economies. As a country, we borrow money from abroad to fuel our current consumption of products manufactured abroad. Spending money you do not have on products you do not make can only lead to cheapening the value of that money against other currencies.

The dollar is also likely to lose its value as a reserve currency. Each country holds on to foreign currency as a reserve to protect its trade and currency regime. Also, many international companies hold foreign currency reserves and foreign asset reserves to hedge their business risks. At the start of 1999, more than half of these reserves were U.S. dollars. As the Euro gains in importance in trade and finance, dollars will be sold and Euros held in reserve. As economies other than the Euro group grow faster than the U.S. economy, their currencies will become more important as reserves as well.

These long-term processes are very beneficial if you invest in foreign stocks and emerging market stocks. Even if the stock markets are flat, over time you will make money on the currency. Short-term fluctuations will cause you to question these trends. But as you are lifetime investors, you will see many benefits from them if you stay fully invested and do not market-time or raise cash in your foreign stock or emerging market stock portfolios.

Staying fully invested will also lead to one of the best benefits of non–U.S. stocks. Non–U.S. stocks are excellent investments for retired investors because they can have up years when all your other asset classes have down years.

Foreign and Emerging Markets Are Not Correlated with U.S. Assets

You will benefit from both foreign stocks and emerging market stocks in years when all your other asset classes are flat or down.

Foreign Stocks versus U.S. Assets

Since most large foreign companies have significant sales in the United States and since foreign businesses and consumers are significant buyers of American goods and services, the return on foreign stocks is somewhat correlated to the returns on U.S. stocks.

Most years when the U.S. stock market is up, foreign stocks are up. Most years the United States is down, foreign stocks are down. But the correlation is not as tight as that between large-cap U.S. stocks and small-cap U.S. stocks. Diversification into foreign stocks is still quite significant.

Since the introduction of the European Common Market, Europe's exchange rate mechanism, and now the Euro, European economies and stock markets have become more correlated with Germany and less with the United States. The exception is the United Kingdom, which continues to have significant trade and investment in the United States. The U.K. stock market is more correlated with the U.S. market than with other European stock markets. The Canadian market is even more closely correlated with the U.S. market because of the significant trade links, though the correlation is still not as great as that between U.S. small and large stocks.

There is very little correlation between Japanese stocks and U.S. stocks. While U.S. stocks more than tripled in the 1990s, Japanese stocks lost more than half their value. But in the 1950–1990 period, Japanese stocks far outperformed U.S. stocks. Today, with Japanese stocks very cheap and U.S. stocks very expensive, it is likely there will be many years in the next thirty when Japanese stocks will be up and U.S. stocks flat or down. Japan holds one third of the world's savings, almost entirely in low-interest savings accounts. If any significant amount of this money makes its way into the Japanese stock market, there could be a rally lasting many years.

Foreign stocks have very little correlation to returns on other U.S. assets. A portfolio holding U.S. bonds, U.S. real estate, and foreign stocks is much more diversified than a portfolio of U.S. bonds, U.S. real estate, and U.S. stocks. The first portfolio is less likely to have down years than the second. When structuring a portfolio, choosing foreign stocks over U.S. small-cap or large-cap stocks can provide steadier performance without reducing your return.

Emerging Market Stocks versus U.S. Assets
Emerging market stock returns are rarely correlated with U.S. stock returns. Most emerging market business is local or regional.

In 1993 the typical emerging market was up 70% while the U.S. stock market was up about 13%. In 1995 the typical emerging market was down 5% while the U.S. stock market was up about 35%. In 1998 the typical emerging market was down more than 20% while the U.S. stock market was up more than 20%. This lack of correlation is very beneficial to you. Since you are looking for a steady long-term return on your total portfolio, it is important to own some asset class or classes that are not correlated to the others. This increases the likelihood that when the United States is in the tank, for example, because interest rates have risen by 3% or more, and your U.S. stocks, U.S. bonds, and U.S. real estate are all off, some other asset like emerging market stocks can keep you going. Foreign stocks can also serve this function but not to the extent of emerging market stocks.

Emerging markets that trade a lot with the United States or have currencies linked to the U.S. dollar are more correlated with U.S. markets than the others, but the correlation is still slight. Currently, only Hong Kong and Argentina have currencies directly linked to the dollar. Often currencies that are tied to the U.S. dollar do not stay that way. A political or economic crisis can lead to a floating exchange rate overnight. The Mexican peso has been linked and unlinked with the U.S. dollar many times. Under NAFTA, Mexico may someday ride the same economic and market cycles as the U.S., but this is many years off.

Volatility in Emerging Market Stocks

Unfortunately, emerging market stocks are also very volatile. They can be and often are up 50% one year and down 25% the next. And there are no guarantees that the up years will occur when the U.S. market is down and vice versa. Foreign stocks are more volatile than U.S. stocks but nothing like emerging market stocks. In recent years, large-company U.S. stocks have typically swung up or down 25%. Mexican stocks have swung up or down 70%.

The great volatility in emerging market stocks does not mean they are unsafe investments. In fact most of the best investments in emerging market stocks are conservatively managed, monopoly or near-monopoly businesses that will grow regardless of the fluctuations in the stock market. Some of these companies are practically sure things over the long haul. For example, there are telephone companies that have government-protected market share in growing economies where currently one in ten households has a phone but one in three can now afford a phone. There are rock and cement companies that own all the available supply in countries rapidly building their infrastructure.

The fluctuation in the stock price of these businesses is sometimes due to currency fluctuations and local politics. Local politics were particularly negative for emerging markets when the Soviet Union was promoting civil wars and socialist regimes around the world. With the end of the Soviet Union, one big factor of volatility has been removed. There is also political volatility as dictatorships give way to various stages of democracy. Though these developments create volatility, they also lead to positive long-term stock returns.

In recent years, the whims of international mutual funds, pension funds, and hedge funds have been the biggest cause of volatility. Many emerging markets have inactive local stock markets. Some shares trade less than once a month. When big American, European, and Japanese investors buy huge quantities of stock or currency or dump huge quantities of stock or currency, these small markets are overwhelmed.

None of these causes of volatility will ultimately prevent large, dominant local companies from growing and their stock prices eventually reflecting that growth. While emerging market stock prices have moved up with great volatility over the last twenty-five years, foreign direct investment in emerging markets has increased steadily year after year. The confidence of direct investors in emerging markets can be shared by stock investors as well. Long term they can expect the highest returns of all the liquid asset classes.

Diversify as Stock Markets Can Disappear

Diversifying is very important in emerging market investing. In the United States, companies can suddenly go into bankruptcy and the stock become worthless. But entire countries can also go bankrupt and their stocks disappear.

Stocks are pieces of paper or electronic blips on computer screens that can be sold in a stock market for cash. History has shown that markets disappear and the pieces of paper or electronic blips cannot be unloaded at any price. The New York Stock Exchange has been open since 1792. But in Europe, stock markets have disappeared at least twice in the 1900s. Many emerging markets are only now getting their first stock markets. There are no guarantees they will last. Companies can be nationalized and their stocks made worthless even though the business continues and the market remains open for other stocks.

It is a mistake, though, to see all emerging stock markets as the same. Some, like those in Singapore and Hong Kong, are highly developed and liquid. The average citizen of these countries is much more likely to own stock than the average German. The key is to own many stocks in many different emerging markets. This will be discussed further below. Through diversification, you will have some great stocks and countries, some awful stocks and countries, and a solid thirty-year return.

Emerging market stock returns are not correlated with returns on other U.S. asset classes. If you want to pick an asset class to diversify an all–U.S. portfolio, emerging market stocks are your best choice. For example, the returns on emerging market stocks and U.S. real estate are on completely different cycles. Both are subject to local economic conditions. Any similarity in their cycles is coincidence. If all your U.S. assets decline, you may still get terrific returns on your Polish stocks.

How Much Should You Invest in Foreign and Emerging Market Stocks?

Whereas U.S. stocks have outperformed their long-term trends over the past ten years, foreign stocks and emerging market stocks have underperformed their trends. There is a modest interest by investors in foreign stocks and emerging market stocks, but nothing like the flood of funds into U.S. stocks. Foreign stocks and emerging market stocks are not as ignored as U.S. real estate is right now. But if I had to guess where markets are likely to do better than their long-term averages over the next ten years, I would certainly put emerging market stocks and foreign stocks ahead of U.S. stocks.

Opportunity to Invest in Young People

As very long-term investors, there is a danger in investing in an all–U.S. portfolio. The danger is as follows: in twenty years or so, the baby boom generation will retire and begin selling off assets to meet their expenses. All their assets will be U.S. assets. As the generations following the baby boom are much smaller, there will be fewer U.S. buyers than sellers of these assets. All U.S. asset prices will therefore decline, and the decline will last for more than a decade. No investors will make their living expenses anymore, much less their inflation adjustment.

This could happen in the United States. Owning substantial non–U.S. assets is the solution. Outside the United States, the demographic situation is very different.

Investing internationally allows you to own stock in many nations with young populations that will reach their prime investment buying years just as U.S. baby boomers retire. Though there will be ups and downs, many Asian, South American, and even African investments will have tremendous decades between now and 2050. For example, India, Indonesia, Brazil, and Argentina will have huge investment buying middle classes in 2025. The best way to take advantage of these buyers in the future is to purchase emerging market stocks now.

Most readers will do well by putting significant amounts of their assets in either foreign stocks or emerging market stocks. But do not put more than one third of your assets in non–U.S. stocks. However, the 5% to 10% that many advisors recommend is not worth your time and effort. If 95% of your assets have a down year and only your 5% in emerging market stocks have an up year, you are not likely to make your inflation target. If you have five asset classes and one fifth or 20% are invested in emerging market stocks, you could break even with decent returns in the emerging markets.

If you intend to use non–U.S. stocks as one of your asset classes, an investment of up to one third of your portfolio is appropriate. Here is how to make that purchase.

How to Buy Foreign Stocks and Emerging Market Stocks

To get the full benefits of international investing there are two reasonable choices:

1. Use the best mutual fund or money manager available.
2. Buy individual stocks either as American depository receipts (ADRs) or through local country brokerage accounts.

U.S. Multinational Companies Are Not the Same

There is a notion pushed on the public by commissioned brokers and others that buying stock of multinational companies is the same as investing in foreign and emerging market companies. This is not true. U.S.–based multinational company stocks perform in line with the U.S. market. Their returns are nearly identical. Why? These stocks dominate the Dow Jones Industrial Average, the Standard and Poor's 500, and all the other U.S. large-cap indexes and markets. Buying these stocks provides no asset class diversification from buying U.S. stocks. Buying foreign and emerging market mutual funds does provide diversification.

Mutual Funds

Whereas managed mutual funds are not appropriate for living off your assets when investing in the U.S. stock market, they are a very good choice for investing in foreign and emerging markets. These markets are not yet dominated by institutional investors. There is an opportunity for good money managers to outperform index funds on a regular basis. Here is how to pick and monitor international funds that meet your needs.

- Buy broad-based funds. Every country has its own economic and stock market peculiarities. In some countries small stocks have done better over long time periods. In others large stocks and conglomerates have not just done better but have monopolies. In some countries only certain stocks and stock funds can be purchased by outsiders. Currencies fluctuate, politicians come and go. Selecting individual country funds or industry funds would require extensive research of local economies and trends. Choosing between small-cap funds and large-cap funds in foreign markets and emerging markets complicates the process without adding to your returns. It is best to hire a mutual fund manager with many years of experience, a huge worldwide staff, and contacts. Based on their extensive research, let them make the decisions on how to allocate between countries, regions, industries, and stock sizes.

- Buy only no-load funds. Be sure the fund has no load of any kind.
- Begin by making a list of no-load foreign stock funds or emerging market funds that have been in existence at least ten years. Then make the following comparisons. Compare foreign funds to foreign funds and emerging market funds to emerging market funds. Morningstar is a good source of data.
- Compare the results of each for the past ten years to the average foreign or emerging market fund and not to EAFE. Select the five funds with the highest ten-year returns.
- Make sure each of these five funds has a local presence in most of the markets in which it owns stock. Eliminate any funds that do not.
- Make sure these five funds have the same management team in place that produced the ten-year record. Eliminate any funds that do not.
- Rank your five funds in terms of turnover, the lowest turnover being the highest ranking. Many countries withhold taxes on sales of stock by foreigners, and many foreign brokers charge much higher fees than U.S. brokers. In taxable accounts, you will already be creating capital gains as you sell shares of the fund to live, so keeping taxes and expenses low is important.
- Rank your funds in terms of management fees, the lowest fees being the highest ranking. Due to the expense of running a worldwide company, management fees already are high for foreign mutual funds. So look for low turnover and low management fees.

- Study the criteria set out for U.S. mutual funds beginning on page 226. Eliminate any funds that do not meet these criteria.
- From the funds not eliminated, buy up to three funds ranked first by return, second by turnover, and third by management fees.
- It may be difficult to fill your list of no-load emerging market funds. Very few have been around more than ten years. If you have difficulty finding funds that have been around for ten years, look for managers who have been investing actively in emerging markets more than ten years.
- Compare returns of less than ten years to the same-year returns of the other funds you find. For example, compare a return from 1994–1999 with the same return even if one of the funds has been in existence since 1989.
- Do not compare the records of broad-based emerging market funds with the records of regional or single-country funds. This is often done in the magazines.
- Due to the size of international markets, it is fine to select two or three funds in each category. There are so many stocks and so much opportunity to find great bargains in international investing that it is unlikely that your funds will cancel out each other's results and become an expensive index fund. However, do not buy more than three funds. You will want to monitor your international funds quarterly, paying attention to changes in management and country allocation. If you own too many funds, this process will be time consuming and confusing.
- There are several things to watch for when monitoring your international funds. Make sure the fund holds only a small amount of cash, 10% or less of assets. Holding 5% in cash would be ideal. You do not want a market-timer or cash raiser.
- Avoid funds that hedge currency to a significant degree. Twenty percent of assets is significant.
- When funds change managers, they often change investment styles. New managers may start raising cash and market-timing. If you see this, immediately change funds. New managers may start shifting from emerging market stocks to foreign stocks or vice versa. Usually this just happens at the edges, 5%

to 10% of the portfolio, and does not have a big effect on the returns. But some funds have changed character entirely and gone from 90% foreign stocks to 90% emerging market stocks.

- How can you tell the fund has changed character? Every six months you will get a list of all the stocks owned by the fund, the percentage in each country, plus the cash and bond position. Keep a chart of this. Do not rely on the written report that precedes this information. Often the report will say something like, "we reduced your exposure to Japan as prospects have deteriorated there." Yet your chart will show that Japan went from 30% to 29%. With the Japanese market down 10%, no change in the Japan position should have reduced Japan to 27% of the fund. The fund must have bought stock in Japan to keep above 27%. Or the report says nothing about Latin America, but your chart shows the fund went from all foreign stocks to 10% Mexico and 10% Argentina just before those two markets crashed.

- Chart your fund's country weighting all the years you own it. This will alert you to any change in character in the fund. In 1989 many foreign funds had more than 50% of their assets in Japan. If you knew that and did not want to own a Japan fund, you could have gotten out. In 1999, many foreign funds have as much as 80% of their assets in Europe. If you kept your chart and did not want a Europe fund, you could have gotten out in 1998.

By 2010 Index Funds Will Outperform

Index funds would be ideal for foreign stock, but there are no adequate ones. The major foreign stock index is the EAFE. This index, put together by Morgan Stanley, contains 1200 stocks and is more than one third Japan. Most experts believe that Japan is overweighted in the index and that 1200 stocks is too many to hold in an index fund. A few quasi-index funds try to imitate the EAFE by owning a few hundred representative stocks, but these too are heavily Japanese. Eventually, an adequate index fund will be developed that will be a good investment for you. The institutional investors who predominantly buy big stocks will soon dominate foreign stock buying. Then the advantages of low fees and no turnover will make index funds the best long-term holding. But it is many years before emerging stock index funds will make sense.

Emerging market stocks indexes are new. Emerging market stock index funds are even newer. No one believes an adequate index fund for emerging market stocks has yet been developed. As there are restrictions on foreigners investing in markets such as Chile, India, and Korea, many indexes exclude these countries. Yet you as long-term investors will do especially well in these countries.

Emerging markets are inefficient markets where outperforming the average is not just possible but likely. In the United States, 80% of mutual funds underperform an index fund. In emerging markets, even if there were an adequate index developed, it is quite likely that most professional money managers would outperform the index. Most local investors in emerging countries are not sophisticated and information is often available only to a few investors. Sophisticated, aggressive investors have a real advantage in these markets.

Foreign stocks also are not efficiently priced. In Germany and most of continental Europe, investors favor bonds over stocks. This has resulted in little first-class stock research in Europe. The few professional money managers who do their research have an advantage. But this is changing rapidly.

The postwar European generation now understands the long-term advantage of stocks over bonds. Many family-owned businesses are becoming public as the founders die or retire. And all countries are privatizing by floating stock of once government-controlled businesses. By 2010, it is likely that European markets will be dominated by institutional investors forced to buy primarily large-cap stocks as in the United States today. This will then give the advantage to the lowest fee and lowest turnover strategy, the index fund.

Japan should see a similar transformation. As the deregulation of the financial system allows more and better research organizations to compete in Japan, they will first outperform other investors and then become the norm. The Japanese public will soon realize postal savings will not get them through retirement and will return to the stock market they left in 1989. By 2010, indexes will have the advantage of lower fees and lower turnover.

Similar trends can be expected in the emerging markets. Therefore, for any new additions to your foreign stock funds and emerging market funds after the year 2005, buy index funds.

Money Managers

Investing through a money manager is also an appropriate way to buy foreign and emerging market stocks. Be sure to use a money manager who specializes in international stocks and has done so for at least ten years. They are scarce but can be found. Do not let a U.S. stock manager handle individual international stocks for you. Those who dabble in international stocks and would be willing to put together a portfolio for you are to be avoided. If they want to buy Japanese stocks for you, take them to a Japanese restaurant to discuss it. If they cannot speak fluent Japanese to the waiter they have no chance of understanding a Japanese stock report.

Go back to page 90 and review the criteria beginning there for selecting a money manager for U.S. stocks. Adjust the criteria as follows:

- Look for large firms with significant international offices and contacts rather than local firms.
- Compare the firm's ten-year results to a large international mutual fund and not to EAFE. This comparison will give you a realistic idea of what you could be getting with an alternative strategy.
- Many of the large international mutual fund houses have individual money managers. Consider these money managers for international investments, though not for U.S. stocks.

If neither mutual funds nor money managers meet your needs for buying foreign and emerging market stocks, consider buying individual stocks yourself.

Individual Stocks

This is the area where more money can be made than any other discussed in this book. There are unbelievable opportunities in individual stocks outside the United States. With enough research and travel, it is realistic to achieve returns of 20% a year over the long term. But for every opportunity to make outstanding returns, there are equal opportunities to lose money.

Foreign investing is very complicated. Accounting rules, labor relations, and borrowing costs are different in every country. Government regulation differs widely, as do requirements for disclosing information to shareholders. Taxes, consumer preferences, political stability, and inflation rates are different in every country. Business management differs, and so do share settlement rules, share custody rules, and stock analysis. Morality in business and government is different in every country. All these factors and more affect stock prices.

Here is how to buy individual non–U.S. stocks without losing your family, friends, and sanity.

- Turn the rest of your assets over to a money manager or put them in mutual funds or other long-term passive investments. Buy only individual foreign stocks and emerging market stocks if you plan on spending the bulk of your time in this area. The rewards can be large. But there is a huge amount to learn in order to do this successfully.

- Do not put everything into these asset classes. It is difficult to live off individual foreign stocks and emerging market stocks alone because of settlement delays and tax-withholding problems. Also, individual stocks are more volatile than broad-based mutual funds. Stay with three to five asset classes. Spend your time here because you enjoy it, find it fascinating even, and hope to achieve fabulous returns. But do not risk it all. Remember Japan spent the entire 1990s in a bear market. The world's best investors have ten-year losses in Japan.

- Buy at least five stocks in ten different counties. This amount of diversification will ensure an average return in spite of potential stock liquidations, political crisis, currency collapse, bizarre accounting rules, and so on. This is your international humility portfolio.

- Start with some mutual funds to ensure you are getting an average return while you do your research. Phase into fifty

stocks over a few years. Then, a few years later, as you understand what you are doing, pare your list down to no fewer
than twenty. With twenty stocks, you will not get the average
return from international investing. If your research and theories are good, you could get 20% or more per year on your
investments.

- It is best to open a foreign stock account and buy stock in foreign and emerging market companies directly. This will
lessen the influence of the U.S. market on the price of the
stocks you buy. It will also give you access to many more bargains. Most foreign and emerging market stocks are neither
ADRs nor pink sheet ADRs.

- There are two types of stock that can be purchased from U.S.
brokers. The first are standard American depository receipts.
These ADRs must file financial statements that comply with
U.S. generally accepted accounting principles. This is helpful. Unfortunately, three fourths of all ADRs are the second
type, pink sheet ADRs. These companies only need to file an
English translation of their annual reports within six months
of the end of their fiscal year. These annual reports may
make no sense to you. Companies with booming sales show
consistent losses. Why? Expenses that we capitalize and take
over many years are written off immediately to avoid current
taxes. Reserves are set up for contingencies that do not seem
real, again to avoid taxes or to assuage local politicians who
are clamoring about the gouging of the people by the company or the industry.

- Although ADRs represent shares of foreign and emerging
market companies, they often trade as if they were U.S.
stocks. The ADRs of the largest international companies
tend to go up and down with the U.S. market. Many U.S.
mutual funds, pension plans, and other large investors own
ADRs. When they have to put hundreds of millions of dollars in the market in a bull run, they buy ADRs just as indis-
criminately as they buy U.S. stocks. When they panic, they
sell ADRs just like they sell everything else. Ultimately, the

underlying business of the company will determine its stock price. But this can take many years.

- You must have a local contact. Only locals and experienced foreigners who spend considerable time in the local environment will do well. For example, a study by the International Monetary Fund showed that before the Mexican markets collapsed at the end of 1994, local Mexican investors sold out. It was foreign investors who were too late and took losses in dollar terms of 50% and more. Interestingly, several emerging market funds that spend substantial time in Mexico also sold out early. But big U.S. stock mutual funds that were dabbling in Mexico got hurt.

- There is excellent information available on overseas stocks. But you have to go there to get it. The Internet will not do. Certain locals have the best information. It is not like the United States. Here most information is so widely dispersed as to be meaningless. Hundreds of analysts have run the same numbers hundreds of different times on every company. The only remaining advantage you can have in U.S. investing is the humility to buy an index fund.

- Do not rely solely on company reports, news reports, company visits, and local contacts for your research. There are many knowledgeable analysts and stock pickers who have contacts and experience that can benefit you. For example, John Dessauer prints a monthly newsletter of his international stock picks. These reports are not free but can more than pay for themselves in time savings and insight. Use all the help you can get in this area. This investing is both tricky and rewarding. Do not hesitate to go back to mutual funds if you get overwhelmed. This is what I did. You will still get good returns. You can phase back to individual stocks later.

chapter seven

Real Estate

Real estate is a very big subject. The value of all commercial real estate in the U.S. is more than $8 trillion. It is very important that you focus on what you want to get from this asset class. The business is dominated by people looking for 6% commissions, management fees, finder's fees, and loan fees. You need to have clear goals so you can minimize these fees and maximize your returns. Let's start with the big question.

Is Real Estate Appropriate for a Retired Investor?

Most investors these days are focused on stocks. There are many arguments as to why the bull market in U.S. stocks and foreign stocks has decades to go. The main argument is that the baby boomer generation in the United States and Europe is now saving for retirement rather than spending and they will put all their savings in stocks and bonds, driving up those markets for twenty years. Now it is true that some baby boomers are saving for retirement. Some, however, are not. But there is no reason to believe that the savers will put all their savings in stocks and bonds. This has not been the case with prior generations.

Many generations have believed that the surest path to retirement security is to buy income-producing real estate. My grandmother's generation, who saw stock prices decline by 90% between 1929 and 1933, retired on income-producing real estate and bonds. My grandmother lived comfortably more than twenty-five years on the cash flow from the Piggly Wiggly building. But she was not a blind faith believer in real estate. In the 1970s when real estate was considered a sure thing, as stocks are today, she reminded every-one of the 1930s. "The Doctor and I," she used to say, "built our dream house for $42,000 in 1927. When we sold it in 1938 we got only $18,000." My father's generation, who saw both bonds and stocks lose more than 60% of their value in the 1970s, also retired on income-producing real estate.

At the end of a bad investment cycle, real estate is a better asset class than stocks. When a corporation goes under, all that is left is an empty bank account. When a building goes under, what is left is an empty building.

An investment in retirement housing today should produce good returns until the demise of the baby boom generation. An investment in U.S. stocks now will have questionable returns as soon as the baby boomers retire and begin selling shares to make their mortgage and rent payments on their retirement housing. Real estate can be an excellent retirement investment.

Your Five Requirements

Real estate is an excellent retirement asset if it can meet five criteria.

1. A different cycle than your other asset classes.
2. A predictable total return over your lifetime of 10% or more per year.
3. Lower tax expenses than other assets held in taxable accounts.
4. The availability of easy, low-cost management if you wish to spend your time elsewhere.
5. The possibility of larger gains if you spend more time on these assets.

A Different Cycle Than Other Asset Classes

In general, real estate and stocks of the same country are on different cycles. There is a fundamental reason. Real estate is the second biggest expense of business after wages. When real estate prices and rents are down, profits have room to move up. When profits rise, stock prices rise. When real estate prices and rents are up, profits get squeezed. When profits are squeezed, stock prices go down.

Real estate returns are primarily determined by local market conditions. (This will be discussed in more detail starting on page 143.) Each market has different conditions that will determine returns. The office market in major California cities did poorly in the 1980s because of oversupply. The housing market soared. Lack of land, neighborhood groups, and zoning restrictions kept the supply of housing down while a robust economy and huge population growth increased the demand. Stock prices are primarily subject to national economic conditions. There is no significant correlation between the returns on a strip shopping center in Cleveland and an S&P 500 index fund. An individual property can be its own market. An office building with long-term leases can provide excellent returns when the building next door is losing tenants daily to the local recession.

In the 1970s and early 1980s, it was believed that real estate did best in times of high inflation and stocks did best in times of low inflation. Real estate was supposed to always do better than inflation. When the office vacancy rate in many cities rose above 20% in the mid-1980s, the price of office buildings began to decline. Yet new office buildings planned in the early 1980s and financed in the mid-1980s were being built. Most of these office buildings are worth less today than the cost of building them, yet inflation has gone up every year since 1980. The laws of supply and demand determine the price of assets, not inflation. Inflation is a result of supply and demand not a cause of it. In order to keep pace with inflation, you need to invest in assets that have good supply and demand characteristics.

Real estate returns are subject to the supply and demand of investment capital. (Beginning on page 80 I discussed this in some detail.) Since the economy every year produces a limited amount of excess capital that can be used for investments, rarely do all asset classes rise together. When one asset class does well, it gets press coverage and this leads to more demand. Institutions as well as individuals are investing in stocks today. Fifteen years ago institutions and individuals were investing in real estate. Over ten- to fifteen-year periods, the demand for one asset class can build to excess while another asset class is ignored. Then the popular class collapses and the other surges. I have no ability to predict when the shifts will occur. All you have to know is that over your lifetime, the shift will occur many times. Your best strategy is to stay invested in both asset classes at all times.

Real estate and bonds are on similar cycles. Real estate is a capital-intensive business. Most buildings are purchased with borrowed money. Borrowing costs affect both bonds and real estate. When interest rates increase, both bond owners and real estate owners are hurt. When interest rates decline, both bond owners and real estate owners benefit. However, real estate is subject to many more factors than bonds. For example, the price of lumber or the supply of construction workers affects real estate prices and not bonds. The real estate and bond cycles are related but not the same.

U.S. real estate and foreign stocks and emerging market stocks are on completely different cycles. There are very few factors that affect both asset classes equally. The most diversified portfolio you could own would be part real estate, part emerging market stocks.

The main problem with real estate investment trusts (REITs) for the retired investor is that they are publicly traded stocks. Their returns are correlated with the returns on U.S. stocks. In a retirement portfolio that owns no other U.S. stocks, REITs are a good diversifier. However, they are an excellent vehicle for someone saving for retirement. For this reason, REITs will primarily be discussed in Chapter 11 with limited reference made in this chapter.

A Long-term 10% Per Year

There is little agreement about long-term total returns from real estate. This is because there are many types of real estate held in many different ownership vehicles with many different leverage levels over many different time periods.

You are interested in the return on your investment. If you invest $100,000 in a building costing $1,000,000, you are interested in the return on your $100,000, not the return on the $1,000,000 building. If the other $900,000 of the building was purchased with a mortgage, then you have a leveraged ownership. If the value of the building increases 5% to $1,050,000, the return on your investment is $50,000 or 50%. The mortgage remains at $900,000. If the $900,000 interest in the building is owned by nine other partners, $100,000 each, then you have a partnership interest in the building. If the value increases 5% to $1,050,000, your share of the increase is one-tenth or $5,000. The return on your investment is 5%. If you have a partnership and a mortgage, the return on your investment is different than either of these. If a publicly traded REIT owns the building, and you purchase $100,000 of REIT shares, the return is determined by the stock market price of your shares.

Real estate return studies show estimated total returns from specific, limited classes of real estate without regard to leverage. For example, studies of office building prices in the 1970s showed them far outperforming stocks, returning around 15% per year. Studies of the 1980s showed returns closer to 5% a year. But these studies did not account for different leverage levels or ownership structures. Other studies showed that returns on office buildings held in limited partnerships in the 1980s were negative. High commissions, management expenses, and large mortgages during periods of high vacancies sunk many limited partnerships. Other studies showed that office buildings that were bought for all cash had positive, though small, returns during the 1980s. With no mortgage payments, the rents more than covered expenses, and the owners had the flexibility to lower rents to meet market conditions and to keep their buildings fully occupied. With no mortgage, there was no possibility of foreclosure when the property value dropped from the original purchase price.

Studies of long-term returns on real estate tend to look only at office and industrial buildings. As individual buildings tend to be held for long periods of time, most of the studies deal with all the properties sold during a given year and not gains or losses on the exact properties sold in prior years. The duration of the studies also affects their outcome. Few go back before the 1950s. Those that end in the mid-1980s show very high returns. Those that look only at the last ten years show very low returns. The amount of leverage the properties held is rarely taken into account.

All the studies make one point quite clear. Long-term returns from real estate of 10% a year are very likely. This makes sense. There are two sources of gain from real estate, rent and price. In some markets, rent alone can run as high as 10% of purchase price. As economies and populations grow, the demand for space grows. Thus rents can be increased. As building supply costs and construction wages increase, the replacement cost of existing buildings increases. Old buildings sell at or near the price of new buildings. The value of the land under the building also grows as the community around the site develops, making the land a more desirable location. Obviously, sites can also deteriorate, economies can be devastated, markets can be overbuilt, and so on. But these are not the general trends in the United States. You need to be selective.

Your best strategy is to find property types, leverage levels, and forms of ownership and management that have the best chance of returning 10% a year long term. You need to consider that prices and rents can go up 50% as well as down 50% over any two- to three-year period, even though such volatility is not the norm in real estate. The key is to take on low levels of debt, pay close attention to market supply and demand conditions, and use real estate tax benefits.

Low Leverage

The biggest mistake I have made in real estate has been taking on too much leverage, meaning too much mortgage and not enough down payment. I failed to understand the effect leverage would have on my goals. I fooled myself into believing that it would not matter because the loans were nonrecourse. On nonrecourse loans, if the properties fail to liquidate for more than the value of the loan, I am not liable for the deficit. Nonetheless, I lost all of my equity in this property. The property consistently had occupancy rates above 90% for the years I owned it. While occupancy levels stayed high, rents declined below the level of expenses. The major expense was the mortgage payment.

Refinancing at lower mortgage rates and obtaining a lower tax appraisal helped reduce the expenses, but I still lost the property to the bank. The return on my investment was a negative 100%.

The problem was not the investment but me. I failed to understand my own goals, so I was not in a suitably structured investment. I did not realize that I wanted 10% per year *total return*. The structure of the investment was for capital appreciation or, in this case, depreciation. There never was any possibility of income. The rents barely covered all the expenses to begin with. I never received a dime of the rent. Then when the rents declined, the general partner stopped paying the mortgage and the bank foreclosed. My only hope to make 10% a year was if the value of the property had gone up. That also failed to happen. To get a 10% return on your *investment* in real estate, you must watch your leverage.

If a property is bought for all cash, zero leverage, then there are no lender fees to pay and no mortgage payments. Your investment in the property will not be threatened by bank foreclosure. Your only worry to equity is market fluctuations. But by having no mortgage payment, you will have smaller expenses. Repairs, maintenance, management fees, taxes, and insurance are typically a fraction of mortgage payments. Thus most of the rents paid will go right into your pocket. For example, an all-cash, direct investment in several single-family homes could return more than 10% long term. In many markets today, a $100,000 home can be rented for $700 per month or $8,400 per year. This is a return of 8.4% per year on an investment of $100,000. Expenses, including vacancies, taxes, insurance, and repairs, should run no more than 2.4% a year. This house could be expected to appreciate in value 4% per year long term simply due to the rising replacement costs of building new homes. Rent increases should keep pace with expense increases. This adds up to a long-term return of 10%, as illustrated below.

INCOME/EXPENSE ITEM	$ AMOUNT	% OF $100,000
Rent	$8,400	8.4%
Expenses	($2,400)	(2.4%)
Average appreciation	$4,000	4.0%
Total	**$10,000**	**10.0%**

Unfortunately, you give up potential capital gains and potential rent receipts in an all-cash deal. To average 10% return on your investment long term, it is necessary to have years when you do better than 10% to offset the years when you do worse than 10%. If you buy a property partially with your money and partially with the bank's money, you can increase the amount of property you buy, thereby increasing the amount of potential gains. For example, if you invested $100,000 of your money and $100,000 of the bank's money in a luxury duplex on a large lot costing $200,000, you could potentially get a greater return. In this example, assume you would get double the rents and have double the non-mortgage expenses. Also assume double the appreciation. In the real world, your rents would not necessarily be double, but neither would your expenses. (Possibly a luxury duplex on a large lot would produce double the rent and have double the expenses of an ordinary, detached, single-family house.) The additional cost would be a mortgage payment. A $100,000 mortgage at 7.5% interest would cost only $7,500 per year. For the purpose of simplicity, let's leave out the effect of principal payments on your return. Here is how the return on your $100,000 investment is calculated.

INCOME/EXPENSE ITEM	$ AMOUNT	% OF $100,000
Rent	$16,800	16.8%
Expenses	($4,800)	(4.8%)
Mortgage payment	($7,500)	(7.5%)
Average appreciation of 4%	$8,000	8.0%
Total	**$12,500**	**12.5%**

By simply borrowing money from the bank, you have increased your return from 10% to 12.5%. Note that these simple examples do not take into account loan fees, principal payments, income taxes, and many other important considerations that will be discussed below. The point is that by borrowing money you can increase your potential return. So the temptation is to borrow more. What if you were to buy an exclusive five-unit townhouse complex, put down $100,000, and borrow $400,000? The chart below summarizes the potential results.

INCOME/EXPENSE ITEM	$ AMOUNT	% OF $100,000
Rent	$42,000	42%
Expenses	($12,000)	(12%)
Mortgage payment	($30,000)	(30%)
Average appreciation of 4%	$20,000	20%
Total	**$20,000**	**20%**

By buying a five-unit development, you have doubled your potential return to 20% a year. This seems to be the ideal way to go. But there are problems. Remember, you are looking for 10% a year long term, over ten years or more. What if during that ten years one or more of the townhouses becomes difficult to rent? What if there is an environmental problem with the lot or the local economy goes into recession, tenants lose their jobs and move out, and there are no new tenants around until the economy picks up again a year from now? You are counting on $42,000 of rent to pay $42,000 of expenses and mortgage payments. Most local economies go into recession twice every ten years. It is likely you will either miss some mortgage payments or have to pay the mortgage and expenses from your other assets. You do not have any room to reduce rents.

Note that now your entire return is based on the assumption that the value of the complex will increase. Rent is totally used up by expenses and mortgage payments. Your return is based on the assumption the complex goes up 4% a year for a total 20% return on your $100,000. This is a hope, not a fact like the receipt of a rent check each month. In a local recession, it is possible for the value of a townhouse to drop more than 20%. In Texas in the 1983–1986 recession, prices and rents dropped 50%. In Southern California from 1990–1994, prices dropped 50% and rents dropped 25%. If you are not making the mortgage payments and the house is worth less than the mortgage, you will likely give the property back to the bank and lose the $100,000 invested in the complex.

Your best bet to achieve 10% long term is 50% leverage. This is playing the odds. Part income return, part appreciation return, and a higher total return than an all-cash purchase. One problem with the all-cash property is it will eventually be sold. While you own it, the rent far exceeds the expenses. It is unlikely that it will ever be necessary to pay expenses out of your other income. But on sale, more than 6% of the value of the property will have to be paid to the real estate agent and others. We have assumed appreciation of 4% a year. But this must be offset in the final year by a negative 6%. Buying the duplex and shooting for a 12.5% return will give you a cushion to pay real estate agents and others on the sale of the property. The duplex also has a good cushion of rents over your expenses and mortgage. If necessary, you can reduce rents in a recession and still stay fully occupied. If prices decline 50% in a severe recession, you are in little danger of losing the duplex. If prices rise in a boom, you have two units instead of one and will benefit. Additionally, a mortgage that is not due on sale can increase the value of your property in certain markets. For example, if your assumable mortgage is for 7.5%, and at the time you sell the property, current rates are 12%, a buyer would offer more for your property with your mortgage than without it. If rates are lower than 7.5% when you sell, it will not decrease the price any. The buyer will simply obtain other financing.

A final problem with excessive leverage is it makes it difficult to live off a property. You need cash out of your properties every year to pay your living expenses and taxes. Mortgage principal payments and price appreciation, if it occurs, should function well as your inflation reinvestment. But if you have too much leverage and do not receive any cash from your properties, you will have to take living expenses from your other assets. Over time this will change your asset allocation. This has happened to me a few times. What I have done is sell a building and live off the proceeds entirely for more than a year and taken nothing from my other assets during that time. It would have been simpler and less risky if I just used less leverage.

The biggest obstacle to keeping leverage to 50% of the purchase price is ego, not finances. Many of you know the bank will loan you 80% to 90%. You know the risks of recession. You have seen friends and relatives forfeit properties. You have all read about the downfall of the Donald Trumps. But you need "more." It is not to show the neighbors or your parents, many deceased, who you are. You are not braggarts and you have given up trying to blatantly get Dad's approval. You need to prove to yourself that you can buy a 100-unit apartment. You need to show yourself what you can do with all this money. When you could buy 20 units with 50% down and make 10% a year the rest of your life, you do not. The loan officer says that with your assets, 10% down is fine. The plan becomes to buy the 100-unit apartment now, take the profits in five years, and then buy a 250-unit apartment. Why sit on 20 units for twenty years when you could have 250 units? The issue is not money. The issue is not whether you have enough money. The real issue is: are *you* enough?

Everyone in the transaction benefits from large leverage except you. A larger mortgage means more points, interest, and other fees for the lender. A larger mortgage means more property to manage for the property manager, and it means you can take a bigger property off the seller's hands. There will be pressure from your property manager, from your lender, and from the seller to use a lot of leverage. You must know yourself and your needs here and stick to what is right for you.

Note that in the examples and in the real world it is rare to be able to borrow money at an interest rate below the rate of return on current net income from your investment. The examples assumed current income of 8.4% and current expenses of 2.4% for net current income of 6.0%. Yet you are willing to borrow money at 7.5%. If conditions stay the same, if rents do not go up, if the property does not appreciate, if you cannot refinance at a lower rate, etc., you are losing money on every interest payment you make. It is important to realize this. When you borrow money to buy real estate, you are willing to gamble that a current loss can be turned into a future gain. The larger the mortgage and the higher the interest rate, the bigger the gamble. Be clear as to what you are trying to prove when you borrow money to buy real estate. A lifetime return of 10% per year is available in most real estate markets in the country. With a large mortgage you can turn a sure thing into a big gamble.

Estimated Values

In the preceding examples, I used estimated appreciation to determine the returns each year. One difference between real estate investing and stock investing is that prices in real estate are unknown until an actual sale takes place. With stocks, you can get a quote instantly. With real estate you need to rely on estimates and appraisals. You are looking for a steady 10% a year. Rent is more exact and predictable than appraised values. The more you get your returns from the net operating income (rents less real estate taxes, insurance, management fees, and other expenses) on your properties, the steadier the returns will be. The more your returns come from appreciation, the more volatile they will be. With high leverage, all your return is from appreciation. If you have difficulty living in the question, keep the leverage in your real estate to a minimum.

Lower Taxes

One of the advantages of real estate is that the cash you receive every month, the net operating income (rents less real estate taxes, insurance, management fees, and other expenses), is not fully taxed like dividends on stock. For properties you own directly, the taxable income from the rents is reduced by the depreciation of the property, which can partially or wholly eliminate taxes on that income. The cash you receive from your real estate will go further than the dividends you receive from your stocks and the interest income you receive from taxable bonds. In addition, the gains on the sale of your real estate are taxed at low capital gains rates. Real estate investment trust dividend payments are also partially tax sheltered. Even if you were to average 8% a year from your real estate, the tax savings could make this the equivalent of 10% you receive from your other investments.

Easy, Low-Cost Management

The main area where stock and bond investing is clearly better for your needs is the availability of easy, low-cost management. There is nothing in real estate that works as well as no-load, minuscule-fee index funds. Within the world of real estate, some options are better than others.

Self-Management

Self-management is not what the nuns are trying to get the kids in Catholic school to do. This refers to buying and managing properties yourself. Before you make a purchase, you need to consider how much of your time will be required. If you buy only a few units, management is fairly simple.

Commercial properties are easier to manage than residential. There are fewer middle-of-the-night calls about the plumbing. The bookkeeping is simple. Collect rents and pay taxes, insurance, and mortgages. Auto-deduct accounts can be set up with the rent automatically being taken from the tenant's account and the taxes, insurance, and mortgage payments being automatically transferred to an escrow account. Set up the utilities to be auto-deducted as well and there will be even less bookkeeping to do.

You have to screen tenants and market the properties. Marketing properties is simple. Post a sign, run an ad. If you get nothing, reduce the rent, and try again. You have to decide between the convenience of long-term leases and the potential gains of short leases and future rent increases.

The hardest part of self-management is accepting market rents that are lower than what you expected to get. Assuming you have 50% or less leverage, this is an ego deflation problem more than a financial problem. The tenants have looked at ten other sites and get to choose what rent they are willing to pay. It is best to stay fully leased. One month's rent is 8.3% of a year's rent; two months' rent is 16.6%. It is better to reduce the rent 16.6% than to go three months without a tenant and lose 24.9%.

A few units can be managed in less than five hours a week. But if you are going to own many units or out-of-state properties, it becomes a full-time job. In this case, consider a property manager.

Professional Property Management

The up-front cost of property management is generally reasonable. The costs of incompetent management can be extreme. A common property management contract for an established building is 5% of gross rents. For a turnaround property or a speculative property, you might pay 10% of gross rents and 10% of profits on sale of the property. A vacation rental property, which mostly rents on weekends and holidays, may cost 25% of gross rents.

Management is full service and comes with all the accounting you will need to prepare your taxes. In the examples starting on page 130, I estimated expenses without including management fees. If you subtracted management fees of 10% of gross rents, you would still find that a return of 10% a year is possible using 50% leverage. In the second example, the gross rent is $16,800 a year. Subtracting 10% will reduce your potential return by 1.68% to around 11%. So it is reasonable to say for that example that using management would not be so expensive as to prevent you from reaching your goals. Generally this is true in real estate.

Real estate managers are easy to find. They are listed in the Yellow Pages and any realtor will know several. The difficulty is finding competent real estate management. Incompetent management will cost much more than 10% of gross rents.

What separates good management from bad management is how they perform in a bad market. In a good market, all managers look good. Tenants are everywhere, rents are rising, prices are rising. In a bad market, every expense has to be looked at. Rents have to be reduced. Marketing is crucial.

Interview several property managers before you pick one. Ask the property manager what mistakes she has made in the past and what she is doing differently now. Every property manager makes mistakes. What you are looking for is someone who can admit his or her mistakes, learn from them, and not repeat them. Many so-called professional managers lack the ability to accept market realities. In tough markets, they must reduce rents to keep buildings fully occupied, toss out delinquent or underperforming tenants, and take losses on remodeling.

There are two keys to finding good management. First, you must analyze your property to determine what type of management it needs. Then screen candidates to determine if they can meet those needs.

Property managers do many things. They market the space. They screen tenants and check credit. They close tenants. They maintain the property. They supervise improvements. They pay expenses and keep the books. An empty building will need experts in marketing the space and closing tenants. A full building will need good, reasonable maintenance and good bookkeeping. A half-empty building will need all this. Determine what your property will need most. Then screen the managers who are available.

Look at the properties they are already managing. Talk to the owners and the tenants. Find out what they did to keep buildings fully occupied and expenses down in the last bad real estate market. Avoid retired business people and retired realtors who have gone into real estate management because they were bored. You need full-time, dedicated people. You do not need a genius. Real estate is a simple business. Get examples of their bookkeeping, and see if it makes sense to you. Ask how they check credit and when has their system failed. Everybody rents to a deadbeat now and then. If they deny they ever have, they are not likely to be learning from their mistakes. Avoid big egos. When it is time to reduce rents and start a marketing campaign, they have to act quickly. Big egos can take years to deflate, and this can cost you a lot of money. Retired realtors who represent themselves as "knowing the market" can be a liability. They must respond to the market, not outthink it.

If you do not want to manage properties yourself or to hire and supervise managers, then institutional management is available.

Institutional Management

Both real estate investment trusts (REITs) and real estate limited partnerships (RELPs) are managed by professionals. One of the problems with RELPs is that the management's interest and your interest are opposed. Management often is more interested in collecting large fees and commissions than in improving property performance. Another disadvantage of RELPs is they are not publicly traded. There is very little information available on their past performance that has not been prepared by the managers themselves. For these reasons and others stated below, do not buy RELPs. REITs often offer the opposite.

The managers of many REITs own substantial portions of the stock. This is a good sign that their interests and yours are aligned. Also REITs are publicly traded stocks. There are many sources of information available to judge past performance and estimate future performance. If performance is disappointing, you can sell the stock. With a RELP there is usually no market to sell into, and it is nearly impossible to get rid of management no matter how incompetent.

You are looking for easy, low-cost management. Hiring a property manager, you have to periodically meet with him or her and discuss matters. You need to make decisions about improvements, rent increases, and evictions. Things come up. Storms destroy roofs. Insurance claims have to be dealt with, etc. With a REIT, there is nothing to do once you have selected the REIT. Part of the REIT selection process, which will be more fully discussed in Chapter 11, is to find competent management. After this has been found, you simply read quarterly reports and annual reports to see if things are going okay.

Larger Gains If You Devote More Time

Real estate, like emerging market stocks, is a vast investment area that has not been fully analyzed, documented, computerized, and understood. Drive down any commercial street and most of the buildings' financials are known only by the building owners. For some buildings, even the owners pay attention only to their tax records. Yet the financials of at least 10,000 U.S. stocks are known to anyone who has an interest.

The possibilities of finding undiscovered gems in real estate are vastly greater than the possibilities of finding undiscovered U.S. stocks. In 1989 I had a conversation with a friend in Denver who told me his parents had just bought a two-bedroom, two-bath condo in a nice building in a good neighborhood for $25,000. The same condo in the same building had sold for $65,000 five years before. Now if Denver was going to turn into a ghost town, even $25,000 was too much. But my research indicated Denver was headed the other way. In fact I thought the entire city, with the exception of the office towers, was a real estate gem. I told many people to buy there. Only one did. My subsequent Denver investments tripled in five years. The other guy who invested there did even better. Yet all the time people come to me with stock tips both for themselves and for me. I check them out and have yet to find an undiscovered gem. The possibilities to make extra returns with extra effort in real estate are much better than in U.S. stocks.

There are many properties available even in mediocre markets that are not being competently managed, such as strip shopping centers owned by groups of doctors or lawyers who just wanted tax benefits in the early 1980s and never spent any time marketing the property and have below-market leases. Properties inherited by widows or children who know nothing about the properties. Owner-occupied properties where the owner is not in real estate, has no knowledge of the real estate market, and is retiring and closing the business.

If you spend time looking, you will find many gems. Underperforming buildings are easy to spot. The roofs are shedding, the paint is peeling, and there is trash and dead wood in the parking lot. There are not thousands of mutual fund managers looking over every property on every street. There are no huge databases hooked to Dow Jones, Bloomberg, Reuters, or the Internet. Spending time in this area can be very profitable.

Real estate is a good investment for a retired investor. The question then becomes how much to invest in real estate.

How Much Should You Invest in Real Estate?

A properly structured real estate portfolio can be expected to provide a tax advantage return of more than 10% per year long term. However, there have been ten-year periods when it was very difficult in many markets to make a positive return in real estate. You certainly do not want all of your assets in real estate. But real estate is an excellent diversifier. Real estate returns are local market-driven. An apartment house in St. Louis can have a wonderful decade while the Dow slumps, the emerging markets submerge, bonds are doing no better than passbook savings accounts, and Houston apartments are half vacant. On the other hand, an apartment in St. Louis can require calls to the fire department at 2:00 a.m. and trips to the dump on Sunday.

If you want a good return but do not want a part-time job, put up to one third of your assets in real estate. If you are willing to work part-time, put up to half your assets in real estate. But never more than half.

How to Buy Real Estate That Fits Your Needs

Your best choice is to buy individual properties. Whether you will manage the property you buy or hire a property manager, the selection process is the same.

Once the property has been selected, the type of manager you will need to be or will need to hire will be determined by your analysis of the market. For example, if you choose to buy an apartment complex that has a low vacancy rate, you or your manager will need good marketing and closing skills. But if you buy an apartment complex that is full, you or your manager will need to be good at keeping maintenance expenses down, keeping existing tenants happy, and keeping the books.

The selection process is a matter of finding a property likely to give you a total return of 10% per year or better. You must be selective. Fewer than one in ten properties in your price range will meet your needs. Learn what not to buy.

Properties to Avoid

Avoid the property development business. This is only for full-time real estate people. Everybody wants to have his or her name on a new building or a new section of town. The Gillette Edmunds Towers or Edmunds Estates sounds good to me. But humility works better. Development is a long-term process. When you start planning the project, the market may be good. When you finish building, you may just be part of the overbuilding problem. Even if you hit the market right, you still need to keep your costs down to make a profit. To be successful at development requires putting together a whole team of architects, builders, lawyers, accountants, property managers, salespeople, and so on. You want to live on your investments, not under them. The thrill of watching a building go up, of turning a vacant lot into a happening place with your name on it is great. This is, however, an expensive thrill and has put many independently wealthy individuals into bankruptcy and has led to suicide for a few others.

Do not buy land. Land pays no rent yet requires annual tax payments.

Do not kid yourself that your vacation home is a real estate investment. Simply adding up your annual expenses to own and maintain this property should indicate that you have an annual deficit from this asset and not an annual income. The pleasure you get from a vacation home can be worth more than the cost. But that still does not make it an investment.

The Humility Real Estate Portfolio

The humility real estate portfolio consists of three or more developed buildings with at least five years of operating history in three or more markets purchased with 50% leverage.

Three buildings in three markets is minimum diversification. Putting all your real estate money into one property is a mistake. No matter how good the property looks, there are things you cannot see because they have not happened yet. Hedge against the unknown.

Divide your real estate money into three or more parts and look for appropriate buildings. Some of the buildings will do better than you dreamed of, and some will do worse, but on average you will get a 10% total return a year. Putting everything on one big, towering building will not add meaning to your life. It will only add risk.

How to Find the Right Market

There are many pockets of real estate today where supply is tightening and demand is good.

Many real estate supply and demand statistics are sketchy and unreliable. Most are compiled by realtor groups that have an interest in making the market look better than it really is. There is no Dow Jones Industrial Average or New York Stock Exchange volume statistics for real estate available to the general buyer. The worst source of information is realtors themselves. They do not consciously lie. It is more a process of rationalization. They discount the negative news and enhance the positive news to improve their chances of selling. A lie detector test would not work on these salespeople.

The best source of information is potential buyers and potential tenants. If you are told that there is a shortage of warehouse space in the market you are looking at and that the tenants in the warehouse office park you are interested in are paying below market rent—meaning you can raise rents after you buy without losing tenants—check your source. If you got that from a realtor, doubt it. Get the names of the last five people who tried to rent space in the park and the names of five actual tenants, and ask them how much space is out there and what it is going for. Ask them, "Do you know of any new building going on, who is building it, and what are they asking for it?" These ten experts have all looked at spaces in the last months and talked to leasing agents and compared what they have seen to what they have heard. They know the real market. Then go try to rent space yourself at other parks. The supply and demand characteristics will become obvious to you quite quickly. Confirm your conclusions with any available public information.

The Institute of Real Estate Management in Chicago publishes annual income and expense analysis for apartments and office buildings for major cities. There are a few other private consulting firms that have detailed figures if you can afford their fees. If you are interested in individual homes, the Office of Federal Housing Enterprise Oversight publishes quarterly figures on housing prices in all fifty states. These figures are based on repeat single-family home sales, which is much more accurate than the National Association of Realtors' figures.

Spend some time studying the local economy. You all want to buy something nearby. This may be a mistake. The chances are only 1 in 50 that you live in the best state to invest in and maybe 1 in a 1000 that you live in the best city. If the supply of buildings is more than adequate where you live, then you need to see clear signs the demand is going to pick up. Spend some time studying the economy of other cities. Are the prospects better in Denver,

Dallas, Boston, or LA than where you live? If those economies look better and the supply of buildings is tight, real estate will do better there. How do you find out? Call friends in other cities. Go to the library or the Internet. Get the Sunday papers from other cities and look at the real estate sections, the business sections, and the rest of the paper. Read the local papers on the Web.

Look for depressed markets that no one else is interested in. The market could simply be a category of real estate like apartments, office warehouses, or retail space. Or a market could be a whole town, state, or region like the oil region. (I will suggest several ways to buy outside your state below.)

For each depressed market, make a list of reasons why this market will come back. The best market to buy in is not the "hottest" market. The best market is the one with the best supply and demand characteristics. Hot markets are often the worst to buy in and the best to sell in. In hot markets demand for space has been greater than supply for a long time. Prices have risen enough to increase the supply dramatically and eliminate many buyers. The next direction for prices will be down.

You are not looking for the market where Jane Doe doubled her money in two years and John Doe made five times his investment in seven years. You are looking for the market where Jane sold for a loss, John gave his property back to the bank, and people think you are a fool to waste the cost of a long distance call much less the price of an airline ticket and a hotel. In the right market, the property owner is reluctant to tell you what the property appraised for five years ago because she thinks it will discourage you as much as it discourages her. She only sees one future direction, down.

Avoid the market where they are building like crazy, new banks are springing up to get in on the financing, and real estate is a can't lose proposition. When the tenants in the apartments just completed are all construction workers on the apartments still going up, it is not going to end well.

Do not look for "location, location, location." Look for "dislocation, dislocation, dislocation." Rockefeller Center is considered the best location in the world. The property went bankrupt, and investors lost billions. You cannot afford that mistake. There was once a theory that certain locations would do well regardless of supply and demand. So-called "trophy" properties would never lose their value. Rockefeller Center was *the* trophy property. In Manhattan, market prices and taxes got so high that tenants went elsewhere. Major corporations cut staff. Demand decreased at the same time as huge new buildings were being built. The tenants in the trophy properties were offered a year of free rent and 30% less than current rent a few blocks away. They moved. E-mail, faxes, and computers made it possible to leave the state and still stay in direct contact with customers. Supply and demand are the only factors that determine price. In New York, new buildings and electronic communications permanently increased the supply of suitable buildings. Corporate restructuring and recession reduced the demand. The demand for any one location is not constant. The trophy went to the realtor who collected a massive commission by selling Rockefeller Center as the "location, location, location."

The Questions to Answer Before You Buy

Look at a minimum of ten buildings thoroughly before you make an offer. If you are using a property company to help you find a building, make sure they get you data on at least ten buildings and not just the deal they have got for you. Begin looking within a half-hour drive of your principal residence. Though it is not likely you will find what you are looking for in your area, at least you will develop a procedure for analyzing properties. If the property company has nothing in your area that works for you, thank them and let them go.

There will be sales pressure from the realtors showing properties. Be sure to tell them and yourself that you are looking both in-state and out-of-state before you buy anything. If you need to convince yourself, buy a plane ticket to another likely city before you begin looking in your own town.

You are looking for three or more buildings that you will own for five to twenty-five years. There is no hurry to buy. These properties will be a part of your life for a long time. The biggest mistake I have made has always been buying without checking out all possible alternatives. If you buy well, you will never have a problem selling later. If you buy poorly, it will be very difficult to unload your mistake on someone else. Be thorough!

To pick a property you need to answer the following:

- How much gross rent can you get from this building if it were fully occupied?
- What is your likely vacancy rate?
- What are your likely operating expenses, including property management fees, if any?
- At the potential purchase price, what will be your net mortgage payment including interest and principal?
- How much can you expect this property to appreciate per year over the next few years?
- At the potential purchase price, what is your expected total return from this investment?
- If the return is too low, what other markets and property types should you look at, and how should you go about that?
- What special terms do you need in your offer and financing arrangement?
- Is there a property manager available to run this building, and what does he see that you are missing?
- What are you missing and who else should you consult? What other questions should you ask?
- Having answered these questions, how much are you willing to pay for this property?
- What property management issues are likely to arise during ownership?
- When do you sell and what expenses and tax considerations should you take into account?

The answer to these questions will determine if you can get 10% a year from your investment. In order to understand the questions and answers we will use an example. Assume you are offered a small town, 20-unit Class B office building for $500,000 with a $250,000 mortgage at 8.5% a year for thirty years. Below are the expected results from the first year of operation.

GROSS RENT	20 UNITS AT $5,000 A YEAR	$100,000
+ Other income	8 parking spaces at $500 a year	$4,000
− Vacancies	2 units at $5,000 a year	($10,000)
= Net rents		$94,000
− Operating expenses	Tax, insurance, repairs, etc.	($54,000)
= Net operating income		$40,000
− Debt service	$250,000 mortgage at 8.5%	($23,000)
+ Loan principal	Early year	$2,000
= Income		$19,000

You are investing $250,000 and can expect $19,000 of income or about 7.5% a year.

The local economy has been hit hard for the last five years due to the shutdown of several area factories. However, new businesses are starting to move in to take advantage of the cheap, educated labor force and the low costs of doing business and living in the area. You expect to be 100% leased soon and to raise rents on tenants renewing leases in the next five years. But realistically, if you sold at the end of one year, realtor commissions would more than eliminate your profits. You estimate a zero return from appreciation the first year.

An accurate estimate of your return from appreciation would use this simple formula: ((Estimated sales price − Sales expenses) minus Purchase price) divided by Investment expressed as a %= % return from appreciation.

Your total return can be calculated as follows: Total return = Return from income + Return from appreciation. In our example, the first-year total return is estimated as 7.5% + 0 = 7.5%.

These are the estimated first-year figures. Should you buy this building? Let's go through the list of questions above.

How Much Gross Rent Can You Expect?

The gross rent is the amount you would receive if the property were fully occupied and all tenants were current on their rent. Rarely are buildings 100% leased, so you will need to estimate this number. Do not use the seller's estimates. If the seller believed his own numbers, he would not be selling the building.

Unfortunately, there is nothing besides ethics and a vague possibility of a lawsuit to prevent the seller from inventing numbers. Ask to see actual rent rolls on the property, but let go of the idea that you will get the same rent. Go out and survey rents in the area yourself or buy a rent survey done by a local property management company or another professional real estate analyst. Also talk to as many tenants as you can. Are the tenants wanting improvements in their space without rent increases? If so, it is likely the rent is already too high. But if tenants have no complaints, "Everything is just fine, you are not going to raise the rent are you?" then rents are probably too low. If the tenants are too happy, you can expect to find rents are below those across the street and could be raised without losing anyone.

You want to estimate your gross rents for the next five years. If there is potential to increase rents, use those figures. If there is a possibility that rents will have to come down, use those figures. Using multiple estimates is good because your actual results will vary over time. If you own a property five years, the odds of a recession in your market one of those years are very good. Also estimate other income sources from the property if any are likely. Parking fees or club dues can be a source of extra income.

Go back to the example. Your talks with tenants, the owner, and the property manager of the building across the street reveal that rents are cheap in this building. No one ever complains about anything. Tenants have been lost because the economy was bad but not because anyone thought the rent was too high. The building across the street lost tenants to this building and decided to lower rents. The elderly lady who owned the building before her children inherited it did not raise rent for at least ten years. The children had big plans for a remodel but decided to sell instead. On the other hand, no one in town thinks the current recession is over. They have all seen their homes lose value, and they are surprised anyone has any interest in buying any real estate at all. You think the economy has turned. Your best guess is the same rent for the first two years of operation and then 5% increases a year for the next three years.

Vacancy Rate

The vacancy rate and the rental rate are related. If you raise the rent, you may lose tenants and vice versa. The trick is to maximize both.

Starting with the actual vacancy rate in the building you are looking at, the question is whether this rate will improve or decline with your ownership. If you intend to immediately raise rents, what effect will that have on the vacancy rate? If rents in the building are below market rents, you can expect low turnover and a low vacancy rate. If rents are not below market, then you should expect to lose tenants.

Many buyers expect to raise rents, create vacancies, make upgrades during the vacancies, and then increase rents. This strategy will work only if there is a market for upgraded units. Going from shabby office suites to luxury office suites will not work if all the tenants in the area are small businesses and not highly paid lawyers and money managers.

Never use a zero vacancy rate in your estimates. Simply in transition from one tenant to another you lose rent.

A marketing strategy is the key to keep vacancies low. If you or your property manager can figure out why there are vacancies, then you can come up with a plan to fill them. If the rent is above market, then you must calculate the effect of lowering rent. If well advertised, you will fill your vacancies, but you will have to lower rent on each renewing lease as well. If you do not lower rent on renewing leases, you will lose more tenants. But often the problem is not the rents. Sometimes the location is a problem. There is no drive-by traffic because you are in the woods outside town. You will need an ad campaign and your ads should emphasize quiet, beauty, privacy, and exclusiveness all at market rent. The problem could be quality or extras like apartment swimming pools. You will need to plug in estimates for improvements under operating expenses to see how these costs net against increased rents.

Going back to the example, you have two vacancies at the moment. While you do not think you can raise rents for two years, there appears to be enough traffic to fill at least one of those vacancies by the end of the year and to keep to an average of one vacancy a year for the next several years.

Operating Expenses

Get as much information as you can on the current operating expenses of the building. These include real estate taxes, insurance, utilities, improvements, maintenance, repairs, office supplies, credit reports, bank fees, management fees, and other miscellaneous expenses. Going over the expenses item by item, look where they could be reduced or expected to increase. An experienced property manager could help you analyze these numbers.

Sometimes real estate taxes are too high because the property is on the tax rolls at the price the previous owner paid and you can get a reduction. Other times your purchase price will trigger an increase in the tax appraisal.

Always get three bids for the insurance. Very often money can be saved here.

Utilities will usually go up over time but there may be an opportunity to have the units separately metered and pass these expenses on to the tenants.

Improvements should not be done unless you have strong evidence that you can raise rents or get a better sales price or the improvements are required to keep existing tenants in place. Get a professional to look at the roof, the plumbing, and everything else that may need repair or replacement. Odd, expensive things happen. I've had hailstorms ruin roofs, cities order trees to be removed at my expense, and cracks mysteriously appear in foundations. Always estimate high for repairs and maintenance because stuff happens.

Estimate management fees even if you plan to manage the building yourself. You may soon change your mind, so you do not want to own a building that will make sense only if you manage it yourself.

Operating expenses vary dramatically by property type. In some office warehouses and other office buildings, every time you put in a new tenant you may have to spend a year's rent to remodel the space. Apartments rarely require more than paint and an occasional carpet. Restaurants are extremely expensive to rent. Some retail space also requires considerable expense.

There may be times when you would be better off leaving a space empty while waiting for the market to improve than incurring marketing expenses that are unlikely to result in a profitable rental. Be sure to budget for these expenses. If the building has had the same tenants for a long time, these expenses will not show up on the accounts you are shown. If the tenants leave, you will not only incur remodeling expenses but lose rent while the new tenant search takes place and the remodeling is completed.

Looking at the example, your research shows that you are paying less than the previous owner for the building and can get the taxes and insurance down. Your management fees, 5% of gross rents, will be about the same as the previous owner's, as the current manager has made a bid to stay on and all her competitors are willing to work for the same fee. If your manager gets another unit rented and negotiates rent increases, thereafter management fees will increase proportionately, as will utilities. Maintenance has been low this year. It was high the year before. The owner put on a new roof, built a new fence, painted common areas, and made other repairs the prior year to get the place ready to sell. You decide to use a higher number for maintenance and repair next year than the current year to compensate for likely electrical and plumbing problems. However, lower taxes and insurance should offset any maintenance and repair increases for the next five years.

What Will Be Your Net Mortgage Payments Accounting for Both Interest and Principal?

A 50% mortgage, as discussed above, works best for you. Sometimes it is prudent to buy one property with no mortgage and another with 5% down so your average leverage is about 50%. Any property that you buy where there is a possibility, even remote, of selling off units or pieces of land separately from the whole requires special terms in the purchase agreement and financing agreement. Partial release clauses or separate financing for separate parts of the property may be required. Talk to an experienced real estate attorney and have her draft the agreements. When mortgage rates are high, you can sometimes obtain seller financing or assume an existing mortgage.

The complexities of financing are beyond this chapter. But shop around and get advice. With 50% down, you will have no trouble qualifying. But the wrong terms can still destroy your returns. If you buy an apartment house and later decide to sell off the units as condos, you could be prevented by the mortgage holder. You need to secure releases of each unit from securing the loan. Be aware that commercial loans are generally 1% higher than home loans and usually for shorter duration.

In the example, you have decided to use a $250,000, 8.5%, thirty-year mortgage with no points or fees, as opposed to paying points and fees for an 8.125% loan. You are not sure you really want to be a landlord, so you would rather save on fees now and pay a higher interest rate if you decide to stay with it. Some part of every mortgage payment is principal. Every principal payment increases your equity in the property. You estimate your principal will increase $2,000 per year.

Income, without adding back loan principal, is the money you will live on while you still own the building. If, over a period of years, you can increase rents and keep operating expenses low, you may never need to worry about price appreciation, real estate commissions and other huge selling expenses, finding new properties, like kind exchanges, and so on. Theoretically, you may never need to sell some properties the rest of your life if the income rises to 10% of your investment and continues to increase as fast as your living expenses. If you pay off the mortgage over the years, then your income will increase even more. This is the great advantage of real estate for those living off their investments. While bonds pay out substantial income, the amount is fixed and cannot rise with your living expenses. Stocks pay out dividends that can rise over time, but these days it is rare that dividends are even half of the total return from stocks. Stocks have to be periodically sold to receive the 10% to 14% you need to live off. However, markets will come along that make it prudent to sell one building and buy another. These issues will be discussed below.

In the example, income as you estimate it for the first five years is summarized below.

	YEAR 1	YEAR 2	YEAR 3	YEAR 4	YEAR 5
Gross rent	$100,000	$100,000	$105,000	$110,000	$116,000
Other income	$4,000	$4,000	$4,000	$4,000	$4,000
Vacancies	($10,000	($5,000)	($5,000)	($5,000)	($6,000)
Net rent	$94,000	$99,000	$104,000	$109,000	$114,000
Operating expense	($54,000)	($55,000)	($56,000)	($57,000)	($58,000)
Net operating income	$40,000	$44,000	$48,000	$52,000	$56,000
Debt service	($23,000)	($23,000)	($23,000)	($23,000)	($23,000)
Loan principal	$2,000	$2,000	$2,000	$2,000	$2,000
Income	$19,000	$23,000	$27,000	$31,000	$35,000

Based on your assumptions, income will increase each year. In year 5, you will be getting 17% a year ($35,000) on your $250,000 investment just from income.

When your first analysis looks so promising, it is prudent to question your assumptions. Your primary assumption is that the five-year recession is over, business will pick up in the community, and you will be able to take advantage of it with occupancy increases in year 2 and rent increases beginning in year 3. What if the recession lingers five more years? It would be best to run your numbers with no increases in rent or occupancy and look at that. What if a major repair to the plumbing becomes necessary?

Play the "what if?" game to see how much you trust your numbers. Do you trust them enough to invest $250,000 on them? How low could rents go? Are you looking at a future ghost town or just a lingering recession? A possible scenario might be no rent or occupancy increases coupled with an unbudgeted, uninsured $50,000 repair. If you spread the cost over five years, you would be looking at an average income of $9,000 a year or less than 4% on your $250,000 investment.

After you have estimated your return from income, estimate any price appreciation.

Price Appreciation

There are three factors to look at here. First, projecting your numbers out five years, what is a buyer then likely to pay for this building? Second, what are your selling expenses likely to be, including any necessary repairs? Third, what will conditions be like from a supply and demand perspective? No matter how good your numbers are, if the market is then overbuilt you won't get your price.

Projections must be real. When Rockefeller Plaza sold to a REIT in 1985, the promoters were projecting rent increases for the next ten years. When it went bankrupt in 1995, rents were below those of 1985.

If you can guesstimate reasonable rents and expenses five years out, you can assume a buyer will likely pay the same ratio of price to net operating income that you did. For example, you are paying $500,000 for a building with a net operating income of $40,000 in year 1. This is a net income multiplier of 12.5 ($500,000/$40,000). If net operating income is $56,000 in year 5, a buyer is likely to pay $700,000 ($56,000 × 12.5). But if net operating income is $30,000 in year 5 due to a large uninsured repair and no occupancy or rent increases, a buyer could be assumed to pay only $375,000 ($30,000 × 12.5).

Once you are comfortable with some likely selling prices, you must subtract selling expenses. These differ by state and city but can run as high as 10% of the selling price and are rarely below 7%. Realtor commissions are the largest item followed by closing fees including title insurance, document prep, etc. For difficult-to-sell properties, it may be necessary to pay for ads not provided by the realtor and bonus commissions to motivate the realtor.

Most of these expenses can be saved if you sell yourself. Reading a few books and using an attorney to advise you will reduce your risks of being bilked. In a strong market, marketing will not be an issue. In a tough selling environment, it is better to pay for the best salesperson you can find.

Once you have your numbers, the question becomes what will the market then be like? You are buying based on your projections of what will happen over the five years following your date of purchase. If ten new buildings in the area are under construction at the end of that five years, a new buyer is going to have to assume either lower rents to keep the building occupied, or lower occupancy at the same rent, or both. If there is no new construction and competitive buildings have been converted to other uses, a new buyer might assume higher occupancy and rents than those of year 5. Interest rates also play a big role. If mortgage rates are higher in year 5 than in year 1, a new buyer is not going to pay the same net income multiplier that you did. Estimating interest rates five years from now is not possible. Be aware that there is uncertainty as to what a buyer will pay five years from now.

Some markets are not affected as much by changes in interest rates and net operating income as others. Single-family homes are affected mostly by general economic conditions. People do not buy homes based on what they would rent for. They buy them based on their current income, family size, and sense of job security. Projecting the selling price of a home five years from now is projecting the state of the economy five years from now. It is also impossible to predict the state of the economy five years from now.

The best you can do to arrive at a selling price five years from now is to play with your numbers and assumptions and guess. If you know something about how prices got to be where they are now, you can sometimes look at trends to the future.

The overbuilt office markets of 1986 got that way because of reckless bank lending, heroic rent projections from promoters, tax shelter possibilities, the inflation hedge, location, location, location myths, and a long recovery from the 1980–1982 recession. Today there are still heroic rent projections but no buildings going up. The myths and the lending are gone. A growing economy has filled some vacancies. A slow improvement seems possible.

If your numbers showed an office building doubling in price over the next five years, you should doubt it. If your numbers showed price increases of 1% to 3% a year, you could feel comfortable. Oil state apartment markets were destroyed in the 1980s. In Houston they stripped apartment buildings of their pipes and wiring and left them to rot. Nothing new was built for a decade. In the 1990s a comeback has been strong. New units are on the drawing board. Apartment REITs have been hot. In 1990 projections of

5% to 10% rent increases were accurate and rare. In 1999 projections of 5% to 10% rent increases are common and likely inaccurate. If your numbers showed an apartment building bought in Oklahoma City in 1999 will double in value by 2004, you need to rethink your assumptions.

In the example, assume that your projections of rising rents and higher occupancy will be accurate but that by year 5 interest rates will likely be higher because today's interest rates are at historic lows. In addition a few other buildings nearby that have been neglected will be fixed up and become competitors. You think a buyer will pay 11 times your net operating income of $56,000 or $616,000. You expect selling expenses of about $49,000 or 8%. This should leave you with a profit on sale of $67,000 or 27% on your $250,000 investment.

Compare Your Estimates to Other Markets and Property Types

If nothing you look at locally seems likely to do better than 10% a year total return, it is time to start reading the Sunday papers of other cities. The business pages and the real estate sections will give you an idea what is going on. Call out-of-state friends and tell them straight out that you are looking for bad real estate markets that have stabilized and have potential to go up. Subscribe to real estate magazines.

When you have found a potential market, call realtors and property managers there and tell them that you are planning a trip to look at properties and want all the historical data available on the buildings you will be looking at. Let it be known that you will be making your own projections of future results but would be happy to see anything they have come up with for comparison. Then fly out there and spend a few days looking around. Get a local map and mark the properties you have seen on the map. Come home, analyze your data, watch your ego soar as you think you have found a gem, or feel your ego drop when you think it is hopeless.

Visit another city or revisit the first one and look at other properties. Check out apartments, office warehouses, offices, single-family homes, strip centers, everything that looks promising. Take about six months. Use a property manager for out-of-state property. Give him an incentive to do well. I have paid 10% of gross rents plus the right to list the property and 10% of net sales profits as a bonus. This kept them focused even when my phone calls did not.

Let go of the idea that buying out-of-state from a realtor you do not know or, using a property manager you do not know, is more risky than buying next to your favorite restaurant across town. Your research has shown that buying across town is buying into an over-priced, overbuilt market that is at the end of a long growth period. Yes, everybody at the country club will know it is your building. When you take them to lunch at the restaurant you can point out your property. Nobody in Springfield, where the real buys are, has ever heard of you. It is important to separate investment decisions from ego boosters.

The pride of ownership can get in the way of rational decision making. Few people show off their stock portfolios, but many people show off their real estate. I once showed a client several great buys a few thousand miles from his home. He thought it too risky. Instead he bought a second home in a nearby resort area. Six years later when he tired of the second home, he sold it for a loss. The risky properties would have quadrupled his investment by then. He wanted to show off the second home to his friends. When that wore off, he still had to pay taxes, insurance, utilities, and mortgage payments with no rent coming in and no prospects of appreciation. This case might seem exceptional, but it is really the norm.

Many people who live off their investments get lost in the myths surrounding real estate and fail to spend enough time analyzing what they are doing. There is a myth that most great fortunes were made in real estate and not in stocks or bonds. Certainly, before 1900 this was true. But today it may or may not be true. The problem is the buyer who believes this myth is more interested in the association with great fortunes than the analysis of individual properties. I have seen buyers' maps of the properties they own in a given town that are supposed to show what a great fortune they have amassed. On closer examination, these maps often show that they have cornered the market on bad real estate in a given area. The numbers reveal that they would have been better off financially in CDs. But CDs have no association with the great real estate empires of the past.

Once you have found a good prospect, you need to consider the legal details of the purchase.

Special Terms

For anything more complicated than single-family homes, be sure a lawyer has reviewed your offer, your leases, and your contract with your property manager. If you have plans to further develop the property, to sell off parts, or to refinance after a balloon payment, or to do anything at all in the future other than just collect rent, use a lawyer. Avoiding a $100,000 lawsuit five years from now is well worth $5,000 in legal fees today.

While you are looking for a lawyer, also look for a property manager.

Discuss with Your Property Manager

Most property managers will not understand your investment philosophy. They are used to looking at the details and not the big picture. Before you buy a building, be sure you have a property manager that understands why you want it and who can enhance your return. If you are looking for current income from existing tenants, you do not want a property manager aggressively marketing the property or wanting to add on. Rather you want to keep the current tenants happy with the least possible expense. If you are looking for capital gains from a future sale, then you need a manager who can bring in the tenants and get the leases signed that will make the sale possible. An experienced manager in the style you are looking for will have ideas to help you reach your goals.

Do Not Stop Asking Questions and Getting Help

Before you buy, bring in every expert you can think of. You will want to have all parts of the building and land inspected. You need to know about any permits required for operating a business or remodeling. Expenses come out of nowhere. A future buyer's financial institution may require the roof to be in top condition before it will approve the financing. Is there any reason to talk to a structural engineer, an environmental consultant, an architect, a landscape architect, a tax authority, or anyone else? When in doubt, put out the money and talk to them. A few bucks now can save a lot of bucks later. You may own this building for the next thirty years.

Now that you have done all your research, how much are you willing to offer for the property?

The Offer

Price is not always the critical issue. When interest rates were particularly high, I was looking at properties that purportedly had assumable loans. My offer stated that "if the loans were assumable, then I would pay x dollars. If not assumable, the seller would have to finance at x interest rate. If not, no offer." Before you make an offer, list the most important considerations to make the deal for you. If you are going to need special financing or the right to sell off parcels or guarantees as to the condition of the soil or whatever, these need to come before price. Have your lawyer draft your offer, not your realtor, if there are many terms that need to be negotiated besides price. You have to convince the seller that your offer is reasonable. Be prepared with suggestions that may alleviate his concerns and not hurt your position.

The Price

There is no rule about offering x % below the list price. Figure out what you are willing to pay and offer less. Negotiate up to your number. Do not agree above your number just to close the deal. There are thousands of properties out there. Let this one go if you do not get your price and terms. You have learned something from the process. Perhaps this city is overpriced and it is best to look elsewhere. The next time you will be more efficient with your analysis and negotiations. But do not overpay. If you are counting on a good market to bail you out, you are going to get the opportunity for an even bigger lesson.

The property in our example is listed for $500,000. It looks very promising, based on the analysis you have done. Should you offer $490,000 and be prepared to pay another $10,000? Your most reliable projections are for year 1 results. You expect to get a 7.5% total return the first year. But you need 10% a year to live on. Your projections show that in later years you will do much better than 10%. It would be best to look at other properties to see if there are any that show a better possibility of giving you a 10% return the first year that also have good prospects for future years. (When I had great confidence in my projections, I bought properties that had a return of substantially less than 10% the first year. Some of these have worked out exceptionally well, and some have not.) If, after comparing your example to many other properties, it looks to be the best and you continue to have confidence in your projections, then make an offer.

Once you have bought a property, your real problems begin.

Management Issues During Ownership

The five issues that come up are filling vacancies, changing rents and leases, maintaining the property, making improvements, and preparing the property for sale. For most of you, the issues around buying and selling the properties are the most exciting. But it is the other issues that determine whether you can live off your buildings or not. If vacancies are not filled or expenses get too high, you will not be able to pay your personal bills. You must pay attention to these matters. If you are using a property manager, have regular meetings or phone conversations. Study the reports you get. If you get a notion there might be a problem, there is a problem.

It is better to act sooner rather than later. I let myself be convinced by a property manager that there was no point getting rid of a delinquent tenant because supposedly: (1) the market was so bad that I could not replace her and, (2) the improvements I would have to make to attract a new tenant were so costly that it would take a year to break even. So the delinquent tenant became a non-paying tenant, and the losses mounted without any marketing or improvements. Finally the tenant was ousted and improvements made for a new tenant. The loss of rent was about five times what the ultimate improvement expenses cost. My thinking was "the property manager knows best, he is there every day, I am an airline flight away, go with his judgment." This thinking is often valid on issues such as improvements to fix up the place and make it more attractive to prospective tenants. But in the matter of allowing a tenant to stay who is delinquent, the owner needs to decide and decide quickly.

The on-site manager should be asking prospects what they are looking for and what would make your building work for them. Often simple things like paint or plants in the hallways, new carpets, trash cans, or shade trees in the parking lot can make a big difference at little cost.

There always comes a time with every property that you feel the need to sell. Before incurring expenses to prepare a property for sale, interview several brokers and see what their prospective marketing plans will consist of. Then make repairs and improvements that fit in with the plan you have decided on.

Selling and Tax Issues

The best time to sell is when the current property appears to have little prospect of returning 10% a year for the next five years, based on its current appraised value, and you have located another property that does appear to have what you are looking for. The second best time to sell is when the current property does not have good prospects and you have decided to reinvest the sales proceeds in another asset class. The third best time to sell is when the current property does not have good prospects and you have decided to use the sale proceeds for living expenses. Never sell when, based on the current appraisal, your property has good prospects of returning 10% a year for the next five years. Selling expenses and tax consequences are so large that it is never a good idea to trade in and out of different properties, hoping to make quick profits.

An advantage of staying with the same property for many years is that you get better and better at understanding an individual market and working with your property manager, accountant, and tenants. You will find more and more ways to save money, keep tenants happy, and increase rents. Of course when markets start getting overbuilt or the local economy heads into a long slide, the best management in the world will not make you money. But most recessions last a year or two and many affect only certain property types. Generally, overbuilding has a much more devastating effect on a real estate market than recession.

If you intend to reinvest in a new property once you sell, talk to a tax advisor before entering into a contract to either sell or buy. If structured right, you can postpone all the capital gains taxes from the sale of the current property.

Individual properties are a superior asset class for retired investors. But they require substantial time and attention. If you want some of the benefits of real estate without spending more than a few hours a week, and have less than one sixth of your assets in U.S. stocks, REITs would be appropriate for you. The section beginning on page 235 explains how to purchase REITs. If a predictable return is more important to you than a large return, consider the next chapter on fixed income investments.

chapter eight

Fixed Income
Investments

Fixed income investments include bonds, CDs, money market funds, and treasury bills. Fixed income investments pay a fixed amount to the owner at fixed intervals for a fixed time period, after which the owner is entitled to receive the face amount of the investment. For example, the owner of a $100,000 five-year corporate bond will receive $2,000 of interest every three months for five years and then the face amount of $100,000. An owner of $100,000 of corporate stock may receive a dividend check every quarter if the corporation votes to send one, but the owner has no right to demand any dividend. After five years the owner of stock will get whatever price the market offers for the stock, sometimes far more than $100,000 and sometimes far less. The certainties of fixed income investments are their greatest appeal and their greatest liability for the long-term investor.

Advantages and Disadvantages of Fixed Income Assets for Retired Investors

Throughout this book I have discussed the short-term unpredictability of investing and have suggested strategies to deal with it. Fixed income investing is very simple and predictable. As long as you stay with high-quality investments, you can plan to the dollar the amounts you will receive to live on over any given time period. The problem is the amounts you will receive to live on will be low. If you look at the list on page 51 , you will notice that six of the seven lowest returns available are from fixed income investments. Given the need to reinvest to preserve your lifestyle in an inflationary world, some of these returns are simply too low for most of you to live on the rest of your lives. If your cost of living increases 3% a year and you are getting 3% a year on your treasury bills, the only way you can protect your assets from inflation is to reinvest that 3% and spend nothing on living expenses. If you expect a 2% increase in your living expenses and you have a very large portfolio or very low expenses, a 3% return may work. But very few people will fit this category. However, if your target investment return is 7% (you have a large portfolio, low expenses) including a 2% inflation adjustment, you might be tempted to invest it all in bonds paying 7% and not worry about market fluctuations. Is this a good idea?

Predictability versus Volatility

Predictability is the greatest appeal of fixed income investing. Predictability is not lack of volatility. A thirty-year, 6% treasury bond is both highly predictable and highly volatile. It is a certainty that every year for thirty years the U.S. government will pay the owner of this bond 6% of the face value, and at the end of thirty years the owner will receive the face value of the bond. But should the owner of the bond wish to sell it at any time during those thirty years, the price will be highly volatile. The owner could receive as little as half the face value or as much as twice the face value.

The volatility of a fixed income security depends on its time to maturity and its coupon or stated interest rate. Some securities, such as money market funds, are not volatile. They can be cashed in at any time for exactly their cost. Such investments are often referred to as "cash" even though they pay interest, unlike the dollar bills in your wallets. Their interest rate varies from day to day, but the price of the security is always the same. Securities with maturities of less than a year, such as treasury bills or six-month brokered CDs, have very little volatility. They can be bought and sold for roughly the same price throughout their life. As security maturities go from one year to thirty years, their volatility increases greatly. In addition, intermediate and long-term securities with low coupon rates are more volatile than those with high coupon rates.

A twenty-year, AA corporate bond with a 4% coupon will be more volatile than a twenty-year, AA corporate bond with a 10% coupon. One strategy, discussed in detail below, for using highly volatile bonds to live off is to rely on their predictability rather than their volatility.

Predictability has value in the investing world. For paying fixed expenses, fixed income lets inexperienced investors sleep at night. Knowing when and how much cash you will receive for the next thirty years allows for planning that simply is not possible with a portfolio of all real estate or all stock. Many investors, including most of the large pension funds, endowment funds, and insurance companies, are willing to exchange lower long-term returns for predictability.

After owning bonds for about five years, I realized that a portfolio of five different high-return asset classes that excluded bonds had both high predictability and high returns. Over a period of years, I sold my fixed income investments and added to my real estate, international, and emerging market stocks. But in doing so, I gave up another benefit of fixed income securities. I reduced my protection against deflation.

Government Bonds Are the Best Deflation Investment

The other appeal of fixed income investments is that they perform the best of any asset classes in periods of deflation. If you are considering a substantial investment in fixed income securities, you must have a good understanding of inflation and deflation.

We have not seen real deflation in the United States since the 1930s. From the peak of inflation in the mid teens in 1981 until the present 2% level, the United States has been experiencing disinflation, meaning that the rate of inflation has been declining. But all these years there has been some inflation. Deflation means that the general price level in the economy declines for at least six months. It can be measured by declines in the consumer price indexes or declines in wider price indexes, including consumer prices, producer prices, government prices, and so forth. Within a balanced economy, prices of some goods are always going up and other prices are going down. These trends affect individual companies and industries, but they do not affect entire asset classes like the stock market or the bond market.

Deflation is caused by lack of demand. When an economy has more productive capacity than demand for its products, prices decline. Inflation is caused by excessive demand. When demand for an economy's output exceeds supply, prices rise. The cure for deflation includes lower interest rates and lower taxes. The cure for excessive inflation includes higher interest rates but not higher taxes.

Deflation destroys corporate profits. As prices fall faster than costs, corporations lose money. Stock prices decline sharply during deflation. Interest rates decline, but corporations often are unable to make their bond payments because they have no profits and can sell their assets only at a loss. Government bonds do well. If tax revenues decline, governments simply print money to make bond payments.

In Japan in the 1990s, prices of many goods have been declining such that the average cost of living has gone down. Many companies have been forced to sell goods for less than they cost to make. For this and other reasons, the stock market dropped from 39,000 to 14,000. Meanwhile, the government bond market soared. Ten-year government bond rates dropped from 8% to 1%. Japanese investors living off long-term government bonds in the 1990s found that their income bought more each year and left more to reinvest. Housing prices particularly dropped. In some neighborhoods, the Japanese bond investor could have gotten a house for less than half what it sold for in 1989. A Japanese stock investor would have had less than half his assets left to buy a house.

Japan has had a general price decline. This is devastating for an economy and its stock market. There are deflationary periods that do not hurt an economy or stocks. At times of rapid productivity improvement, prices decline because it is cheaper to produce goods and services. If these productivity improvements apply to enough parts of the economy, there will be brief periods when price indexes decline. This happened briefly in the United States in the 1950s as the war factories and manpower were shifted into highly productive economic uses. It also happened in the 1920s when new technology made production of goods much more efficient than previously. During these brief periods of deflation, stocks were better investments than government bonds. But during the 1930s, when we had general price deflation, government bonds were a far better investment than stocks.

To protect against deflation, it is necessary to own long-term central government bonds. When short-term bonds come due, you will get your principal back but you will not be able to reinvest at a decent rate of interest or at all. With a long-term bond, your rate of interest will remain the same during the entire deflationary period. But if you do not own central government bonds, there is a great risk of default. With many corporations going under in deflationary times, even highly rated corporate bonds may not survive. And state and local government bonds are also more vulnerable than treasuries as state and local governments do not have the ability to print money if necessary to pay bond holders.

In my opinion, for the next twenty years, the probability of 2% to 4% inflation is very high, the probabilities of 0% to 2% inflation and 4% to 10% inflation are low, and the probability of deflation is very low.

High Inflation

The probabilities of high inflation are low because most of the typical causes of high inflation are not now present in the economy and are unlikely to reappear in the future. The Federal Reserve and large bondholders have learned to raise interest rates with authority anytime inflation appears to be rising. Wage demands are unlikely to be successful in this era of corporate downsizing and ever cheaper and more productive technology. While energy prices should continue to rise over the next twenty years, this is not likely to lead to excess money supply as it did in the 1970s. Then international banks with OPEC assets flowing in lent recklessly to Latin American countries desperate to keep up their standards of living in an inflationary world. This lending multiplied the effects of energy price increases. Today OPEC desperately needs to spend its earnings on capital investments, Latin

America has tamed its excess borrowing needs, and the emerging economies of Asia are huge savers with no need for loans from the United States.

There will, however, be inflation in the next twenty-five years. The retirement of the baby boom generation guarantees this. Demand for large segments of goods and services will at least stay even when they retire. Demand may even go up as the excess workers now have time to consume. Supply of goods and services will decrease as these workers no longer produce. This will drive up prices. Meanwhile, demand for U.S. stocks, bonds, and other over-owned retirement investments will decline and supply will increase as baby boomers sell investments to buy goods and services. This will drive down prices of these investments and allow excess money supply to flow into goods and services. There will be price inflation in the goods and services used by retirees and perhaps general price inflation. Do not overcommit to bonds. High inflation can destroy bond returns. So can high taxes.

If your gross return from a bond is 7% but you lose one third of that to taxes, your after-tax return will be less than 5%. If you must save 3% for the future, you must live on a return of 2%. For this reason, many investment advisors recommend tax-free municipal bonds for retired investors. Is this a good idea?

The Municipal Bond Myth

Many bonds issued by state and local governments are free of federal, state, and local income taxes. This is a very positive feature of any investment. However, many people living off their investments have given far too much weight to this tax-free feature. It is my theory that they are motivated by dislike of taxes rather than any rational expectation of outperforming other asset classes. Below I will explain how to determine whether municipal bonds are a better asset for you than treasury bonds or corporate bonds. That is an important comparison to make. But for any long-term investor, real estate, large U.S. stocks, small U.S. stocks, foreign stocks, emerging market stocks, and many other asset classes have always and will always produce higher before-tax and after-tax total returns than municipal bonds.

This is especially true for investors living off their assets. As there are many tax advantages from living off assets, such as no tax on returns of capital, lower tax rates on capital gains, and tax deferral from depreciating real estate, it is not required that anyone living off his or her investments pay the highest tax rates. Since municipals often pay as much as 40% less interest than corporate bonds, their tax benefits only compensate taxpayers in the highest brackets.

Municipal bonds are not the risk-free asset that their promoters claim. There is considerable political risk in municipal bonds. Currently, flat tax proposals include provisions making the interest on municipal bonds federally taxable. Since 1986, Congress has narrowed the federal tax-free status of municipal bonds and could end that status at any time. This would cause a permanent drop of 25% to 33% in the value of municipal bonds. You would not want to have all your assets in this one asset class. In addition, municipal bonds have never been free from capital gains taxes. Plus municipal bonds bought for more than their original issue price are subject to severe capital gains tax penalties that do not apply to other premium bonds.

Do not overcommit to municipal bonds. Bonds are, however, excellent investments in times of deflation, if you feel a long-term deflation is coming. They also add predictability to your portfolio. How do bonds fit into a diversified portfolio of three to five asset classes?

Correlation with Other Asset Classes

There are two ways to make money from long-term fixed income securities and only one way to make money from short-term fixed income investments. The only way to benefit from short-term bills and money market funds is to collect interest. For every dollar invested, you receive back a dollar plus interest. If interest rates rise, you do better with money market funds, and if they decline, you do worse.

Long-term bonds pay interest and can go up and down in value. If you buy a newly issued long-term bond paying 9% and over a period of time long-term rates decline to 6%, you will collect your

9% over that time period and you can also sell your bond for much more than you paid for it. If you bought a newly issued 6% bond and rates rose to 9%, you would still collect 6%, but if you sold before maturity you would get back substantially less than you paid for the bond. Long-term bonds do well when interest rates decline, and they do poorly when interest rates rise.

The returns on long-term bonds are highly correlated with the returns on stocks of the same country. Declining interest rates lower borrowing costs for businesses, which raises their profits and stock prices. This is particularly true in financial and other businesses that borrow huge sums at low rates and lend out at higher rates. Rising interest rates hurt businesses and stock prices as they raise borrowing costs and reduce profits. So stock prices and long-term bond prices generally move in the same direction.

Long-term bond prices and real estate prices are somewhat correlated. Borrowing costs are an important element of the real estate business. But as long-term interest rates declined from the mid-1980s to the mid-1990s and long-term bonds rallied, commercial real estate experienced a severe recession. This is because real estate is more influenced by the supply and demand characteristics of its local market than by interest rates. The correlation between bond prices and real estate is moderate.

Long-term bond prices in the United States are only moderately correlated to foreign stock prices and are not correlated to emerging market stock prices. Trade flows between the U.S. and major foreign economies have been increasing for many years such that changes in our interest rates can have an effect on company profits in Germany or Japan. If German imports are being financed by an American bank or if a Japanese auto maker needs dollars to build an American auto plant, then U.S. interest rates will affect their profits and therefore their stock price.

Changes in U.S. interest rates also affect the price of the dollar versus the Euro or the Japanese yen. Sometimes a rise in U.S. interest rates will lead to a rise in the dollar that will reduce the value of foreign assets denominated in foreign currencies held by U.S. investors. Thus a rise in U.S. interest rates can hurt both your bond holdings and your foreign stock holdings. But not always; there are many times that a rise in U.S. interest rates leads to a decline in the value of the dollar and thus an increase in the value of your foreign holdings.

The influence of U.S. interest rates on emerging markets is even more erratic than the influence on foreign markets. Some emerging market currencies are pegged to the dollar by their country's central banks. But as the low-cost producers of many goods worldwide, their trade profits, and thus stock prices, depend on worldwide demand and not U.S. interest rates. Their huge savings rates and access to Japanese capital allow them to finance expansion without regard to U.S. interest rates.

Returns on short-term fixed income securities are generally the opposite of those on other asset classes. High interest rates lead to high money market returns, low bond prices, low stock prices, and often low real estate prices, and at times to low foreign stock returns.

Fixed income securities can add diversity to your portfolio. How much should you invest in fixed income securities?

How Much Should You Invest in Bonds?

As I have stated, in my opinion, for the next twenty years, the probability of 2% to 4% inflation is very high, the probabilities of 0% to 2% inflation and 4% to 10% inflation are low, and the probability of deflation is very low. In this environment, it would be prudent not to rely too much on bonds as a hedge against deflation. Foreign stocks and emerging market stocks can do well when there is deflation at home and have much better long-term returns. While Japan suffered deflation in the early 1990s, bonds were not the best investments for Japanese investors. Non-Japanese stocks did quite well for Japanese investors, despite the rise of the yen against many currencies. In fact, by 1999 many Japanese stocks had higher yields than Japanese government bonds. If deflation continues, stocks may provide better returns in Japan than government bonds.

Do not substitute real estate for bonds as a hedge against deflation. If there is a mortgage to pay, the payments will not decrease, yet deflation may lead to lower rents. Nor is it likely that the market value of the building will remain intact in a severe deflation. In the 1929 to 1933 deflation, real estate values declined as much as stock values, and the typical stock lost 90%. A building with no mortgage may be able to keep a positive cash flow in a severe deflation, provided real estate taxes can be reduced to meet current appraised values and insurance and other costs can be similarly reduced. But a government bond and foreign stocks would be much better investments.

If inflation takes hold again, you do not want to be caught with a large bond position. In a fast-rising inflationary environment, the best investment is a money market fund or other security with a dollar-for-dollar redemption value that has a daily or weekly adjusted rate of interest. High inflation leads to high interest rates. Bonds do poorly when interest rates rise because their fixed rates will be lower than what is currently being offered on the market. A bond with a coupon of 6% loses substantial value when bonds with coupons of 10% become available. The cash value of a money market fund that can be redeemed at one dollar for each dollar invested stays even and pays a higher rate of interest as rates rise.

If you have a high need for predictability, invest up to half of your assets in bonds, provided the average return on your portfolio meets your target investment return. If you expect long-term deflation or want to add some predictability to your income stream, invest up to one third of your assets in bonds. However, it is reasonable for many of you with three to five asset classes to own no bonds.

How Much Should You Invest in Short-term Securities?

The long-term returns from money market funds and CDs are about 4% a year and from treasury bills about 3% a year. This is rarely enough to live on. Yet the best-selling asset allocations continue to recommend 5% to 20% of your assets should be in short-term securities. This makes no sense for you. You need income to pay your expenses. A 3% to 4% return long term is not enough.

Short-term securities' strongest appeal is during high inflation. There are few other good investments during times of rising inflation. Gold, when the supply available is not excessive, has historically stayed even with inflation. Real estate was once thought to be a good inflation hedge but, as discussed in Chapter 7, if there is excess supply or insufficient demand, real estate can do poorly in times of high inflation. Stocks get hurt in times of high inflation because most businesses are unable to raise their prices enough to compensate for their rising wage, supply, and capital costs. For stock prices to stay flat, profits must at least rise as much as the rate of inflation. Declining profits and losses will lead to plunging stock prices. International stocks can do well in times of high U.S. inflation if the dollar declines and the inflation stays in the United States. But if the inflation is worldwide, international stocks will not fare well either. Short-term securities are your best bet during sustained high inflation.

The amount of cash to keep on hand is both an asset allocation issue and a practical living problem. Between a money market fund and a checking account, I keep one to four months' living expenses in cash. When the level gets down to about a month's living expenses, I sell something. I have plenty of liquid assets, so I can raise funds quickly when necessary. Each person needs to decide for him- or herself how much cash to hold for living expenses. For the long-term investor with other liquid assets, the smallest tolerable living expense account is the best.

Use short-term securities primarily for current expense accounts. Even if you expect severe inflation, do not invest more than one sixth of your assets in short-term securities. The total of bonds and short-term securities in your portfolio should never exceed 50%.

How to Invest in Short-term Securities

There are many types of short-term securities. Make comparisons and pick those that best suit your needs. If you make a mistake, don't worry. If you wait until maturity, a year or less, you can switch to another short-term security without costs or tax liability.

When comparing short-term securities, it is important to compare the effective rate of interest or yield on one security with the yield on another security. Some securities like treasury bills are sold at a discount and have no stated interest rate. But T-bills have a yield. Other securities have a stated interest rate but are not compounded. The interest on some securities is compounded daily. The more often interest is compounded, the higher the yield. Because of compounding, two products with the same stated interest rate and term can have different yields. With short-term securities you want high yield and high liquidity.

Money market funds have checking account privileges and yields above those of savings accounts, money market deposit accounts, and most CDs and T-bills that are six months or shorter to termination. Avoid money market deposit accounts. These are bank accounts that are supposed to compete with money market mutual funds but never pay as much interest. The name of these accounts often leads investors to believe they are buying mutual funds.

There are many types of money market funds with many different yields. It is best to look for a money market fund that has had one of the highest yields for many years. Often fund families offer money market funds for limited periods of time that have all their expenses paid by the fund family and not the money market fund. As a result, the yield is often higher than that of other money market funds for a short period of time. Once the fund family is no longer waiving the fees, these money market funds generally fall into the worst yield group. It is best to stay with consistent winners than trying to scramble back and forth between funds with waived fees every few months.

There are money market funds that hold corporate securities, those that hold treasury bills, those that hold municipal securities, and those that hold combinations. The interest on corporate securities is fully taxable. The interest on treasury bills is exempt from state and local taxes. The interest on municipal securities is exempt from federal, state, and local taxes. But corporate securities pay higher interest rates than treasury bills, which pay higher interest rates than municipal short-term securities.

All money market funds are safe. There is virtually no risk of losing your investment in any form of money market fund. The only question is whether your taxes are high enough to warrant accepting lower returns from T-bill funds or municipal money market funds.

CDs with six months or more to termination often have higher yields than money market funds. If the FDIC insures the bank that issues the CD, there is no risk of losing your investment. The problem with using CDs to fund living expenses is that they are not liquid. If you need the cash before the CD matures, you will lose your interest. There are, however, CDs that can be bought and sold from a brokerage house that do not need to be held until maturity. As the broker earns his commission from the issuing bank and the broker has CDs from all over the country, you can get both liquidity and a higher yield from this form of purchase. Note that brokers do sell CDs from uninsured banks with higher yields. These are not worth the risk.

The interest on both standard CDs and brokered CDs is not paid until the CD matures. For tax purposes, there is no tax liability until the interest is paid. Thus you can defer taxes on the interest for the length of the CD plus the number of months until your estimated tax payments or final tax payments are due. For example, if you buy an eighteen-month CD on July 20 that pays interest on January 20 of the second following year, the taxes on the interest will not be due until April 15 of that second year, when your next estimated tax payment is due. The longer and more often you can defer paying taxes on your income, the longer and more often you will be able to compound your return from reinvesting that income.

Treasury bills are considered the safest short-term investment. These are direct obligations of the U.S. government. CDs are just insured by the FDIC, a government agency. If you are using short-term securities for one sixth of your portfolio, then the absolute security of T-bills may appeal to you. They are less liquid than treasury bill money market funds. But the returns over time should be higher because you are not paying fees for fund management. Individual T-bills can take a few weeks to sell on the open market if bought directly through the Treasury. If the bills are bought through a dealer bank, they can be sold at any time, provided you pay whatever transaction fees are charged by the bank.

If you want to own T-bills to fund living expenses, use a T-bill money market fund. If you are holding T-bills as a long-term investment, buy direct from the Treasury and automatically roll them over when they come due so you do not lose income between bills.

How to Invest in Bonds

Investing in bonds is more complicated than investing in short-term securities. There are many issues to deal with. The bond market is highly volatile. Every bond has several features to consider. Reinvestment risk is a big factor in achieving your target return. You can do the investing yourself or you can hire a money manager or a mutual fund manager to do it for you. And there is a myriad of new bondlike products coming to market every year.

I will show you some simple strategies to resolve these issues. If these strategies are applied, most investors can manage their own bond portfolio without ending up like Orange County. I will also discuss the pros and cons of mutual funds and money managers who, for a fee, will manage a bond portfolio for you.

Bonds are an asset class that you need to be both predictable and secure. I have discussed predictability. Security involves the ability of the debtor to pay both interest and principal in full over the entire term of the bond. Even though a corporate bond has a fixed payment schedule, it is not guaranteed that the payments will be made. If the corporation goes into bankruptcy, you will likely lose some or all of the interest and principal payments owed to you. Since bonds pay less than most other asset classes, it is especially important that the amount they do pay be secure. Over the long haul, the best you can do with bonds is receive the face amount of the bond and all interest payments. The return on stocks or real estate is unlimited. For example, $1,000 invested in Wal-Mart when it went public in 1970 is worth more than $2,000,000 today; $1,000 invested in a thirty-year government bond in 1970 is worth $1,000 today, plus any reinvested interest payments. Yet the downside is the same in bonds, stocks, and real estate. A $1,000 investment can become zero in all three.

It is expected that stocks or real estate will have bad years when the returns are lower than what you need to live off. This is tolerable because in good years stocks and real estate will provide far more than is needed for your living expenses. This in not true with bonds. A few bad years of bond defaults are rarely followed by years strong enough to make up the deficits. In the 1980s low-quality, high-yield bonds became in vogue on the theory that, over time, high yields would more than compensate for defaults. Unfortunately, the results proved otherwise. The theory was based on a study of bonds in the boom years following the Depression and World War II. Those years were an exception to the norm that prevailed in the 1980s. The loss of capital from defaults was far worse than expected, and many investors not only failed to compensate with high yields but in fact suffered many years of negative total returns. When investing in bonds, safety is the first requirement.

There is, however, a range of safe bonds to invest in. Treasury bonds do not default. These bonds are issued directly by the U.S. government. Bonds issued by agencies of the U.S. government will not default either. These agencies include the Federal Home Loan Bank, the Government National Mortgage Association, Student Loan Marketing, and the Inter-American Development Bank. Agency bonds pay a bit higher interest than treasury bonds but for all practical purposes are just as secure.

Corporate and municipal government bonds can be highly secure or on the verge of default. Fortunately, you do not need to figure out for yourselves where they are on the risk scale. Standard and Poor's and Moody's rate all the liquid bonds for you. The highest-rated bonds are AAA (S&P terminology versus Aaa for Moody's). The next highest is AA, followed by A, BBB, BB, B, CCC, CC, C and D. Bonds rated A and above have a very low risk of default. Bonds rated BBB and below have a risk of default.

There are two rules to follow if you are managing your bond portfolio yourself. Always know what your bonds are rated and never invest in bonds rated lower than A. If you are using a money manager or a mutual fund that works full-time in bond investing, it is okay to invest in S&P BBB or Moody's Baa bonds, but never any lower grade. Over the long haul, investing in lower grades will not pay off for you.

Do-It-Yourself Strategies

You are looking for income to live on and to reinvest to offset inflation. There are no new income products that have been invented in the last fifteen years that work any better for you than bonds. All sorts of leveraged, derivative, swapped, floating rate, variable, inverse, collateralized, reserve, zero coupon, whole life, annuity, whiter than white products are sold. Despite the salespeople's claims, these products have yet to prove themselves over a lifetime of investing. Many have led to spectacular bankruptcies like that of Orange County in 1994. Keeping it simple in this area also keeps it cheap. In addition to the untested risks of these products, there are high and sometimes hidden commissions to pay. Companies that sell these products are getting rich. Consumers are not benefiting.

You need a system to get high interest over a lifetime. You need to reinvest some interest every year and your principal when your bonds come due. But the interest rates available change from day to day and year to year. And many bonds that appear to offer a good interest rate for many years get called. Here is how to achieve a livable, long-term return from bonds.

Avoid callable bonds. Most long-term corporate and municipal bonds are callable. This means the corporation or municipality issuing the bonds can buy the bond back either at face value or a higher price. If your bond has a particularly high yield and it gets called at a time when interest rates are low, you will get your money back but not have the option of reinvesting at the high rate. For example, if you bought a callable corporate bond in 1981 paying 14% for thirty years, you would be happy today to still hold that bond. Unfortunately, most corporate bonds issued for thirty years are callable after five to seven years. As interest rates in the late 1980s were much lower than 14%, the corporation issuing the bond would have called it in by paying you the face amount and possibly a little more. You would have to buy another bond to keep interest checks coming but at much lower rates. It is common for intermediate-term bonds up to ten years to be noncallable. Treasuries are rarely callable.

Stay away from mortgages. Mortgages are not good investments for you because they are freely callable. Anytime the mortgage payer sees that interest rates have gone down, they can refinance. If you own thirty-year, fixed-rate mortgages, either individually or in a fund, you may think that you are set for thirty years. But it is unlikely that you will collect on any of these mortgages for that long. They will all be either refinanced when rates go down or paid off when property is sold. And if rates go up, you will be stuck accepting the lower thirty-year rates as long as rates remain above the rates you are getting. This is a bad bargain.

Do not invest in bonds with a longer term than ten years. As a rule, interest rates are higher for longer-term bonds. But the differences between ten-year bonds and thirty-year bonds are generally less than .5% and at times as little as .1%. Long-term studies of returns on ten-year bonds and thirty-year bonds have shown very little difference in total returns.

For the most predicable, secure return, use the basic humility bond portfolio: five or more treasury or agency bonds in equal amounts spread over ten or more years at equal intervals. You will average 6% from long-term treasury bonds even if today the best you can do is 5%. Interest rates fluctuate. Generally, long-term rates are higher than short-term rates. But long-term rates are sometimes lower than short-term rates, and sometimes all rates are lower than your target return. Other times, all rates are higher than your target return. The best strategy is to buy bonds with different maturities and each time a bond matures, reinvest in a bond with a longer maturity than any you have left. This way you are assured of good average rates over a lifetime. Assume, for example, that you have $250,000 to invest in bonds and you are looking for an extremely secure 6% return. You could set up a ladder that looks like this:

AMOUNT	MATURITY	TYPE	INTEREST
$50,000	10 yr.	Treasury	6.5%
$50,000	8 yr.	Treasury	6.5%
$50,000	6 yr.	Treasury	6%
$50,000	4 yr.	Treasury	6%
$50,000	2 yr.	Treasury	5%

This ladder would give you an interest rate of 6% for two years. At the end of two years, you would have $50,000 in cash and 8- ,6- ,

4-, and 2-year bonds. Since the bond that just paid off had the lowest coupon, 5%, you need to reinvest your $50,000 at only 5% to get an average return of 6% for the next two years. If interest rates were then 5% or higher on treasury bonds, you would simply buy a $50,000, ten-year treasury. If interest rates on ten-year treasuries were lower than 5%, you should buy a ten-year treasury or agency bond at whatever rate is available. Two years later, ten-year treasuries or agencies may be paying high enough interest rates to bring your average interest sufficiently above 6% to make up for the two years of lower returns. When followed over time, this strategy will never compromise your security needs and will result in your reaching your target return. There is no call risk and no credit risk. Since your target investment return of 6% is the long-term average return for ten-year treasuries, there will be as many years when you reinvest at rates higher than you need as there will be years when you reinvest at rates lower than you need.

Do not overdiversify. One purpose of diversification is to reduce the effect on the portfolio from defaults. For example, a junk bond fund will buy one hundred different bonds on the premise that three or four bonds will go into default over time but the returns on the other ninety-six or ninety-seven bonds will be high enough to compensate. Treasuries and agencies do not default. You want to buy five bonds not to prevent defaults but to spread out your maturities over ten years.

Keep expenses as low as possible by buying only five bonds and holding each to maturity. Since bonds provide among the lowest returns of the asset classes, it is important to keep as much of that return as possible. Incurring 1% expenses on an asset that returns 6% is much more devastating to your lifestyle than incurring 1% expenses on an asset that returns 14%. The commissions, service charges, and dealer spreads charged on the purchase of bonds are a percentage of the purchase price. The higher the purchase price, the lower the percentage for commissions, service charges, and spreads. Thus buying five bonds for $50,000 each will result in lower commissions than buying ten bonds at $25,000 each or buying twenty bonds at $12,500 each. Holding bonds to maturity results in no commission. Selling bonds prior to maturity incurs a sales commission.

Set up your humility portfolio now, regardless of current interest rates. You might believe that it is silly right now to buy bonds. It is very clear to you that interest rates are low. If you just leave your money in a money market fund and wait a few years, rates will be much higher. Then you can put everything into bonds paying at least 3% more than today and have plenty of income to live on. The problem is, it is not possible to predict interest rates. Even economists who believe it is not possible to predict interest rates believe it is possible *sometimes* to predict interest rates. While they concede that over long periods of time one cannot consistently predict interest rates, there are times when it is clear that interest rates are extremely low or extremely high. I disagree even with this premise. In 1974 AAA long bond rates were the highest in history, 8.5%. Very conservative economists thought they could not go higher and advised investors to go heavily into long-term bonds. By January, 1982 these bonds had lost almost half of their value as long AAA rates were then as high as 16%. Predicting that rates were headed higher still and that Paul Volker was incapable of stopping inflation, I sold a portfolio of bonds bought in 1974 and started a ladder with the proceeds. Rates peaked in 1982. I was dead wrong about my interest rate prediction. At least with a ladder, a large percent of my bonds were long-term. I got a high average return for the rest of the 1980s.

Each time a bond matures, buy a new one immediately. Do not time the market even a day. If it looks like you made a mistake, wait. You will get another chance to buy in two years.

Do not trade bonds. Trading bonds can destroy your after-tax returns. As you cannot predict interest rates, you are just as likely to incur trading losses as trading gains. You will be stuck many years with less money to reinvest due to your losses and no offsetting tax breaks. This is because capital losses can be deducted against ordinary income only up to $3,000 a year. Also, by incurring large capital gains taxes now, rather than ordinary taxes over many years, you are reducing your funds available for reinvestment and thus penalizing your future returns. You will also have substantial trading costs.

For higher returns, set up a corporate bond ladder. The humility strategy can be set up for any type of bonds your asset allocation requires. If you are looking for 7% a year from corporate bonds, you can set up a ladder of AAA bonds that will give you that return over the long haul.

Use ten bonds in a corporate ladder. Do not use more than ten bonds because the sales commissions will mount up. Ten bonds will compensate for default risk and downgrades. The biggest problem with the corporate ladder is downgrades. Sometimes a AAA bond gets knocked down to AA or A or even into the Bs. This can be caused by a gradual deterioration of the company's finances or by a sudden takeover or leveraged buyout of the company. Assuming the downgrade is not severe, that is, not below A, and the company appears capable of making all payments till maturity, then it would be reasonable simply to hold the bond until maturity. A bonds are nearly as secure as AAA, so a downgrade to A should not affect your sleep or your current and future income. There is also the possibility of an upgrade to AA or AAA in the future. A downgrade to BBB is not a disaster. These bonds are still highly secure and could some day be upgraded again.

Sell bonds downgraded below BBB. A downgrade below BBB could affect both your sleep and your current and future income. Take your loss and reinvest. This is why it is useful to own ten corporate bonds. Downgrades from AAA to below BBB are very rare. But should one occur, it would affect only 10% of your portfolio and would rarely involve a loss of more than 25% of the pre-downgrade value of the bond.

If you are in a high tax bracket during retirement, use a municipal bond ladder. The municipal bond ladder consists of ten bonds. Though AAA municipal bonds are highly secure, downgrades and defaults happen.

Determine if your tax bracket really justifies municipal bonds before you buy any. When you are living off your investments, your tax situation is much different than when you are working for salary or commissions. The best strategy is to sit down with your tax advisor and go over the likely capital gains and ordinary income for the next few years from all your nonbond asset classes. Then construct a ladder of currently available treasuries, a ladder of currently available corporates, and a ladder of currently available municipals and plug the interest payments into your estimates for the next few years. Remember treasuries are exempt from state and local taxes while municipal bonds are exempt from state, local, and federal taxes. If the tax savings more than compensate for the lower rates on municipal bonds, then buy them.

Do not buy other states' municipal bonds. Some states do not have a large municipal bond market, and other states' finances are in poor shape. It is often argued that if you come from such a state, it is best to construct a portfolio of multi-state municipal bonds. This is true only if there are not enough AAA bonds available to construct your ladder. If there are AAA bonds, then you can be confident of their security regardless of the state's finances or the size of the state market. These bonds are rated AAA for a reason. Some states whose finances are a wreck still offer AAA bonds because the bonds are insured for all principal and interest payments by an independent insurance company. Other AAA municipal bonds have been prefunded, meaning that cash or treasuries have been set aside to pay off the bonds' interest and principal when it comes due, so there is no risk.

Determine how to meet your annual inflation adjustment from each interest payment. If your personal inflation outlook requires you to reinvest 3% each year and you are receiving 6%, then you will need to reinvest half of each interest payment. If you are expecting 2% inflation and getting 7% in interest, then you need to reinvest two sevenths of every interest payment. Using a ladder, you always want to reinvest at ten-year maturities since over time this will give you the best yield. But most individual ten-year bonds are sold only in denominations of $10,000 and higher. So you need either to save up your reinvestment interest until it, combined with any maturity proceeds, equals $10,000 or use another approach.

Save in either a money market account or a bond fund. (Bond funds will be discussed starting on page 188.) If you use a ten-year bond fund, you will get a return equal to that of buying ten-year bonds less the bond fund's expenses and fees. If you use a money market account, you will have lower interest over time than a ten-year bond fund but also lower expenses.

Live with a simple ladder for a few years and see how it works. Then you might want to consider a few ideas for getting better yield without compromising your security.

Ideas for Increasing Returns

Here are a few ways to juice up the returns on your bonds without taking excessive risks.

1. Use agencies instead of treasuries. Agency bonds can pay as much as .5% more than treasuries. I know of no instances of agencies ever missing or even delaying interest payments, much less defaulting. A .5% increase in yield on a large portfolio of bonds over many years can make a big difference. This doesn't mean you need to buy all agency bonds. You could buy agencies only in years when ten-year treasuries are yielding below some set rate, say 6%.

2. There are two types of municipal bonds. General obligation bonds are secured by the tax base of the municipal government. These bonds are highly secure. Revenue bonds are secured by specific projects, real estate, or leases. If the project goes bad, then you do not have a call on the general tax base. As a result, general obligation bonds pay less than revenue bonds. But not all revenue bonds are the same. There are revenue bonds that are rated AAA and are insured and still pay more than general obligation bonds. It is worthwhile to look at insured, AAA revenue bonds.

3. Use A-rated corporates for higher returns. As many A-rated corporates get upgraded to AA as get downgraded to BBB. The risks are not all on the downside.

4. Many studies have shown that ten-year bonds do about the same long term as thirty-year bonds. But some studies indicate there is added yield for every year of maturity. The difference in the studies is based on the years studied. Logically, longer-term bonds ought to pay more than shorter-term bonds even if this has not historically been true. They are

riskier. Lengthening your ladder could result in higher yield. A ladder of fifteen years, twelve years, nine years, six years, and three years might do better than your standard ladder over time. There is little possibility that it will do worse.

5. Consider an occasional trade. Large segments of the bond market are not very liquid. Many bonds are traded less than once a month. Less liquid bonds tend to have higher yields than more liquid bonds. This is a great advantage to investors like you who buy bonds and hold them to maturity. Every once in a while, it is useful to call up your broker and get a real offer or two on the bond you are holding and get a real price for any substantially identical bonds available. In municipal and corporate bonds, you will almost always find that you can get the same rating and/or insurance coverage on another bond that has a higher yield. Even after commissions. Trade only when there are little or no taxable gains or losses, in other words, when current interest rates are about where they were when you bought your bonds. When my broker first suggested this strategy to me, I thought he was just looking for commissions. But, in fact, I was twice able to increase yields after commissions. There are also yield differences between different industries. Utility bonds often pay more than food company bonds, even though both may have the same rating. Different industries come in and out of favor with bond investors. You are not fashion conscious. You only want to get your interest and principal payments on time. Simply choose the highest-yielding bonds.

For most of you, the humility portfolio is the best choice. It is simple, secure, low-cost, and tax efficient. But if you do not want to do it yourself, consider bond funds and money managers.

Bond Funds and Money Managers

There are as many types of bond funds as there are bonds. There are treasury bond funds, convertible bond funds, government guaranteed mortgage funds, single state municipal bond funds, etc. Bond funds come in different average maturities from long-term to short-term. Bond funds have a few advantages and many disadvantages.

Advantages of Bond Funds

Bond fund managers are buying bonds constantly. Interest payments that are not being paid out to the fund shareholders are being reinvested every day. If you are investing in a bond fund that has a yield of 7% and you need only 4% to live on and want to reinvest the rest, a bond fund is very convenient. You simply take your 4% and the rest is automatically reinvested for you no matter how small the amount. There are no commissions or dealer spreads on buying and selling no-load bond funds. To reinvest in individual bonds often requires that you save up as much as $10,000 to buy one bond.

Bond fund managers are highly experienced in evaluating risks and bond intricacies. If you find calls, credit risk, discounts, interest rate risk, and the like overwhelming, then hire an expert to figure out all these things. If you want to own risky bonds believing that they will pay off over the long haul but do not have the time or desire or expertise to evaluate companies, then use a bond fund.

Disadvantages of Bond Funds

The biggest disadvantage of bond funds is the expenses. The typical bond fund has expenses of 1%. A buy and hold treasury fund may have expenses as low as 0.6% and a junk bond fund may have expenses of 2%. Municipal bond funds typically have expenses around 0.8%. Considering that bonds are already low-return assets, expenses like these can make it impossible for you to live off your interest and reinvest to offset inflation. If your expected 5% return from municipal bonds is reduced to 4% by expenses, you will have a hard time living off the interest even if the interest is tax-free.

Another disadvantage of bond funds is that bond managers actively trade. This can both create tax problems for you and lead to poor results. Unless the manager is exceptional, over the years his trades will lead to as many capital gains as capital losses. As discussed beginning on page 177, this will lead to a loss of capital over time.

Unfortunately, bond fund managers have also found more devastating ways to lose capital. Hired, they believe, to outperform the market, many engage in leverage and derivative practices that lead to large losses and severe underperformance. Leverage is very expensive; interest must be paid on loans. These interest expenses can bring total fund expenses to the 2% to 3% level. In a municipal bond fund, that can cut your interest income in half. Other bond funds have invested in foreign bonds. Due to large expenses and currency fluctuations, these moves rarely work as well.

Another drawback is that bond funds rarely hold a bond to maturity. This adds to your taxes and increases bond fund expenses.

Bond funds all hold cash, which reduces returns. Some hold cash as an attempt to time the market. Others hold cash to be able to make redemptions. Whatever the reason, holding cash will reduce the total return of the fund.

There are also some accounting gimmicks used by bond funds that can cost investors money. Many funds buy premium bonds. These are bonds that sell for more than the face value of the bonds. When the bonds mature, the fund realizes a loss as it does not receive its purchase price, only the face value. Thus the value of the bond fund or the payout from the fund or both will suddenly be reduced. Some funds account for this loss annually rather than suddenly when the bond matures. Either way, investors should be aware of how many premium bonds the fund owns and how this will affect future returns.

Since bond funds are perpetual and have constant turnover, they do not have the predictability of individual bonds. With individual bonds, you know exactly when you will get your interest payments and when you will get your investment back. The interest payments from bond funds vary from day to day, depending on the composition of the fund. The value of the fund shares varies from day to day. It is very difficult to plan your spending based on likely receipts from a bond fund.

Selecting a Bond Fund

Begin by compiling a list of no-load intermediate- and long-term bond funds with at least ten-year records. Long-term funds generally hold bonds that mature between seven and thirty years. Intermediate-term funds hold bonds that mature between three and ten years.

- Find the funds with the lowest expenses. There are some bond index funds available that have low expenses. Some have expenses below 0.2% a year.
- From the lowest expense funds, determine which have very low turnover and never engage in leverage or buy derivatives or foreign bonds. Occasionally, there is a mutual fund manager on a streak whose market timing, derivatives, and leverage practices are always working out. As these streaks often come to an end dramatically, it is best for you to avoid these funds.
- From the funds that have made the cut so far, pick the one with the best ten-year record.
- Look closely at index funds before buying. More than 70% of general bond funds do worse than bond index funds. They have low turnover and never engage in leverage or buy derivatives or foreign bonds. They do, however, have much more turnover than a ladder. Indexes of bonds are changed to reflect a preset maturity so the bonds in the index funds have to be sold to mimic the index. Index funds buy only the most highly liquid bonds, as those are the bonds in the index. Often bonds that are less liquid, but are just as secure, are available at higher yields. Here you have to decide if the low expenses and low turnover of an index fund compensate for the lower yields. Generally they do. A fund holding less liquid bonds will often have expenses 1% higher than those of an index fund, yet the bonds will yield only 0.5% more than the bonds in the index.
- If there is little difference between several funds, pick the ladder fund with low expenses over the index fund. These are funds that own bonds with staggered maturities, hold them to maturity, and reinvest the proceeds in the longest

maturities. Although these funds do not have the predictability of the humility bond portfolio, they are more predictable than most bond funds. The staggered maturities keep the share values from making the wide fluctuations of a long-term bond fund. By holding bonds to maturity, the yield on these funds does not fluctuate widely. But as these funds are always taking in new money and liquidating old shareholders, there is turnover in the portfolio and always some cash on hand not being reinvested at the long end.

• Compare your first choice fund with any closed-end funds available. There are times when closed-end funds trade at sufficient discounts to net asset value to give you a good yield advantage over open-ended bond funds. Look for closed-end funds that are managed the same way as desirable open-ended funds. Look for low expenses, no leverage or derivatives, experienced management, low turnover—preferably a ladder fund. Closed-end bond fund managers have abused leverage and derivatives even more than open-ended bond fund managers. Do a lot of research before placing an order.

If bond funds do not fit your needs, consider using a money manager to invest in bonds for you.

Money Managers

Money managers can be used to manage a bond portfolio if it is large enough. Generally, money managers require at least $250,000 of bonds, and some require much more. Go back to the discussion on how to pick a money manager in Chapter 5. The main difference between bond managers and stock managers is fees. Whereas 1.5% to 1% is normal for managing stocks, that would be robbery for managing bonds. Bonds are relatively easy to manage. A fee of 0.5% is the maximum you should be willing to pay for a bond manager. Also, be certain that you are hiring a buy and hold manager. You do not want a trader or a market timer or any leverage or derivatives of any kind.

Anyone connected to any insurance company in any capacity is not a money manager, no matter what they tell you or their literature says. Insurance companies sell many fixed income products.

None fit your needs. The salesperson may promise to watch your portfolio for you for free. You cannot afford this.

You want a money manager who can find small-issue high-quality bonds at low dealer spreads that yield more than the big issues. If he or she can explain to you what is going on when interest rates shoot up and keep you focused on the long term, that is an added bonus. Occasionally, your money manager may trade into better bonds, but that should not happen more than once a year. Most of your bonds should be held to maturity. Your bond manager should be very aware of your tax situation and make trades, if any, with the tax consequences in mind.

Besides bonds, stocks, real estate, foreign stocks, and emerging market stocks, you might look at other asset classes for your portfolio. The next chapter shows you how to determine if other asset classes work for you.

chapter nine

What Else Works?

There are hundreds of asset classes today, and many more will be invented over the next thirty years. If your portfolio is going to produce for the rest of your life, you must have guidelines to analyze any asset class to determine if it meets your needs. Here are six general guidelines to consider before you make an investment.

The Six Guidelines

1. The asset class must be on a different cycle than your other assets. Since a substantial part of your living expenses comes from appreciation and appreciation is less predictable than "income," you need several different asset classes to ensure some appreciation every year. If you own small U.S. stocks and large U.S. stocks, you would get no benefit from shifting money into mid-size U.S. stocks. If the market crashed, all would decline, and if the market boomed, all would do well. Since you need to live off your money each year, you need assets that have different cycles so that your average return will be at least moderately positive each year.

2. You need a reasonably certain positive return over your lifetime large enough to pay expenses plus an inflation premium. Las Vegas or the horses would not work because

there the predictable return over time is negative. Other investments lack certainty because there is no history to look at. Brokerage houses and insurance companies are constantly coming up with new products, but no one knows how they will perform over time. Until products have been through recessions and booms, high inflation and high interest rates, low inflation and low interest rates, war and peace, and Democrats and Republicans, no one knows how they will perform. Real estate and bonds have been tested for centuries and have had large positive returns. Some investments have appeal for the next year or two but are unpredictable beyond that. Others, like gold, have a very long history, but do not return enough to live off.

3. The investment should provide enough easily accessible cash to pay monthly expenses. At times you can afford to invest in an illiquid asset if you can get your living expenses from your other assets. But when you do this, you start to use up your other assets and thereby change your asset allocation. It is best to stay with assets that can immediately contribute to your living expenses. Sometimes the problem is not the asset but the structure of your purchase. For example, it is commonly thought that land is not a good asset for a retiree. But if the purchase is structured right, lots can be sold off from time to time to produce living expenses.

4. It is important that easy, low-cost management be available. Some assets are sold with such high commissions and expenses that it would take extraordinary performance to make them pay off. Since extraordinary performance is unlikely, it is best to stay away from these assets. The RELPs sold in the 1980s are a good example, as are many loaded mutual funds sold today. Other assets have great potential and no fees because they must be managed by the buyer. Often small businesses you must manage yourself because paying a manager would eat up all the profits. This guideline can be ignored if you plan on spending substantial time on this asset rather than hiring someone to manage it for you. In that case, it is important that you have managers for

all your other assets so you can take the time necessary to run this business.

5. If you are going to spend more time on the asset, it must be one that has a possibility of creating large gains. Turning a small business into a large business can create large gains. But spending time on a portfolio of options is not likely to increase returns and may, in fact, create losses.

6. Finally, it is important that the investment creates little or no taxable income for the investor each year. Generally, each time an underlying investment is sold it creates taxable gains. It is possible to owe more in taxes from an investment than the amount of cash you receive from the investment for living expenses. Over time, paying large taxes erodes your capital and hurts your ability to reinvest to offset inflation. Your investment must produce a return to live off and to re-invest. Look for opportunities to live off principal and capital gains rather than fully taxable income. This will keep taxes on living expenses to a minimum. Also look for a steadily appreciating asset that can be sold in small pieces. Assets in tax-deferred accounts work here. But taxable assets can also have these characteristics. Taxes are inevitable, but large tax liabilities are avoidable.

Examples of Other Asset Classes

Using these six guidelines, let's examine some currently popular asset classes and determine if they are appropriate for your needs. I will limit the discussion to those I have some experience with.

Venture Capital

Venture capital essentially means investing in firms or products that have not reached commercial success but are believed to have great potential. These are typically thought of as high-tech or biotech firms, but any untested product from new underwear to new hotels can be considered venture capital until it has been proven either a commercial success or a commercial failure.

There are several different ways to invest venture capital. You can invest individually in a firm or product. You can get together with a group of investors and invest together in a firm or product to spread your risks. There are also venture capital pools and funds run by managers. The funds can be anything from biotech funds to real estate "vulture" funds that are put together to buy distressed real estate. Funds are typically structured as limited partnerships with an eight- to twelve-year life.

Some groups accept only "accredited investors," which essentially means that you must have a net worth of at least $1,000,000 and have earned at least $200,000 in each of the last two years. Presumably this is for the benefit of the investor. In fact, it is for the benefit of the promoter. It is highly unlikely that a dentist making more than $200,000 a year who has put away $1,000,000 has had the time or interest to learn enough about investing to separate good prospects from bad. A full-time investor living off $500,000 in assets would have the experience and time to evaluate the investment. The dentist, discovering that she was an "accredited investor," may well get enough of an ego boost to do less diligent research than she should.

Venture capital is on its own cycle. The right new product, even if introduced to the market during a recession, can become a big success. The right product makes its own cycles.

Unfortunately, the predictability of success in venture capital is low. While there are eras when it seems that almost every new innovation is profitable, there are others when nothing is a hit. Venture capital is not the place for steady returns. Many readers of this book will have made your fortune from venture capital. But having made your fortune, it is best to change strategies with the bulk of your assets to preserve them and live off them.

By investing in a venture capital fund or pooling investments with other investors, it is possible to spread the risks. If a fund is involved with ten ventures and nine are failures, it is possible to still make money if the tenth has a better than 1000% return. But that is not predictable.

It is also not possible to get living expenses from venture capital. There is never any current income from venture capital. In some schemes, there is the opposite. Investors are sometimes called on to put in more capital. While some deals are structured to require the company to buy the investor out at future dates at specified prices, these promises can be kept only if the company is a success. You have to have sufficient other resources for living expenses to be able to invest in venture capital.

Management fees for venture capital funds are high, often excessive. Some managements take salaries, costs, and expenses plus large percentages of the profits. Yet you may have no choice but to use this fund. Generally, venture capital funds have either exclusive deals or partnership deals on products and firms. The only way to get a piece of that product or firm is either to put up enough cash to get in on the partnership or to buy into the fund.

There are great possibilities for greater gains if you spend substantial time in this area. In fact, time is more important here than money. Sorting through all the possibilities, both scientific and commercial, is the key to making money in venture capital. That is why this is more appropriate for someone wanting to get rich than for someone who is retired. To properly evaluate a venture capital deal, you need to hire lawyers, accountants, financial analysts, scientists, and other experts to go over all aspects of the deal. You need to spend time at the company talking to the owner and the employees. And, most important, you need to know all the competitive products and companies that could keep this company from being successful. When you buy stock in GE, you know that GE has all these areas and more covered. In a little venture capital deal, you can be sure most of these concerns are not covered.

Venture capital can be favorable to your tax liability. Because venture capital often creates losses in the early years, you may be able to offset some tax liabilities with these losses. The rules depend on the type of venture, the structure of your investment, the dates you invest, and many other factors. It is important to discuss these tax consequences with a tax specialist *before* you invest in a venture capital fund.

Venture capital is better for feeding the ego than feeding the body. Even if a venture fails, it is good conversation at a dinner party. No one is particularly interested in the 20-unit apartment house across from the university that has had 100% occupancy for twenty years. Everyone wants to know about the drug that will cure AIDS, even if it doesn't work.

Hedge Funds

Hedge funds are managed investment pools. Typically the investor must put in substantial assets. A minimum of $250,000 is not unusual. The manager is authorized to invest in a wide variety of assets from stocks and bonds to currencies and all types of derivatives. The typical fee charged is 1% of assets plus 25% of profits annually. In theory, the percentage-of-profits fee is supposed to be an incentive to the manager to make money for the clients.

Hedge funds often are on a different cycle than other asset classes. Some specialize in currencies or commodities futures or sell stock short, all of which have different cycles than other asset classes. A few hedge funds simply invest in U.S. stocks, which are on the same cycle as many U.S. investments. It is important to look at the record of investments made by the hedge fund to see what asset classes have been owned over the years of its existence.

The return on hedge funds is not predictable. Because many use leverage, some always to do very well in up markets and very poorly in down markets. The spectacular returns of some funds in up markets are hedge funds' greatest appeal. Unfortunately, the average hedge fund usually lags the market even in up years. In 1995 the typical hedge fund returned a positive 23% to investors, but this was 12% less than the S&P 500 index funds. Hedge funds are for investors who believe they can get into and out of select asset classes at the right time. These are blatant ego investments. As I have discussed, market timing of this sort is neither possible nor wise. In fact many hedge funds go bankrupt in down markets. Hedge funds were invented in the 1960s, and the bear market that started at the beginning of 1969 and ended in the middle of 1970s put most of them out of business. They have nearly disappeared many times since. The current crop of hedge funds is likely to be severely trimmed by the next bear market.

Hedge funds also have limited liquidity. Many are organized as limited partnerships that can be sold back only to the general partners. Even then the general partners often have discretion as to how long they will make you wait to receive your buyout and at what price. Some will make distributions from time to time but not on a predictable schedule. It would not be possible to keep current on your mortgage payments from what you will receive from a hedge fund.

Perhaps the biggest negative of a hedge fund is the fee structure. Hedge fund management is the route to wealth, not hedge fund investment. Hedge fund managers rarely have more skills than money managers or mutual fund managers or real estate property managers. If a market is up 20% in a given year, a typical hedge fund would also be up 20%, as would a typical money manager. But the hedge fund manager would receive 1% of net asset value and a quarter of the profit. The investors would receive a 14% return, if they could get their hands on it. A typical money manager would receive 1.5% and the client 18.5%, available on demand. The hedge fund promoter will argue that their managers have the long-term track records that make them worth these huge fees. This is never true. If you set their long-term track record against a top money manager or a top mutual fund manager, the hedge fund manager net fees always has a worse record. And many hedge fund managers are not showing you audited records but their own compilation of their record.

Investors in a hedge fund have no control over their taxes. As most funds are limited partnerships, all the taxable transactions entered into by the fund are reportable by the investors. Since hedge funds are generally extremely active traders, it is likely that all gains incurred in any given year will be realized by the fund and taxed to the investors. Thus the investors may not be able to get cash out of the fund yet have to pay taxes on gains incurred by the fund.

There is a possibility to make more money by spending more time in this field. Not by investigating many hedge funds and finding the best but by starting your own. Before I decided to write this book I investigated starting a hedge fund. My conclusion was I was not willing to invest in the types of assets hedge funds typically invest in, nor was I willing to use the leverage they use, nor was I willing to charge the fees they charge. But none of these practices are illegal. If you are interested in hedge funds, you can make a lot of money; not by investing, but by managing. Unfortunately, you are reading the wrong book to learn how to do this.

Buying Part or All of a Profitable Closely Held Business

Small businesses of every kind are available for sale or in need of investors in every town in this country. Before buying into a business, consider the issue of protecting yourself from incurring liability from any losses the business may incur. This is not an issue previously discussed in this book as all the investments considered so far, with the exception of real estate, do not involve the assumption of liability. Buying bonds does not make the bondholder liable if the bond issuer is sued for injuring a customer. With real estate, insurance is taken out to cover all possible liabilities. There are many ways to protect yourself when buying into a small business, including buying insurance, buying only stock, investing as a limited partner, making a loan convertible to stock, and so on. Before investing any money, discuss this issue with an attorney who specializes in this area.

A small business may be on a different cycle than other asset classes. The earnings of a small business are influenced by the general economy, which influences the returns available on stocks and bonds. Some small businesses are on different cycles. A business with a majority of sales to foreign customers may be on a different cycle than the U.S. stock market. A used clothing store or used furniture store may do especially well when the economy is in recession and the stock market is down. This can be determined only by looking at the history of the individual business. As part of your investigation, you will want to look at ten years of financials. Note how the individual business's cycle compares to the economic cycle.

It is only possible business-by-business to determine whether there will be earnings generated over the long-term. It is good to be aware that most businesses that are for sale or looking for investors are in trouble. Sometimes the trouble is not apparent from the books. One business I bought into looked fabulous on paper. But the owners who were looking for investors clearly knew things were not great or they would not have been willing to share their fortune with strangers. If you have ever sold a business, remember all the things that you did not tell the buyer that were of concern to you and that motivated you to sell. Be aware that the seller of this business, while disclosing everything legally required, is not disclosing the whole story. This is the crucial issue in buying a small business. Look only at businesses similar to those you have worked in. If you have no experience in this field, then take a job with the business for at least a year with an option to buy later if you are still interested. This is an ego-busting proposal. Many of you are used to being the boss and want to buy the whole business right away to keep this title. But if you buy the whole thing right away and then have to put it into bankruptcy a few years later, your ego will be crushed even worse. Also stay with existing businesses with at least a ten-year track record. The future of start-ups is too hard to predict. If the business needs loans or other financing in the future, a start-up will not have the track record to get it. You will become the sole bank for the company, further increasing your risks. Do not buy the first business that you hear is for sale. Look at hundreds of businesses before you get involved. Business brokers are helpful. Industry trade journals advertise businesses for sale. Also, you can walk right into any existing business and ask if it is for sale. Always compare figures with those of similar businesses. Again, trade journals and business brokers can lead you to comparable figures. Be careful. Despite good comparables, I have still lost money in small businesses. There is a lot of ego involved in being the owner. Humility is a better place to come from when considering any investment than the belief that you know more than the figures show or more than the market.

Small businesses often eat up cash in the early years rather than provide it for living expenses. This is why it is important to be selective when buying a small business. Only buy into a business that can contribute to your living expenses immediately and that has good prospects for doing so in the future. Do not believe that you will be able to turn around a losing business and make it profitable. The previous owner, with more experience and possibly more at stake than you, for whom it was probably the only source of income, was not able to turn the business around. If you are investing in a small business, rather than owning, be sure to require current income from the investment. A loan to the business convertible to stock is an instrument that worked for me.

A small business investment cannot be tucked into a safety deposit box and forgotten. You either have to manage the business yourself or closely supervise those that do manage the business. Do not get involved in a small business even as a passive investor if you do not plan on spending a lot of time. A passive investment like a loan can go bad quickly in a small business. Do not wait till they miss an interest payment before you get involved. Make sure cash is available in advance to pay your interest and the security for your principal has not been eroded.

It is possible to make a fortune from a small business if you put in enough time and have enough luck. The real question here is: why are you trying to make a fortune? When you have the option of spending as little as ten hours a week monitoring your investments, why are you choosing to work sixty hours a week? The term workaholic comes to mind. If you have made enough money already to be reading this book and yet you still cannot relax, what is going on? The problem is learning to relax and enjoy life, not figuring out how to make more money. It may be that you enjoy business and regret selling yours. It also may be that you enjoy nothing but can stay busy in business so you do not have to sit in a chair and feel how desperate you are to start living. Before you buy a small business, go to at least ten meetings of Workaholics Anonymous and go to at least ten therapy sessions with a therapist who specializes in workaholism. Twenty opportunities to tell the truth about how desperate you feel are worth more than any profits you could make from buying a small business.

The tax consequences of owning or investing in a small business are dependent on the type of business and the form of ownership. Discuss this issue with a tax advisor before you invest any money. Be sure to structure your investment so that if the business goes under you are not liable for the business's debts yet your losses will be tax deductible. The only good thing I can say about the businesses that I have invested in is I got to deduct my losses.

Oil and Natural Gas

There are many ways to invest in oil and natural gas. Do not invest in commodity futures. If you are interested in oil and gas companies, use the suggestions in Chapter 5 on investing in large and small U.S. stocks. There are even oil and gas and other energy company mutual funds available. These can be analyzed like any other mutual funds, as discussed in Chapter 11. Oil and gas interests can also be invested in directly. You can buy a portfolio of mineral interests, or you can invest in producing wells as well as more speculative drilling projects.

Oil is on a different cycle than many other assets. Oil is a worldwide commodity whose price is determined by world supply and demand conditions. If you believe as I do that worldwide economic growth will continue for many decades, then you will understand my belief that demand for oil will grow for many decades as well. The growth in demand will come partially from the developed economies of the United States, Europe, and Japan but primarily from the emerging economies of China, Asia, Latin America, and Central (formerly called Eastern) Europe. The collapse of Russia, Thailand, South Korea, Indonesia, Malaysia, and Brazil in 1997–1998 is only a minor setback in this long-term trend. When China moves from a bicycle economy to a motorcycle economy to an auto economy, the price of oil will go up in Dallas even if Texas is in recession.

Oil is on a world economic demand cycle and not a U.S. or other national demand cycle like U.S. stocks and bonds and U.S. real estate. Natural gas prices are more locally sensitive. Whereas crude oil can be shipped by tanker all over the world, currently natural gas is primarily piped to the nearest users. If the nearest users are in recession, the price of natural gas is likely to go down. Since many users can switch between natural gas, oil, and coal, there is a correlation between the price of natural gas and the price of oil. And natural gas liquid is becoming more available. NGL can be shipped worldwide, but it is expensive to do so. If new technology becomes available to reduce the price of shipping, the price of natural gas will become more and more dependent on world economic cycles and less on local supply and demand conditions.

Many people think that oil and gas wells are short-term investments. In fact, oil and gas wells can produce for forty years and longer. With new recovery techniques available today like deeper drilling and horizontal drilling, it is unknown how long some wells will produce.

It is my belief that the price of both oil and gas will outpace inflation for many decades. Demand is unquestionably rising. Despite recessions and setbacks, India, China, Brazil, Indonesia, and most emerging countries consume twice as much energy per person as they did ten years ago. Yet none of these countries consumes more than 10% of the energy per person of America. Demand will only increase. In the last ten years, worldwide oil and gas consumption has increased by 25%, and there is no reason to believe that will be any less in the next ten years.

There is a myth that supply will keep up with this demand. Consider this: in 1996 Texas for the first time became a net energy importer, producing less total energy resources than it consumed. Or consider this: fifteen years ago there were around 5,000 drilling rigs operating in the United States. Today there are fewer than 1,000. Supply is not keeping up with demand in the United States. Outside of the United States, proven reserves have increased dramatically in the last twenty-five years. Techniques for extracting oil and gas have improved. But few of these new reserves will be cheap to bring online. Almost all are in small fields that are costly to drill and pipe out. Others are inaccessible to the most efficient producers. The vast fields in the Middle East are closed to the major American and European oil companies, and the huge fields in the former Soviet Union are bogged down in legal and political battles. In accessible countries like Venezuela, locals are charging much higher prices for access. And new technologies are much more expensive than the old drill and pump system.

The long-term North American picture for natural gas also looks very promising. The United States is a net importer of natural gas, and all known reserves are either in production or used up. Mexico is a net importer of natural gas as well. Canada is a net exporter of natural gas to the United States, but Canadian reserves are not large compared to the annual demand from the United States. Canadian reserves should run out faster than world oil reserves, thus leaving clean-burning natural gas as a premium product.

If you are one of those investors who believe that demand will grow dramatically but that supply will grow to meet demand, then invest in oil service companies who supply drilling and production equipment to the oil exploration and production companies. If you believe that supply will not meet demand, then invest directly in supply. If you believe as I do that money can be made both ways, invest as I have in both service companies and directly in oil and gas.

Each individual investment in supply must be studied to be sure the reserves are long lived. You do not want to invest in the tail end of old producing properties. Also be sure the investment is structured so your income will rise with increasing oil and gas prices. Some wells are locked into long-term fixed price contracts. These are to be avoided. Discuss any deal with an independent oil analyst before you invest any money. If you cannot find anyone locally, there are plenty of them in Texas and Oklahoma.

Producing partnerships and producing mineral interests are easy to live on. Most pay monthly checks. The only difficulty is reinvestment. The check you receive includes return of principal. Thus it is necessary to reinvest a significant portion of each check to both preserve principal and increase principal as a hedge against future inflation. Reinvestment can be either in a money market fund until significant assets are built up to buy into another partnership or into an oil and gas stock mutual fund. The amount of reinvestment depends on how much you need to live on and for how long. This could be worked out with a financial planner. Generally, expect to reinvest half of each payment. I do not recommend investing in nonproducing interests unless you thoroughly research the venture. Most of the best prospects, the so-called "inside holes," are not available for investors. The other ventures are very speculative.

Management of producing partnerships is relatively simple. Unless you are dealing with older wells that will need to be worked on or redrilled, management has primarily an accounting function. Compare projected costs of partnerships, the lower the better. The real issue is commissions. I know of no no-load partnerships. Look for the deal with the lowest commissions. Spend time looking for other hidden fees as well. If you cannot find a deal with total commissions and fees of less than 5%, do not buy anything. As oil and gas investments become more popular, I expect the 100% no-load houses like Vanguard and T. Rowe Price to offer 100% no-load deals as they did when real estate limited partnerships were all the rage. Stick with a 100% no-load oil and gas stock fund until you can find a partnership that works. The stock fund, unfortunately, will be correlated to the general stock market much more so than a producing partnership.

If you want to work hard on oil and gas investing, it can pay off. There are many drillers looking for investors. Your best approach is to look for prospects first and then see if anyone is interested in drilling there. A dry hole can cost in excess of $100,000. Extensive research is required. Knowledge of geology is important. Finding partners with a good track record and knowledge of the business is even more important.

The taxes on oil and gas investments are quite favorable. There are deductions for expenses as well as a depletion allowance. Part of every check you receive is tax-free, even after you have gotten all your principal back from the investment. Check with a tax advisor before you invest a dime in any deal. Do not rely on the claims of the promoters.

Inflation-Indexed Treasury Bonds

Beginning January 1997 the U.S. Treasury began issuing inflation-indexed treasury bonds. These bonds have a very short history. Five-, ten-, and thirty-year bonds have been issued. Each bond pays interest on principal at a rate of from 3% to 5%. Each year the principal on the bond will be adjusted for the rate of inflation, as measured by the consumer price index. For example, a $1,000 bond paying 4% after a year of 4% inflation will become a $1,040 bond. The 4% interest will then be calculated on the new principal value of $1,040.

The primary advantage of this asset class is that it is on a different cycle than ordinary bonds. As a general rule, when inflation goes up, bond prices go down. With these bonds, by definition, when inflation goes up, prices go up. When inflation declines, normally bond prices go up. With inflation-index-linked bonds, the opposite is true. However, inflation is not the only factor that influences bond prices and interest rates. Supply and demand are the dominant factors. Dumping of U.S. bonds by foreign buyers can force U.S. rates higher, despite low U.S. inflation. In this scenario, both standard bonds and inflation-indexed bonds would be poor investments. It is also possible to have rising demand for credit when inflation is declining. A strong economy with many profitable investment opportunities will lead to business borrowing huge sums to finance expansion. But productivity resulting from expansion can lead to low inflation or even deflation. Credit demand forces interest rates up even when inflation remains low. Again, both standard bonds and inflation-indexed bonds would be bad investments. Huge purchases of U.S. bonds by foreign buyers as a safe haven investment can force U.S. interest rates lower even though there is high U.S. inflation. In this situation, both bonds would be good investments. So inflation-indexed bonds and standard bonds are not on entirely different cycles.

Given the persistence of inflation in the economy, these bonds are likely to produce good returns for the long term. Since they are government issued, there is no risk of default. Whether the amount of the return will be sufficient to live on depends on the individual.

These bonds are ideally structured for those living off their assets and reinvesting part of their returns each year. A system of spending the interest and reinvesting the compounded principal at maturity should work beautifully for many investors living off their assets. If the need arises to sell before maturity, there are some problems. Since these bonds are new, a big and liquid market does not yet exist. Spreads and commissions are determined by the size of the market. At the time of sale, the current rate on competing normal bonds will determine the price available. In most cases, these bonds would be best held to maturity.

If bought directly from the treasury or through banks, fees could be expected to be low. It is ridiculous for anyone living off assets to buy an inflation-indexed bond fund. There is no need for a manager and management expenses and for diversification. These securities will not default. Paying management fees and trading in and out of these bonds is a sure system of reducing both their profitably and their lack of correlation with returns on other bonds.

It is not likely that spending much time in this area will increase returns significantly. Assuming a fairly large, efficient market, there will be few opportunities to profit from other investors' mistakes. The main area of profit will likely be from the government's mistake of setting too high a premium over inflation and allowing inflation to rise too high. The benefits of these mistakes will go to the buy and hold investors and not to the traders.

There is a tax disadvantage to owning these bonds. The annual increase in principal is considered a taxable event even though no cash is distributed to investors. Thus investors will have to pay taxes either from the taxable interest payment or from other income. The tax disadvantage could be overcome if these bonds were held in a tax-deferred account. The interest on these bonds is exempt from state taxes.

Avoid Annuities

Annuities are a poor choice for anyone saving for retirement and a worse choice for anyone who is living off his assets. For those saving for retirement, let me only say that the fees charged by the insurer as commissions, surrender charges, and management far exceed any tax benefits. For anyone living off an annuity, the tax picture is a disaster.

All the earnings on the money withdrawn from the annuity are taxed as ordinary income. This is the reverse of a tax shelter. Earnings that would have been taxed at lower capital gains rates are now taxed at higher rates. And the estate tax picture is also bleak. Your heirs will have to pay taxes on any gains in the annuity on your death whereas with other assets these gains go tax-free.

Even worse, the returns you can expect from fixed or variable annuities are much lower than those from similar assets. Because of high management and other fees, fixed-rate annuities always pay much less than you would receive from a simple ladder of treasury bonds. Because of high management and other fees, variable annuities also pay much less than any stock index mutual fund or average no-load mutual fund.

part three

Investing to Reach Your Magic Number

chapter ten

Designing Your Growth Portfolio

From the calculations you made in Part One, you have determined how much more money you need before you can retire. If you have studied Part Two, you understand the basic principles of investing during retirement. But you are not there yet. In this and the next chapter, I set out some strategies to get you to your magic number quicker.

All the investment strategies in Part Two are appropriate for saving for retirement. If you follow them, you should get steady growth in your investments, leading to a predictable retirement date. You will also be familiar with the investing you need to do in retirement, and your portfolio will be allocated appropriately for retirement. But if Chapter 3 showed your retirement date to be more than ten years away, it would be reasonable to add aggressiveness to your approach. You have time between now and your retirement to ride out the volatility of the aggressive approach.

A Diversified Strategy

You want to increase your returns but you do not want to risk losing it all. The future is not predictable. You cannot predict investment disaster or average returns. No one predicted that Japanese stocks would drop from 39,000 in 1989 to 14,000 in 1998. Based on returns from 1950 to 1989, most would have guessed that by 1998 the Japanese market would have been much higher than 100,000. The Japanese retirees who, in the late 1980s, bet everything on the apparent long-term superiority of Japanese stocks are no longer retired.

After a strong run in the 1980s, I thought the U.S. stock market would be rather dull in the 1990s. The opposite happened. I felt certain that oil and gas would do very well in the second half of the 1990s, and in fact they have declined. Fortunately, I have not invested based on my predictions. I have been in five noncorrelated asset classes and done better in the 1990s than in the very good 1980s.

To avoid disaster, follow the guidelines set out in Chapter 4 for allocating between three to five noncorrelated asset classes. But make these modifications.

If you have more than ten years to retirement, the top five asset classes listed on page 51 should comprise the bulk of your holdings. At least two thirds of your investments should be in real estate, foreign company stocks, U.S. large-company stocks, U.S. small-company stocks, and emerging market stocks. Once you are retired, you may want to cut back on some of these asset classes. That will depend on your target investment return at retirement. By concentrating for now on the top five asset classes, you will have a high target investment return. The lowest expected investment return from these five asset classes is 10%.

However, if you have special knowledge about asset classes not listed, they might also be appropriate. For example, a privately held business that you are involved in may be a better investment for the next ten plus years than anything listed above. Only you can judge that. But start looking for buyers for the business now. If you plan on holding on for ten years and then selling for retirement, you might not get out at the right price or at any price. A downturn in your industry or the local economy just as you want to retire would foil your plan. Selling early at a good price, hiring back as a consultant, and investing the proceeds may prove your surest path to retirement.

Other assets may also be better than the top five listed above. Land, venture capital, oil and gas, art, farms, etc. could work out if you have some special knowledge and experience with these things. Having a fraternity buddy in the business is not special knowledge. Doing substantial research and making a number of previous transactions is special knowledge.

You should also put up to one third of your portfolio in the lower-performing asset classes. Many of these asset classes are on different cycles than the top five asset classes and may turn out to be your best investments over the next decade.

For example, treasury bonds offer good protection against deflation. If you believe the deflation that has taken place in Japan in the 1990s and elsewhere in Asia in the late 1990s could come to the United States, treasury bonds would be a good place to put some of your money. Or you may believe, as some do, that deflation will prevail in Europe over the next decade. If that is the case, then some money in European bonds would do very well. Or maybe you see the opposite, you suspect inflation is coming back. In the 1970s, gold and oil and gas did much better than stocks and bonds, due to inflation. If you sense that this could happen again in the next ten years, put some, but not more than one third of your money, in gold and oil and gas.

There is no need to own cash until retirement. The returns are too low over ten-year periods to justify holding cash as an investment. Whatever forces cause cash to be a good investment will cause some other asset class to be an even better investment. If inflation raises returns on money market funds, gold, oil and gas, short-term bonds, and inflation-indexed bonds will do even better. If deflation hits stocks and cash breaks even, treasuries will do much better than cash. In retirement, you will need cash for expenses and possibly as an asset class. If so, you can build your cash hoard in the last years before retirement, but do not invest in cash now.

Diversify to Cover Your Backside

The returns listed on page 51 are not fixed returns. They are projected future returns based on the average annual returns of the last one hundred years or so. There is no guarantee that these returns will take place again in your lifetime. Treasury bonds have averaged better than 6%. But from 1950 to 1980, a thirty-year period, their total return was closer to 2% a year. From 1981 till 1998 they have returned about 12% a year. Will the next thirty years be like the 1950–1980 period, like the 1981–1998 period, or completely different? There is no way to know. U.S. stocks returned about 2% a year from 1972 to 1982 and 15% a year since 1982. Will the next thirty years be more like the first period or more like the second?

There are investors today who have 100% of their retirement savings in U.S. stocks. Investment advisors support this. They argue that baby boomers looking to retire early will continue to pour money into U.S. stocks for at least ten years, driving up prices. Is this a reasonable approach?

Look at some alternatives. Assume:

1. You can retire in seven years if you are 100% in U.S. stocks and they return 15% a year.
2. You can retire in ten years with a third of your money in U.S. stocks returning 15% and the rest elsewhere returning below average, say 8% a year.
3. You have everything in U.S. stocks, the market goes nowhere for ten years, you do not retire. Inflation increases your expenses. You now need more than ten additional years to retire. In fact, you may never retire.
4. You have one third in U.S. stocks returning nothing for ten years, two thirds elsewhere returning 8%, and you retire in fifteen years.

You must choose both 1 and 3 or both 2 and 4. I recommend 2 and 4 over 1 and 3.

Do Not Put More Than One Third of Your Retirement in U.S. Stocks

Remember the Dow Jones Industrial Average hit 969 in 1965. The high seventeen years later was 1071. That is 10% in seventeen years, and inflation was a killer those years. Everybody's expenses more than doubled those years. But deflation can also kill a stock market. From 1929 to 1933 the market lost 90% as a result of severe deflation. It is insane to put all your retirement money in U.S. stocks. Why risk the chance of never being able to retire if you are wrong?

If the certainty of reaching retirement is more important to you than a small chance of early retirement, do not put more than one third of your money in U.S. stocks. Put something in U.S. stocks and put something in two to four other asset classes. If stocks do well, you will get to retire, and if stocks do not do well, you will still get to retire.

In order to retire, you need to diversify against:

1. U.S. economic growth
2. Inflation
3. Deflation
4. Individual company or property factors

When you set up your portfolio consider all these factors. If the U.S. economy is simply bad over the next decade, can you still retire? Yes, if foreign economies are good and you have money there. If the U.S. economy is bad due to deflation, bonds will work. If it is bad due to inflation, gold and oil and gas may work. If the U.S. economy is good but the stock market is bad, real estate should work. Look at all the possibilities and diversify. Also, diversify within each asset class. Owning one stock, one building, one country fund is too risky.

Set up your portfolio step-by-step:

1. First determine your current asset allocation. See Chapter 4 for examples of how to do this.
2. Second, decide how aggressive you want to be. There is a big difference between going for 12% a year and 8% a year. If you want to retire quickly, you can set up your portfolio to produce 12% a year. But this clearly involves more risk than trying for 8% a year. It makes little sense to shoot for less than 8% a year if you have ten or more years until retirement and expect up to thirty years retired. A long time horizon increases the chances that the highest-returning asset classes will perform as they have in the past. It is not necessary to keep more than one third of your assets in the lower-returning asset classes.

3. Now, pick out asset classes to match your target investment return.

Let's return to the examples in Chapter 3.

Hillary

Hillary inherited $200,000. Based on her fear of losing some or all of her inheritance, she was willing to delay retirement a few years for the certainty of a lower return. Her target investment return was 8%. For her, it is not appropriate to hold two thirds of her assets in the five top-performing asset classes. If she can make 8% a year, she will retire in less than ten years. She needs to set up a portfolio both for the next several years and during her retirement. She is healthy. This is a portfolio to last her at least twenty years. Obviously, she could make changes when appropriate, but it is best now to assume this will be her asset allocation for life. What assets would be appropriate for her to buy? Certainly a portfolio of treasury bonds, corporate bonds, and income-producing real estate might produce 8% for life. Her portfolio might look something like this:

% IN ASSET CLASS	X	EXPECTED RETURN FROM CLASS	=	TARGET RETURN
25% TREASURY BONDS		6%		1.5%
35% CORPORATE BONDS		7%		2.5%
40% REAL ESTATE		10%		4.0%
TOTAL				8%

However, Hillary has 100% of her portfolio in U.S. investments. There have been periods when all U.S. investments did poorly. She could counter this by investing 20% in foreign stocks and 20% in real estate instead of 40% in real estate. It will also be very important to Hillary to keep her investment costs and fees very low. If she has to pay 2% in costs and fees on her investments, she will delay her retirement and have less during retirement. Treasury bonds she could buy on her own without any fees or costs. For corporate bonds, real estate, and foreign stocks she could use no-load index funds or no-load, low-expense, low-turnover funds.

While she is working Hillary could also shelter some income from taxes by funneling as much as possible into IRAs or other plans for which she is eligible. Note: there is no tracing requirement for putting money into IRAs and the other plans. If Hillary is eligible to put money in and deduct it from her income, it does not have to come from her salary. She can put cash she inherited into an IRA and still deduct against her income.

Fred and Ginger

Fred and Ginger are experienced investors. They also need to set up for the long run as they have less than ten years until retirement. They have $425,000 to invest and are looking for 10% a year. Also, they save $24,000 a year. They could put $85,000 in each of the top five investment classes and expect to do better than 10% a year. However, Fred believes U.S. deflation is a real possibility. It could hit U.S. large companies the worst as they have very low profit margins and could collapse if they have to sell their products at declining prices. He believes the Asian economies have already worked through their deflation and will grow by trading with each other, regardless of what happens in the United States. He decides to set up his portfolio with 30% in treasuries, 30% in emerging market stocks, 20% in U.S. small companies, and 20% in a real estate partnership he and four other investors are forming. If Fred starts to believe he is wrong about deflation, he will invest his annual savings in U.S. large-company stocks and move some of his treasury money into other investments.

If You Have High Expenses You'd Better Have High Risk Tolerance

The Beverly Hills couple needs 12% a year for at least thirteen years to make it to retirement. Their best bet is to diversify among only the top five asset classes. These are the most volatile asset classes. Due to their long time horizon, they have a chance to make 12% a year. With 35% in emerging markets, 35% in U.S. small companies, and 10% in U.S. large companies, real estate, and foreign stocks, they could get a return of 12% a year. They will also have to keep their investment costs and expenses low and their taxes low. Everything they can funnel into tax-deferred accounts with discount brokers or no-load mutual funds would be helpful. If they had some type of spiritual awakening and learned to live a simple life, they could retire immediately on low-volatility investments. Since they have high expenses, they need to be able to tolerate high volatility.

Once you have your allocation determined, read the next chapter and refer back to Part Two to decide what form your investments should take. But first consider mistakes to avoid.

Mistakes to Avoid

If you have your allocation set, execute it and you have a good chance to reach your retirement on time. You do not need to be desperate.

Desperately Seeking Savings

Today I see many investors desperately seeking savings. They pile everything into a highly promoted, questionable asset class. This is not just a U.S. phenomenon. The Japanese have gone through a similar thing and are paying dearly for it. The Japanese population is older than ours and has been saving for retirement furiously. They have put almost all their retirement savings in one asset class, postal savings accounts. These are government guaranteed. But the demand has been so strong that today these deposits pay almost no interest. At the start of the 1990s, they paid almost 7%. Will a whole generation of Japanese be able to retire on an investment that cannot increase in value and pays almost no interest? Maybe, if deflation continues. But there is no chance if prices begin to rise even moderately.

In the United States, a whole generation of desperate retirement savers has piled almost everything into the 500 stocks of the S&P 500 index. Many savers do not realize this. They have bought mutual funds but do not realize that half or more of their mutual fund holdings are in the S&P 500 stocks.

Hysteria alone can move asset prices for a decade. Look at the Japanese stock market from 1980 to 1989. Look at the U.S. market from late 1994 till now. But at some point, other investments prove too alluring and the hysteria shifts. In Japan it shifted from stocks to postal savings. In the United States, the gold and real estate hysteria of the 1970s shifted first to money market funds, then to bonds, then to stocks. Piling into the most popular asset class rarely works out in the long run.

Investors desperately seeking savings fail to look at the loads and expenses they are paying for assets. Retirees usually take their time and shop for no-load funds, discount brokers, low expense ratios, underpriced real estate, used cars, and other bargains. The desperate savers buy anything that is put in front of them.

Take your time. It is better to take a year to find the right REIT fund than to jump into the first loaded fund that is sold to you. Loads can run 6.5%, expense ratios can run to 2%, and turnover can increase taxes and decrease performance. Not paying all these expenses for a year and simply leaving your money in a money market fund puts you ahead of the desperate crowd. If you keep looking for a year, you will find the bargains you seek and be rewarded. No-fee IRA accounts are numerous. But you have to look for them. High-fee IRA accounts will find you. Learn to say no and keep looking for bargains.

Market Timing Again

I have already made this point, but I want to make it again. Do not time any market. This means let your profits run. It also means let your losses run. Give them a chance to turn around. If you sell losses, you just lock them in. When you own good investments, ride gains and losses.

The more you trade the greater your expenses. Trading in a tax-deferred account is just as expensive as trading in a taxable account. In any account, it is possible to turn a series of good investments into a loss by active trading. If every trade costs 1% of your capital and you make twelve trades a year, you will lose 12%. Just to break even you need to invest in assets returning 12% a year. If the assets you trade into return a respectable positive 10% a year, you lose 2%.

In taxable accounts, tax considerations may make it prudent to do some trades involving losses. These should be rare—the costs add up too quickly.

How to Turn Positive Returns Negative: Derivatives and Leverage

This is true for saving for retirement as much as during retirement. Let me repeat. A sure method to turn investing into gambling is to buy options and other derivatives or to use leverage.

Never Go Short

If you do not know what it means to short an investment, then all you need to know is do not do it. If you do understand what it is to short an investment, understand this. When you are long, all you can lose is the amount you have invested. When you are short, you can lose the amount invested times the amount of ego that tells you eventually you will be right. If the ego is big enough, you can lose your retirement.

Should You Hire Help?

Yes. Spend more time on your career than your investments. Your time is valuable. Good investment advice is cheap. You can hire the world's greatest foreign stock investor for less than 1% a year and no load. How much better can you do investing yourself than hiring help? If you work at investing in large U.S. companies full time, will you beat an S&P 500 index fund? You should know that 80% of MBAs working at it full time do not.

My son was recently sick for five weeks and three different doctors could not figure out what he had. I decided to research it myself and concluded that he had to have a bacterial sinus infection. I assembled my evidence, took him back to the doctor, and the doctor agreed. Within three days of taking antibiotics, his condition improved, and soon he was healthy. I had beat three doctors at the medicine game. Does this now mean I do not need doctors? That all their training and experience is bunk? Hardly. That would be a life-threatening decision. I could die as a result of trying to be my own doctor from now on. Yet I have seen many an investor pick a good stock, one the pros miss, and conclude that from now on they will do all their own investing. They are risking a secure retirement, their children's education and inheritance, a fund for disasters, and more on the ego-boosting proposition that they can beat professional, highly educated, experienced investors at a complex, difficult, often baffling business.

Is it worth your while to research how the latest tax changes affect your savings plan? Or is it better to just go to an expert and get answers? It takes me days to wade through changes in the tax laws to figure out what applies to me and what I ought to include in this book. And I have an LLM in taxation from NYU. It could take you a week or a month. It would cost only $100 for a short visit to a tax accountant who already has all the answers worked out. Your time is too valuable not to hire help.

Is investing your favorite toy? If so, keep some of your investments under your exclusive control and get help with the rest. But do not compare the results each year. That would certainly take the fun out of it. Remember, you will have more time to do it yourself in retirement. Hire help now, do it yourself later.

Avoid the other extreme as well. Do not ignore the process altogether. Spend a minimum of ten hours a month monitoring your portfolio. Do not believe everything your advisors tell you or all the hype that comes from the mutual fund company or the broker. Keep sight of your long-term goal, retirement, and your short-term goal, x % a year after taxes, fees, and expenses.

There will be setbacks. You will get taken for a ride by some advisors and investment companies along the way. Be especially wary of "advisors" connected to insurance companies that offer "free" services. Hire only advisors who charge on an hourly basis or long-term money managers who charge 1% or less a year. Stay on top of the information you are given and your results. Do not hesitate to make a change in advisors if you suspect problems. It is your money. You owe no loyalty to anyone who is handling your finances for a fee. Your only duty is to pay your bill. Once you have paid, you can switch financial planners, tax accountants, mutual fund houses, realtors, brokers, and anyone else. It is your retirement at stake, not theirs.

Keep track of your annual returns in each asset class and overall. Track your cumulative return. Also, each year redo the formula from Chapters 1 and 3 to see how close you are getting to retirement. If you find after a few years that you are not making your target investment return, consider some changes in your asset allocation. Follow the guidelines in Chapter 4 on when and how to make changes in your asset allocation.

Compare the advice you get to what you read in this book and elsewhere. Question everything. Ask if what you are being told is not just another form of market timing.

Dollar Cost Averaging Is Disguised Market Timing

Most advisors will tell you that dollar cost averaging is the best way to save for retirement. In the retirement savings context, dollar cost averaging means every month you add the same dollar amount to your investments either through a 401(k) or similar plan or in a taxable account. If your monthly contribution is $1,000 and the market is down, $1,000 will buy 100 shares of XYZ mutual fund at $10 a share. If the market is up, $1,000 will buy 80 shares of XYZ at $12.50 a share. Your average cost will be $11.25, not the worst price and not the best price. If you get a bonus at year-end or receive an inheritance, you will phase the money into the markets in equal amounts over a period of months or years in order to get an average cost per share rather than the worst cost or the best cost. This is to be compared to lump sum investing. Lump sum investing means you put everything you have available to invest into the markets as soon as you get it.

In the real world, lump sum investing is better. The sooner you get the money out of your hands and into investments, the better. You will be less tempted to buy a vacation home, a BMW, a boat, an airplane, artwork, or anything else that is more likely to depreciate than appreciate. Over time, your investment results will be better. The sooner you get money into the markets, the more time you will have for your money to grow.

Dollar cost averaging is simply disguised market timing. You delay investing in a systematized way. Every delay you make gives the markets a chance to move up without you and gives you a chance to replace the sofa again or remodel the bathroom for the third time. I know this. I have done it. While I was dollar cost averaging into international markets in the 1980s, the markets were moving up without me, and I remodeled the same kitchen twice with my international stock money. Of course, I lost both the gourmet kitchen and the international investments in my divorce, so it did not matter in the long run.

Regularly putting all you can spare into a savings plan is a good idea. This is not dollar cost averaging. This is lump sum investing, which I advocate. Sometimes the lump sums are small, sometimes they are bigger. The main thing is to get all your excess cash out of your hands and into investments ASAP.

As I write, the U.S. large-stock market appears extremely overvalued. But I do not advocate dollar cost averaging into it. Rather, determine the appropriate asset allocation of U.S. stocks for your portfolio. Then put everything you have available for that asset class in now, before you come up with a worse idea. Leaving your money in a money market fund waiting for a crash does not work. Crashes are rare. Spending binges are a daily ritual in many households.

Investing in Tax-deferred and Taxable Accounts

Tax planning is not the key. It helps. But you can retire successfully without ever using a tax-deferred account. I have never used a tax-deferred account. The key is savings and good investment results.

In general, tax planning will allow you to save more and to compound your returns at higher rates. But some of your deferred taxes will have to be paid in retirement when you may be least able to pay taxes. Still, due to the benefits of increased savings and increased compounding, it is best to put as much as possible into tax-deferred accounts. Once you have reached your limits, continue to save.

It is not likely that you will be able to save enough in your tax-deferred account for an early retirement. It will probably be necessary for you to save in taxable accounts. You may also have money you have received by inheritance, insurance settlement, bonus, or stock options that cannot be funneled into tax-deferred accounts. Should you use the same investments in your taxable accounts as in your tax-deferred accounts? No.

Once you have your asset allocation determined, put the assets that will generate the most taxes in the tax-deferred account and those that are the most tax-efficient in the taxable account. Generally, assets that throw off significant income like bonds and REITs should go in tax-deferred accounts. Also assets with high turnover like some small-cap stock funds or some emerging market funds need to be in tax-deferred accounts. Assets that pay little or no income and have little or no turnover or have their own tax benefits are fine in taxable accounts.

The table below lists some assets that are best suited for taxable and tax-deferred accounts. These are general categories. You must examine the individual asset to determine if it really has the characteristics that make it appropriate. For example, most REITs pay large dividends, and these dividends are about 80% taxable. These REITs should go in tax-deferred accounts. Other REITs are highly leveraged, develop properties, pay small dividends, and their dividends are almost entirely a tax-free return of capital. These are fine in taxable accounts. Individual buildings and other real estate cannot usually be held in tax-deferred accounts.

Assets for Tax-Deferred Accounts	Assets for Taxable Accounts
Managed U.S. stock funds	U.S. stock index funds
Utility and high-dividend stocks	U.S. stock humility portfolio
Most REITs/REIT funds	Return of capital REITs
Bonds	Municipal bonds
Bond funds	Municipal bond funds
Foreign stock funds	Foreign stock index funds
Emerging market stock funds	Emerging market index funds
High-dividend foreign and emerging stocks	Foreign and emerging stock humility portfolio

If you cannot fit all of your high-tax assets into the limits of your tax-deferred accounts, that is fine. Buy those assets anyway if they are right for your asset allocation. In the long run, your asset allocation will have a greater effect on your results than the accounts you hold your assets in. With the right asset allocation, you will have big gains to live on during retirement. With the wrong allocation, you may have nothing to live on, regardless of having saved some taxes along the way.

Remember, when you start to live off your tax-deferred assets, then you will have to pay taxes on your deferred income as well as on your profits. When you start living off your taxable accounts, you will have already paid taxes on the income and on some of the profits, so your tax rate will be lower. In Chapter 2, I suggested that during retirement you want to delay withdrawals from your tax-deferred accounts as long as possible and live on your taxable assets. This will keep your tax rate lower and continue to defer taxes on gains in your tax-deferred accounts. But if you are in the unusual situation of having everything in tax-deferred accounts, then in the last few years before retirement, get some specific advice about your tax situation.

For many tax-deferred accounts, once you begin withdrawing money from them, you must make substantially equal periodic withdrawals the rest of your life or for other specified periods. If the amount of these withdrawals is larger than what you will need to cover your target living allowance, then you will be paying taxes on income you do not need. It might be better to save outside a tax-deferred account for the last years you work in order to avoid triggering these mandatory withdrawals right away. Every situation needs to be looked at in detail with a tax accountant. But if, for example, you retire and then decide to go back to work, it would be a waste to be taxed on withdrawals you do not need at all.

Once you have set up your retirement savings allocation, consider how to invest in each asset class. All the suggestions in Part Two are appropriate. You might also want to increase your returns without taking on a large increase in risk. The next chapter suggests how to charge up your returns within the context of a diversified portfolio.

chapter eleven

Investing for Growth

Part Two showed you how to invest during retirement. All the methods discussed in Part Two are appropriate for someone saving for retirement. But you may wish to get to retirement sooner. In this chapter I will show you several aggressive strategies that could increase your returns.

These strategies are not sold as aggressively by their promoters. But compared to the best bet strategies in Part Two, they are aggressive. For example, large-cap U.S. stock mutual funds are sold as conservative bets on the biggest companies in the world. Yet these funds are more volatile than S&P 500 Index funds, have lower short-term and long-term returns, and are often sold with loads, high fees, and hidden commissions. The only possible reason you should consider such a fund is to attempt to outperform the index. That is an aggressive strategy.

In this chapter I will also discuss how these aggressive strategies can be used by those who are living off their investments. Some of you will not be satisfied by the target investment return you determined appropriate in Chapter 1. Just be aware that by varying from the strategies in Part Two, you increase both the chance of doing better than your target investment return and the chance of doing worse. If you have no interest in going back to work and the lotto tickets aren't working out, you should stay with the strategies in Part Two.

The characteristics to look for in picking retirement savings investments are:

1. The possibility of outperforming the suggested investments in Part Two.
2. Asset classes with a long history of positive returns. Again, avoid newly minted asset classes with no proven track record.
3. Liquidity. The ability to convert the asset into cash or a more appropriate retirement investment when you quit work.
4. Easy, low-cost management while you are busy working on your career.
5. The ability to own the asset in a tax-deferred savings plan or low taxes if the asset must be held in a taxable account.

U.S. Stock Investing Through Managed Mutual Funds

There are several prudent, aggressive ways to buy U.S. stocks. Since you are working full-time, mutual funds are convenient. You probably do not have time to pick out and monitor twenty individual stocks. And you may not have enough assets yet to qualify for an individual money manager. Index funds are appropriate if you can accept a market return. If you want to try to speed up your retirement and are willing to risk slowing it down, managed mutual funds might be just the thing.

Realistically, many of you will buy managed mutual funds regardless of the logic of investing in index funds. These funds are sold aggressively everywhere. There are mutual fund ads in the middle of family TV programs, on billboards, on the classical radio station, on the subway, and stuffed by the hundreds in the mail. Many of you will succumb to the sales pressure. At least follow the guidelines below to improve your chances of buying good funds.

Managed mutual funds' only appeal is as aggressive growth vehicles. For large-cap stocks, only a few funds have beaten the index funds over the last twenty years.

For small-cap stocks, about half the funds beat the indexes and about half do worse. Buying a small-cap index fund is a good way to avoid the risk of picking a terrible small-cap fund. But in the small-cap area, at least you have a decent chance to pick a winner. However, this chance is quickly disappearing. Small-cap mutual funds are growing faster than the number of small-cap stocks listing on the exchanges. By the year 2005, my guess is small-cap index funds will outperform 80% of managed small-cap funds. That ratio of outperformance will continue until the baby boom generation is gone.

Except in an attempt to outperform the indexes, you should avoid managed mutual funds for U.S. stocks. As discussed in Chapter 6, they are appropriate for investing internationally.

Picking small- and large-stock mutual funds is a cross between picking small- and large-stock index funds and picking a money manager. All the information you need can be found in Morningstar at any large business library. If you cannot find that service, work with a fee-based financial planner. Do not use *Money* or any other magazines because they will not have enough information.

If you use a fee-based financial planner to pick funds for you, try to understand what system she is using. Be sure she understands that you are a lifetime investor, will not pay loads, and need to keep taxes to a minimum every year. The advice below is primarily for those who will be picking funds themselves. But if you are using a fee-based financial planner, compare her system to the one described here. Let the planner know if you think she is overlooking something. Let me know if you think I am overlooking something.

Buy Only 100% No Load

Buy only 100% no-load mutual funds. For every good loaded mutual fund there is an equally good no-load mutual fund. You need this money to live on the rest of your life. Do not throw money away on loads. Do not buy funds with 12-b1 fees or any other fee that goes to pay for sales expenses or buying or selling commissions. There is a sales pitch that goes, if you buy loaded funds you will get advice from the broker. Even if you do get good, objective advice, it will be beyond expensive. For example, if you put $100,000 into a loaded fund with 5.75% in loads, you are paying $5,750 for advice. A good, fee-based financial planner can analyze your whole financial picture, set up an asset allocation strategy for you, and pick out no-load funds for you for less than $500. If you invest the $5,250 that you save and make 10% a year on it, or $525 a year, that will more than pay the $100 to $200 a year for all the follow-up investment planning you will need. By going no-load with a fee-based financial planner, you saved at least $5,250 the first year and make up to $425 every year thereafter with objective advice.

Look for Ten-Year-Plus Winners

Buy only funds that have consistently outperformed the relevant index fund for ten years. For large-cap funds, the relevant index is the S&P 500. For small-cap funds, the relevant index is the Russell 2000.

Check how the fund did in the second half of 1987. As of this writing, the second half of 1987 was the last market decline of more than 25%. There will be future declines of more than 25%. You want to have some idea how your fund will perform.

If you cannot find a managed fund consistently better than an index fund, then buy an index fund. Do not fool around with new funds. There are plenty of old, broadly based funds to choose from. You are trying to do better than 10% or 12% a year for more than ten years. Stick with long-term winners. They are the only funds that have even a 50% chance of continuing to be long-term winners. Find five or more funds that have beaten the relevant index for more than ten years.

Factors to Pare Down Your List

Using your list of five or more funds, first check to see if the managers who produced these records are still with the funds. Eliminate the funds with new managers. Long-term winners with new managers are the same as new funds. Large-cap funds with new managers have only a 20% chance of beating the S&P 500, and small-cap funds with new managers only have a 50% chance of beating the Russell 2000.

Buy Low-Fee Large-Cap Funds and High-Fee Small-Cap Funds

Second, check the annual expenses. Low annual expenses are particularly important with a large-cap fund. The expenses on these funds can range from 3% a year to 0.5% a year. Yet the returns on the low-expense funds have been higher over the years. This is because all these funds buy from the same list of 1,000 or so stocks. The main source of difference in their returns is the fees they charge. The larger the fees, the lower the returns over the years. If your inflation adjustment factor is 3%, buying a fund with 0.5% in annual fees versus a fund with 3% in annual fees can go a long way toward keeping you ahead of inflation.

Unfortunately, small-stock funds charge higher fees than large-stock funds. Fees of 2% to 3% are the norm. But, as a rule, the funds with the higher fees have the better returns. This is because there are over 10,000 small stocks. Extensive research pays off with small stocks, not with large stocks. But extensive research is expensive.

Understand the Fund's Style

Third, try to understand why this fund has outperformed over the past ten years. More than likely the fund owns one hundred or more stocks, and yet it has done better than an index fund. What is going on? Is it a value fund, a growth fund, a momentum fund? If you are looking for a large-cap U.S. fund, has it outperformed because it has a lot of small companies and foreign stocks? Call the fund up and ask questions.

The question is: can the fund repeat its past performance in future years? The answer is yes if the outperformance was based on sound strategy. Try to understand the strategy well enough so you can write it down in a paragraph or two.

The best funds have unusual styles run by unusual managers. You are not looking for an index fund with large expenses. The manager must be taking calculated risks every day to outperform an index fund. Some managers find value where others see only risk. They buy stocks in or near bankruptcy. Other managers mix large stocks, small stocks, and foreign stocks. Are you comfortable with this? Do you think it will continue to work in future years? If the outperformance of a large-cap fund was based on small stocks and foreign stocks, then separate those out and see if you still like the fund. Do you want all three asset classes and in the proportions offered in this fund? Maybe you are looking for an outstanding, pure large-cap fund and an outstanding, pure foreign fund. Some managers concentrate on fewer than twenty stocks. Is this too little diversity for you?

Check to see that the fund is still practicing the same style of investing that produced its record. Small-stock funds get popular, accept hundreds of millions of dollars from new investors, and are forced to start buying larger companies. Concentrated funds, those with 75% of their assets in twenty or fewer stocks, get huge influxes of money and end up with 75% of their assets in fifty stocks.

Many times managers are not even aware that their style has changed. Other times fund managers get into fund promotion and fund family procreation and delegate stock picking to others without formally sending out announcements. When a solo fund turns into a family of funds and the star manager appears on all the financial talk shows and in the infomercials, check the trend of the fund's returns closely.

Low Turnover and Low Tax Liabilities Are Important

Study the five funds' turnover records. In taxable accounts, the more the fund turns over its holdings, the higher the capital gains tax you will have to pay for owning the fund. If you continue to hold the fund in retirement, the tax situation gets worse. Since you are going to be periodically selling shares for living expenses, your capital gains tax will already be higher than that of other shareholders.

In taxable accounts, it is also useful to look at each fund's embedded tax gains. When a fund sells shares at a gain, all shareholders are liable for taxes on those gains, regardless of when they became shareholders. If a fund bought IBM for $50 in 1991 and sold it for $100 in 1995, all the 1995 shareholders pay taxes on that gain even if they bought into the fund in 1994. Older funds that have done well and have not realized their gains by selling have the highest potential tax liabilities. This can be a problem if the fund is forced to sell appreciated shares in a crash to meet redemptions. Even if you hold your shares, you could have a large tax liability. When you do sell, you will have lower taxes because you can add to your cost basis the amount of capital that was theoretically distributed to you. But paying taxes early erodes capital, which erodes future returns. In practice, embedded gains are not a huge issue. But when comparing two funds that are otherwise equal, the one with the lowest embedded gains is a better choice.

High Turnover Guarantees Below-Market Returns

Turnover is a bigger problem than embedded gains. Turnover is a problem in tax-deferred accounts and taxable accounts. Significantly, high turnover over time leads to below-market returns.

The typical mutual fund holds one hundred or more stocks. This already creates a great likelihood that the fund will get an index fund return with high expenses. When these one hundred stocks are all replaced and one hundred new stocks bought in a given year, then the fund has owned two hundred stocks that year, further increasing the likelihood of a market return. Researching two hundred stocks increases management expenses more than buying and holding one hundred stocks. And the commissions for buying and selling two hundred stocks are much higher than for holding one hundred stocks. Ideally, you want the fund with the lowest turnover as well as the lowest expenses.

Four out of five funds would have better returns if they did not sell or buy any shares during the year. If you go back and look at their portfolio on January 1 and figure out the return if the portfolio had stayed the same through December 31, four out of five times you discover the fund would have done better by doing nothing. Often in the U.S. stock market, the less you do the better you do. I call this the Do Nothing Rule. It is not true in other stock markets or in other markets, but in the highly picked-over U.S. stock market, four out of five times making any change to a portfolio is a mistake.

If you are already living off your assets but are interested in managed mutual funds to try to outperform the market, low turnover is even more important. You will be periodically selling shares for living expenses. These transactions are unavoidable. Each time you sell shares there will be a tax liability. So finding a very low turnover mutual fund is mandatory.

Buy Only One or Two Funds

Once you have separated the pure funds from the mixed funds and eliminated those with new managers, very high expenses, or high turnover, pick one or two but no more. More than two and you will likely own enough stocks to reproduce an index without the benefit of tiny fees and tiny turnover. Diversification is not a problem here. Mutual funds are already highly diversified. Overdiversification is the thing to watch out for.

When to Switch Funds

If the fund or funds you pick begin to underperform an index fund, then find out why. Have they changed managers or philosophy? If they have done neither, then ask, are they executing their philosophy poorly or is their style of investing currently just out of fashion, soon to come back into fashion? The most common way a fund drifts from its philosophy is by becoming too big. A $100 million small-cap fund becomes a $1 billion fund and cannot find enough good small-cap companies, so it buys either poor small-cap companies or large-cap companies. Or a value fund grows to $1 billion in a rising stock market, cannot find real values, and buys marginal values. On the other hand, the value fund could adhere tightly to its philosophy in a market when growth stocks are all the rage and underperform for a few years. You need to decide if the underperformance is likely to continue or just temporary. A fee-based investment planner could help you analyze the situation.

If You Switch, Switch Rarely and Watch Your Taxes

The biggest advantage of holding mutual funds in tax-deferred accounts is the ability to switch funds without paying taxes. Unfortunately, this advantage is often misused. Some investors rotate in and out of funds as often as fund managers turn over stock. This results in owning the entire market over the course of a few years, yet paying much higher expenses than an index fund. This is a certain formula for not beating an index. Switch funds less than once every five years in tax-deferred accounts to ensure you do not guarantee underperformance.

If you decide to switch in a taxable account to another fund, individual stocks, or a money manager, take a look at your tax situation first. You may need to pay some large capital gains taxes. Or if the results have been dismal, you may have some capital losses you can use. If there are large gains, phase the switch over a period of years. If you are retired by the time you switch, consider living off a larger percent of your stock money to reduce the need to sell other assets for living expenses and further increase your taxes. If there are losses, time your sale with sufficient gains from other parts of your portfolio so you can use them up right away. Over time, inflation reduces the real cost of your taxable gains, but it also reduces the real benefits of your losses. Use your losses as soon as possible.

If you want to outperform markets, it is best to look outside the U.S. stock market. You might consider REITs.

Real Estate Investing Through REITs

Individual buildings are appropriate for anyone saving for retirement. But they require time and effort. If all the questions in Chapter 7 about net operating income, vacancy rates, structuring loans, making improvement, and so on are too much for you, buy REITs. They require less time to manage than properties.

You can buy REITs either individually or in a REIT mutual funds. REITs are run by professionals who have put together a team of lawyers, property managers, accountants, real estate agents, and so on. The REIT employees will check all the tenants' credit and evict all the deadbeats while you sit home and collect dividend checks and read quarterly and annual reports. Yet REITs offer the many qualities you are looking for in a real estate investment.

You are looking for better than 10% a year total return. The REITs that have been in existence for more than twenty years have, on average, done better than 10% a year. There is ample opportunity to do even better. The more than four hundred publicly traded REITs are ignored by most Wall Street analysts. The majority are very small stocks that do not interest the big mutual funds. The possibility of finding great values is high in REIT investing.

REITs are easy to hold. They are traded on the major stock exchanges. Dividends can be sent directly to your brokerage account or to your home.

REITs are a low-profile way to own real estate. It does not feed the ego to own a REIT the way it does to own a landmark building you can show off to friends and family. And REITs are never hot stocks like biotech shares or digital, wireless Internet issues. They tend to be steady, solid, boring long-term investments. No one at the Christmas party will be interested in hearing about your REIT shares. The ego issues to be concerned with in REITs are those of the REIT managers. The section below on when to sell REITs deals with the problem of managers buying more property than the company can afford and other management problems.

One disadvantage of REITs for asset allocation purposes is that their returns are more correlated with U.S. stocks, large and small, than are individual properties. Since REITs are publicly traded stocks, their prices are influenced by the conditions of the general stock market. Whereas a portfolio of individual properties would be on a very different cycle than an S&P 500 index fund, a portfolio of REITs held either individually or in a REIT mutual fund would be on a similar cycle. The correlation is smaller than that between large and small U.S. stocks but greater than that between large U.S. stocks and individual real estate.

There is very little correlation between REITs and foreign stocks. REITs are partially correlated with bonds. Changes in U.S. interest rates have similar effects on both asset classes. REITs with substantial variable rate financing are particularly sensitive to changes in interest rates. REITs with little or no debt are less sensitive to inter-est rate changes. If you own both bonds and REITs, do not buy REITs with variable rate debt or more than 30% debt to total assets.

REIT returns appear to be more volatile than those of individ-ual properties. But this may not actually be the case. REIT prices appear in the paper every business day. Individual property prices can be estimated only by appraisal and are really known only on the sale of the property. At times I have felt it was a disadvantage to know the price of a REIT every day. If the price was lower than what I thought it should be or lower than what I paid, I used to worry that I had made a bad purchase. Today I realize a low price is an opportunity to buy more.

REITs Are Also Good Investments for the Retired

REITs are required by law to pay out 95% of their taxable income excluding capital gains. This makes them especially good assets for living off. REIT shareholders have two tax advantages.

The first tax advantage is that REITs are allowed to deduct div-idends from their taxable income. Other corporations are not. If a REIT makes $1,000,000 and distributes $950,000 to shareholders, it pays taxes only on the $50,000 of earnings it did not distribute. If another corporation makes $1,000,000, it pays taxes on the entire $1,000,000 whether or not it distributes any dividends. Assuming the corporation has a 30% effective tax rate, the maximum available for distribution to shareholders would be $700,000. So REIT share-holders receive full dividends, whereas other shareholders get only what is left after the IRS takes a cut.

The second tax advantage, I have mentioned earlier. Dividends from REITs are generally 25% to 30% tax-free. This is because some of the dividend is considered a return of the investor's capi-tal. This is rarely the case with other stock dividends.

In some cases REIT dividends can be as high as 60% tax-free. There are REITs that sell preferred shares that have fully taxable dividends. As a result, the ordinary shares receive dividends that contain a larger portion of return of capital. Also, some industries have dividends that are more tax-free than others. In recent years, factory outlets, regional malls, and manufactured homes have had dividends that were more than 40% tax-free while self-storage, office buildings, and hotels have had dividends that were 10% or less tax-free.

REITs with high taxable dividends should be purchased in a tax-deferred account, if possible. REITs with low taxable dividends can be held in either taxable or tax-deferred accounts.

Typically, many REITs pay out about 7% a year. Since many REIT dividends are only partially taxable, you get to spend more of the dividend than from other stocks. But REITs make more than 7% a year. Typically, a REIT will earn 10% and distribute only the taxable income, 7%. A REIT's true income, unadjusted for depreciation and other paper losses, is known as funds from operation, or FFO. Earnings and taxable income are not accurate measures of REIT income because REITs have huge paper losses that do not reduce their cash available to distribute to shareholders or to invest in new properties. FFO is the most accurate measure of REIT income.

In Chapter 1, I discussed the need to invest 2% to 4% a year to keep up with inflation. REITs reinvest for you. If the FFO is 10% a year and they pay out 7%, the other 3% is reinvested. This way you are not required to write a check to a new real estate investment or another asset class each year to keep your current asset allocation intact.

Picking Individual REITs

There are two approaches to finding REITs. One is to start looking company by company to find those you like. The other is to decide which markets, either regions or property types, you think are promising and look only at REITs that operate in those markets. Both approaches will lead you to the same companies. If you find a market that has done poorly for many years but you think it has turned up, the best companies would already be making money there. If you find a company with an outstanding record, you will discover that it has done well in good and bad markets. I have discussed how to research markets in Chapter 7.

The National Association of Real Estate Investment Trusts can give you a list of all REITs. Any comprehensive stock service can give you financial and other data on most of these REITs.

You are looking for REITs that will grow for many years. This means you want REITs that both pay a good current dividend and that put some of their cash flow to use maintaining that dividend and for future dividend increases. They will need cash to maintain and market their existing properties and to invest in new properties. Essentially, you want REITs that pay out no more than 80% of their funds from operation.

Some REITs pay out only the legally required 95% of income which is often as little as 55% of funds from operation. These REITs have the lowest dividends. Retaining substantial funds is good as long as they are using the retained funds in a profitable manner. Their long-term record will show the effects of this policy. If for every ten cents per share retained one year, the stock's total return has grown eleven cents per share the next year, the company is making good use of its funds. Such REITs are excellent in taxable accounts as well as tax-deferred accounts.

For people living off their assets, the problem with these low-yielding REITs is that you may need to sell shares from time to time for your living expenses.

Selling REIT shares to meet living expenses does not incur as great costs as selling individual properties to meet living expenses. There are no real estate commissions to pay and no closing costs. But do not trade REITs. The trading costs are great.

Many REITs are very small stocks that rarely trade. The spread between buy and sale prices can be quite large. In these cases it is best to anticipate how much you need to sell your shares for and then list them at that price, even if it is above the current sales price. Wait a few weeks and see if your shares do not get sold. If there are no takers, then come down to the market price. Since REITs trade fairly steadily, you are unlikely to lose much by waiting a few weeks for your price. Use a discount broker to reduce your selling commissions.

Use the same tactic to buy your REITs. Put in a buy order with a discount broker below the current price and wait a few weeks. If your order does not get placed, then buy at the market price if the price is still within the range you deem reasonable.

Leverage Less Than 50%

Overall, your REIT portfolio should have no more than 50% leverage. While it may be prudent to buy some REITs with higher leverage, you want to balance these with REITs with less leverage. For REITs with simple financial structures, the mortgages as a percentage of the historical cost of the properties should not exceed 50%. For complex financial structures, you need to look at other factors.

Many REITs have taken on debt financing besides mortgages. Some have floated bonds or have issued preferred stock. With these REITs, total debt and preferred stock should not exceed equity.

When you see a complicated financial structure, it is a bad sign. It indicates the REIT is scrambling around to finance its deals. A number of REITs recently got in trouble with a form of financing known as "equity forwards." These forwards actually propelled these equities backwards and cost investors as much as half of their investment.

Also, adjustable rate mortgages or other adjustable rate debt is to be avoided. Often rates are highest just when markets are overbuilt, exaggerating future losses. If you can keep your interest expenses steady, you have a better chance of getting through bad markets. Note though, many REITs use lines of credit to buy property and then secure permanent financing later. Lines of credit will appear to be adjustable rate financing until permanent financing replaces it.

One REIT Is Diversification

Owning one REIT already provides diversification. Most REITs own more than one hundred properties. You do not need ten REITs in ten markets. That would give you a small-cap stock correlation. You are buying real estate, not stocks. A single REIT holding is marginally correlated to small-cap stocks and reasonably correlated to one real estate market.

Three to five REITs is the maximum you should buy. One is too few, as management could change or a market could suffer long-term underperformance.

Diversify both by property type and by region. Shopping mall REITs are not all alike. A Southern mall will often do very differently than a Midwest mall. Malls are on different cycles than apartments, which are on different cycles than office buildings. Hospitals have gone from up to down to up, completely independently of other property types. Suburban office markets are different than urban office markets. In 1995 many suburban office markets had lower vacancy rates than urban office markets. In 1999 the opposite was true in many areas.

Do not overpay for existing assets. Buy REITs selling at or below 110% of their currently appraised asset values. This is often known as net asset value (NAV). At times the biggest REITs get hot and sell for much more than 110% of NAV. Be patient. The prices will either decline toward NAV or the NAV will rise. In 1998, prices declined sharply while NAVs rose, creating a good opportunity for those who waited.

Many REIT annual reports contain current property appraisals and NAV figures. Stock analysis services also will provide you with NAVs. No management is worth paying more than 110% of NAV. In Chapter 7, I discussed how to evaluate management. If your evaluation indicates the current management has exceptional abilities, it may be worth paying up to 110% for their services.

Other times, you will find REITs selling considerably below their asset values. Those that I have found have all been small REITs not followed by any Wall Street analysts. They are rarely traded on the exchanges. Some have been in a liquidation stage but have been excellent values even though they had only a few years of existence left. Others appeared to deserve low values as they were converted RELPs that were run down and showed few prospects of returning to prosperity.

Stay with REITs that have been public at least five years and preferably ten years. Often new REITs, even of long-established property groups, are vehicles for current owners to liquidate their holdings and get out of the business. These are generally the most valuable employees. It is also difficult for old managers to learn the skills of running a public business for the first time. The distractions can result in poor financing decisions and excessive property purchases. You need a track record of public ownership to judge the management, the property type, and the region.

FFO Growth Better Than 10% a Year

You are looking to make better than 10% a year from your REIT. If you found a REIT paying a 12% dividend that was maintaining its properties, paying its expenses, and putting away significant funds for future contingencies like rent reductions and tenant departures, you should buy it. But there are few such REITs. In most cases you will be getting your return partially from dividends and partially from capital appreciation. You need REITs with a solid record of growing their funds from operation and with good future prospects.

First examine the growth of the funds from operation per share for the past five to ten years. Though they may not have grown in a straight line, have they, on average, grown by 10% or more a year? Ten percent per year growth in funds from operation is strong growth. Since a REIT is required by law to pay out 95% of its earnings each year, it must grow funds from operation with only a minimum of reinvestment. A REIT that can grow funds from operation 10% a year and pay out a dividend of 7% a year can potentially return 17% a year.

After examining FFO growth, divide the price per share by the current funds from operation per share. Calculate this same ratio, Price/FFO, for prior years. Determine if the stock is selling at or below an average Price/FFO for that stock for the past five to ten years.

Next determine if the stock had a total return of 10% a year or more for the past five to ten years. If FFO has averaged 10% a year or better, the stock is selling at a Price/FFO at or below its average, and the stock has returned 10% a year or more, it is a good candidate for purchase. All you need now is reason to believe that this growth can continue.

Read the company reports indicating how they intend to grow in the future. Are they pursuing the same strategy that worked in the past or are they entering new markets or property types? The same strategy that worked in the past is likely to continue to work, and the management is likely to be expert in this strategy and not another. Developers should continue to develop, acquirers should continue to acquire, buy and hold managers should continue to buy and hold.

Also look at the competition. Has competition ruined the existing strategy? For many years a few factory outlet REITs were growing rapidly, following the same strategy property after property: dirt cheap land a half hour from a major city along a busy freeway, cheap tilt-up concrete construction, many major brand name tenants in true outlet stores. Now there are many factory outlet REITs and other factory outlet developers. Some are building closer and closer to urban centers and mixing discount retailers with factory outlet stores. Competition is tough. The land is more expensive. It is not likely that these REITs can continue to grow as they have in the past.

Visit as many properties as you can. Some REITs own hundreds of buildings. Nevertheless, you are about to become the owner of these properties. You need to see how well they are maintained and what might happen to them in the future. A random sample of a few properties will give you some insights. Talk to tenants to see what is going on with the buildings. Drive the neighborhood and see the competition. Are any new buildings going up? Study the local economy. What are the prospects for this type of property in this economy?

What you will learn from a few random visits will be invaluable. I was looking at an apartment REIT. In the first place, it had not been around very long, but apartments were in great demand. When I found their newest, biggest apartment building, I was impressed. It was right off a new freeway exit in a commuter city. There were vacancies, but they had been renting only a few months. Then I noticed another new apartment house across the street. Driving through the neighborhood, I found more than ten other apartment houses under construction and FOR RENT signs on all the completed projects. Apparently, all the developers got the same tip about the new freeway exit at the same time. I was hoping to find a nice apartment in a high barriers-to-entry neighborhood. This was the opposite. Anyone could build here and had. The overbuilding would lead to high vacancies and low rents. It made me question management's judgment and wonder about the developments I had not seen.

After you have checked out a few properties, check out the management.

Buy REITs with Good Management

Here are some guidelines for finding competent REIT management.

Look for a REIT manager with many years' experience running a publicly traded REIT of this type. There is a big difference between running a publicly traded REIT and running privately owned real estate. Financing is different in a public company. Publicly traded REIT managers need to enhance shareholder value, not just enhance property values.

Be sure the management has specialized in the property type that the REIT owns. Apartment management is much different than office warehouse management, which is much different than hospital management. The annual report, 10-k, and other legal documents available from the REIT will give background information of the management. Check the 10-k to see if there is any potential conflict of interest as well. If a manager of a property also is an owner of a tenant, this will be disclosed. Call the REIT and ask any questions that occur to you. Why did so and so leave his last job? What kind of property was he managing there?

The most important thing to look at is the manager's track record running this REIT. You may never get to ask the manager one on one what happened back in 1988 or 1990, but you can look it up. You are looking for consistent performance from the properties despite what might have happened to the stock price. The measure of consistent performance is funds from operation per share that are gradually moving up year after year. If they are highly erratic, this is a bad sign. Buildings may be deteriorating; new purchases may not be working out; financing problems may have arisen. The record of funds from operations will tell you more about a manager's competence than anything you could learn over lunch. But it is also important to visit the buildings if you are making a significant investment in this manager. Maybe the funds from operation have been good because the manager has not kept up the buildings. Just looking at the condition of the parking lot can tell you a lot. Tenants who have been there a while can also tell you the history of the space. You are interested in the manager's results, not his rap.

One of the difficulties of measuring REIT management is determining what it costs. Compare costs only for similar types of REITs. For example, REITs that buy land and build and lease their own properties have much higher expenses than those that buy only fully leased, built properties. REITs that own shopping centers have higher expenses than REITs that own apartment buildings. The real question is not how high the expenses are but what the results have been. If the expenses seem in line with those of similar companies, then compare just the results. If the expenses seem high and the results are not outstanding, this is a sign that management is draining the property of its cash. This can be covered up for many years with new financing, but eventually this REIT will get into trouble.

Once you find a REIT with good management, good future prospects, selling at or below its average Price/FFO, with a strong past FFO record, buy it. Buy your three to five REITs one at a time as soon as you find them. If you find five immediately, buy them. You have probably hit a low in the market. And if you haven't, over the next thirty years you own these REITs, it will not matter. Interest rates will fluctuate during these years, and the stock market will ebb and flow. Real estate markets will improve and decline. Some of your REITs will be good buys, and some will not be so good. But, on average, you will look back and be impressed at how cheaply you bought these REITs.

When to Sell a REIT

Sell your REIT when it ceases being the company you bought or the reasons you bought it change. If there is a significant change in management and you have no confidence in the new people, sell. When the company dramatically changes strategies, sell. An apartment REIT that buys a huge portfolio of office buildings has changed strategies. There is a big difference between gradually entering new markets and jumping in with huge acquisitions.

If the company makes one major mistake, consider selling. Minor mistakes are to be expected. An extensive remodeling of a major property that does not result in higher rent and higher occupancy is usually a minor mistake. Often management has learned a valuable lesson from the mistake and will do a better job in the future. If you sell, there may be a large tax bill to pay. If there is a pattern of minor mistakes and no evidence of learning, sell. Several more expensive remodels losing tenants and not improving rents are signals to move on. Get out, pay the taxes, and find another REIT. Sell if you bought because the market was underbuilt and now, years later, it is headed for being overbuilt.

If you bought your REIT primarily because it was selling at low valuations and now it is not, consider selling. If you bought it for 60% of appraised asset value and a Price/FFO ratio of 6 and now it sells for 110% of appraised asset value and 11, look at its future prospects. If you sell, there will be tax consequences. If the prospects are decent, hold on. If management has just left and sold its position on the way out, get out too. If a company makes a major acquisition and has no track record for absorbing major acquisitions, get out.

Companies often issue new shares and raise capital with debt financing. This is fine if the money is put to good use. But watch the trend. When the debt significantly exceeds the equity, you will be beyond your 50% leverage rule and will want to get out.

It is normal for a REIT to sell new shares to raise capital so it can buy new properties. Typically, the share price drops just before or after the offering. These equity offerings are not a problem if they are small and the company has a track record of doing well with the proceeds of prior equity offerings. If the money is put to good use, the share price will come back and the dividend will increase. But if the company sells shares worth more than 33% of existing market capital in one year, get out. This is too much dilution, and it is unlikely that they will be able productively to use the new funds. You can also pay a mutual fund manager to do the buying and selling of REITs for you.

REIT Mutual Funds: Simple at a Cost

If this REIT discussion has you thinking about living off the land in a tent, yet you still want to own real estate, here is the simplest solution. Buy a no-load REIT mutual fund. Let the fund manager pick the REITs and let the REIT managers pick the properties. At this writing there are about forty mutual funds that specialize in real estate stocks.

REIT mutual fund returns are correlated to the returns on small-cap U.S. stocks. Almost all REITs are small-cap stocks. Individual properties provide the least correlation to U.S. stock returns. The returns on three to five individual REITs are somewhat correlated to the returns on small-cap stocks. The return on a REIT mutual fund that owns thirty or more REITs is even more correlated to the return on small-cap stocks.

Follow these steps to buy a REIT mutual fund.

- Buy only no-load funds. Paying a load as high as 5.75% would be a big mistake here.
- Eliminate the funds that contain more than 20% non–U.S. REITs. Some funds own foreign real estate companies, and some own building supply companies, and real estate finance companies, and other real estate–related stocks. While these may or may not be good funds or good companies, they do not fit your asset allocation needs. You are looking for a way to own properties.
- Buy funds that have a track record. Of the few funds that have been around more than ten years, most were not REIT funds in their early years. They were general real estate funds. Look only at funds that have been 80% or more in REITs for the last five years. This is a short list. To this short list, add the REIT index fund that began in the summer of 1996 and any other REIT index funds.
- Examine the expense ratio of the remaining funds. You need 10% or better from your real estate. Owning and managing individual properties yourself is the lowest available expense ratio, zero. But this requires considerable time. REITs themselves are generally run efficiently, but not for free. REIT

management is highly paid. Expense to asset ratios run from 3% to as high as 10%. There are economies of scale but also layers of management and employees. Hiring a mutual fund manager adds another layer of expenses. All else being equal, a low mutual fund expense ratio is the deciding factor in picking a REIT mutual fund. In this regard, the REIT index funds have a big advantage. All except for the index funds have expenses of at least 1% a year, and some have expenses above 1.5% a year. The index funds should average expenses of less than 0.3% a year.

- Determine which mutual fund managers added value for the fees they were paid. Compare the records of all the funds year by year and over the entire five-year period. Compare the funds to each other and to the various REIT indexes. If one or two funds have outperformed the others and the indexes, then the managers have added value.

- Learn something about the fund manager's history investing in real estate and REITs. There is an opportunity for a good mutual fund manager to stand out here. The REIT market contains many small stocks that few investors take the time to analyze. As many of these funds are new, the managers sometimes have no track record in this field. They have been assigned by a big mutual fund company to start a new REIT fund. Often they ran another fund that owned a few REITs and management decided, for marketing purposes, to break off into essentially two funds, one all REITs and the other small-cap stocks. While these new managers may prove good at REIT investing, it is better to let them perform awhile before putting your money in their hands.

- Study the fund's management style. Decide if you are comfortable with this style. Some funds believe that REIT management is most important. They will buy REITs with good track records even though they are not currently in the best markets. Other fund managers pick real estate markets and then find REITs operating in those markets. Funds also look primarily at the price of the REIT compared to its NAV and buy the cheapest, regardless of markets or managers. Some funds are not interested in high-yielding REITs. They prefer REITs that pay out as small a portion of FFO as possible and concentrate on growing their assets. Other funds have the opposite approach. There are many new REITs coming to market. Some managers believe they can find bargains here and buy new issues. Others wait for the new issues to prove themselves as public companies. While the latter is definitely my approach, if a mutual fund manager has a good record with new issues, then that is to be in his or her favor.

- Taxes must be considered if you are holding the fund in a taxable account. Some funds turn over more than half their holdings every year, and others are more patient. Turnover will create capital gains that you have to pay taxes on. Dividends are also taxable. REIT dividends are about 25% tax-free. But substantial turnover in a mutual fund can erode this tax advantage. The index funds have almost no turnover.
- Avoid excessive turnover. Excessive turnover is, again, a way to create an index fund with high expenses. If the fund is highly diversified and has turnover above 50% a year, it is definitely a high-expense index fund.
- Look at the number of issues the fund owns. I have suggested that if you buy individual REITs, you buy only three to five. Most funds own at least thirty. Some funds own more than seventy REITs. The more issues the fund owns, the more its returns will be correlated to stock market cycles and the less its returns will be correlated to real estate cycles. You want a fund that owns a small number of companies. A good REIT picker can outperform the REIT index. But not if he loads up on too many companies. Some funds own more stocks than the index. While they may have steady returns over time, they can be expected to underperform the index because they have greater expenses. An index fund would be more desirable.
- Based on these criteria, put your money in either one or two funds. Do not buy more. Then you will guarantee yourself an expensive index fund.

- Sell a fund when managers change and you have no confidence in the new managers. Sell when the prior record appears to be a fluke as the fund is now regularly underperforming the REIT indexes. Real estate cycles can last ten years. One year of underperformance is not a big deal. Wait at least two years to see if things improve. Sell for sure after three bad years.

If paying fund managers and REIT managers to do what you find simple, buying real estate, makes no sense to you, consider individual properties. This time, though, consider using the bank's money as well as your own to get you to retirement soon.

Leveraged Real Estate

A common strategy to speed your way to retirement is to buy leveraged real estate. In Chapter 7, I made it clear that during retirement you do not want to own property with more than 50% leverage. But during your working years, you can afford up to 80% leverage.

The potential advantage of an 80% mortgaged property is enormous. Assuming the cash flow is at least slightly positive, you can make 10% a year on a 2% increase in property values. Assume you put $200,000 down on a $1,000,000 property. If the property increases in value by 2%, that is $20,000. A $20,000 return on $200,000 is 10%. If the property value moves up more than 2% a year, you will move toward retirement quickly. The risks are that the property will not appreciate and the cash flow will not cover the mortgage.

If a tenant moves out and cannot be replaced for a few months, you must still pay the mortgage on the building. If you are retired, the mortgage payment comes from your savings. If it goes on a long time, your retirement could be in jeopardy. If you are working, the mortgage payment can come out of your salary. Instead of saving for retirement those months, you pay another mortgage. That is not a big deal.

Do not buy property with a negative cash flow. If an 80% mortgage guarantees a negative cash flow, either put more cash into the investment or look elsewhere. It is tempting to say that all I need is for the property to appreciate 2% a year to make 10%. Very often when the property will not show a positive cash flow with 20% down, the property and the market are overpriced and you should look elsewhere. Not only will you not get your 2% appreciation, you will likely take a substantial loss. Your 20% down payment is in jeopardy.

If you buy a property with 20% down and hold it until retirement, do you need to sell it to live off? Not necessarily. If you have owned it long enough and the market has been favorable, rents have increased and the positive cash flow is substantial. You may be able to spend plenty of income from the property. It is also possible to avoid selling the property and convert it to a retirement asset by paying down the mortgage. This would increase the cash flow and save the capital gains taxes and real estate commissions you would incur from selling the property.

Unfortunately, not all investments work out. Property markets can crash just like stock markets. A well-diversified portfolio can be thrown off course by global events like the Great Depression, an oil embargo, or the collapse of the East Asian financial system. How do you get to retirement when everything you invest in goes down?

Living Through a

Crash Without

Putting a Bullet Through

Your Head

All markets decline. Sometimes they all decline together.

In the second half of 1987, interest rates in the U.S. rose and the bond market declined. The world's most sophisticated stock investors panicked, sending stock markets everywhere down 30% and more. Meanwhile, real estate markets throughout the United States were plummeting because of overbuilding, new tax legislation, and rising interest rates. Oil and gas prices dropped because of oversupply. There was no place to hide. For investors living off their assets, the decline looked even worse.

Joe, who you thought I retired in Chapter 3, is back as an example. He had $600,000, one half in emerging market stocks, one fourth in small-cap U.S. stocks, and one fourth in real estate. He spends 10% a year. If his investments simply broke even one year, he would lose 10%. But he is in highly volatile emerging market stocks and small-cap stocks. If both declined 20%, his real estate declined 10%, and he spent 10%, he would have a loss of more than 27%. It is very easy for the panicked mind to multiply 27% times 4 and conclude he will be out of money in less than four years.

Fred and Ginger, great savers that they are, would also be likely to despair if all their markets declined at once. They have a chance to retire in five years on the growth of their $425,000 and savings of

$24,000 a year. With 30% in treasuries, 30% in emerging markets, 20% in small-cap U.S. stocks, and 20% in real estate, it is almost impossible that all their investments would decline together. But a severe inflation could knock their treasuries, emerging markets, and small-cap stocks 30% in one year while their real estate, because of bad location, broke even. This would cost them $100,000 and could lead them to believe that the future was just as bleak. In depression they might believe they never will retire and will lose the security of the savings they have built up all these years. Having been through the inflationary 1970s, they don't see going into cash as any help. They feel trapped.

If a retiree spent 8% a year and his assets suffered a decline of 12%, the total loss would be 20%. It is very easy for the panicked mind to multiply 20% times 5 and conclude that in five years he will be completely broke. This was very close to my actual situation in the second half of 1987. The U.S. stock market declined from 2700 in August to 1700 in October. My stocks did somewhat less poorly. My real estate and bonds declined but nowhere near as badly as the U.S. stock market. It was enough to send me into a panic. I remember a BMW license plate declaring that the owner got "OUT2700." (Today investors wish they got in at 2700.) I could not sell everything and put it into a money market fund because I would not make enough to live. I also knew I was no Peter Lynch or Warren Buffett and that I would likely suffer more losses of this magnitude before I died. And as it turned out, the second half of 1987 was nothing compared to 1994 for me as a time for financial loss. But in 1994 I knew, despite all the pain, what to do. In 1987 I did not have a clue.

The trick is to learn how to do nothing meaningful to your investment portfolio while the markets recover. Some markets recover quickly. Others take decades. If you are in three to five non-correlated asset classes, you will do fine financially as long as you can emotionally and spiritually ride out the storm. If you panic and put it all in money market funds, you will set yourself back. If you panic and kill yourself, you will damage everyone you ever met and miss a great opportunity to grow up. Here is how I grew up financially from the age of twenty-nine to today.

How I Survived My Worst Years

From the beginning of 1981 until August 1982 the assets I was living off declined more than 20%, and my wife and I spent about 8%. New to the world of investing, I saw this as an opportunity to fire the trust department that was managing our assets and take decisive steps to prevent anything like this from happening ever again. I had not yet invented the concept of target investment return nor did I know why the trust department had done such a poor job. Fortunately, it did not occur to me that after three more years of losses like this I would be out of money. Professionally, I still thought of myself as a lawyer. If asked what I did for a living, I always said "lawyer." But secretly, I felt that this was my chance to get out of law and into a much more exciting field, investing. I did not yet rely on my assets as part of my identity. I saw the losses of 1981–1982 as paper losses that I would soon remedy. I took everything out of the trust, began managing some of the assets myself, and turned other assets over to a money management firm.

I spent most of August 1987 in Hawaii. I had been on a roll financially since August 1982. There were days in early 1987 when every stock I owned was on the list of new highs. Financially, I thought of myself as some kind of genius. The strategies I had been using were working, and I had hired brilliant people to work for me as well. I had been making more money than many professional athletes were making in publicized salary disputes. My biggest concern was spending enough to show the world how well I was doing.

I spent the first weeks of October 1987 driving around Lake Tahoe with realtors, looking for the appropriate monument to my success. I mentally noted that the market was down from 2700 to 2200 on the Friday before the crash. My fear level was rising, but my ego told me that the market would soon recover and be making new highs again. The Monday of the crash I stared at FNN terrified. Once I tried to call my broker but could not get through. I checked all the earnings news on my computer and found my companies that reported that day had fabulous results and their stock prices were down over 30%. A friend with money in the market called from an airport to ask me what was going on. He had been in Europe and had just heard. I had no response. I did not know where the market was going from 1700. I had no perspective.

Tuesday I woke about 3:30 a.m. and checked on the Tokyo market. Again I stayed in front of FNN all day. Midday I was sure the Great Depression had started. I would have nothing left within a few months. A year or two at most. After the close, I went to buy a new shower curtain. Whereas two days before I would have bought the best they had on the credit card, instead I bought the cheapest, ugliest for cash. Then I went home and opened a bottle of fine wine. Fortunately, I had a large wine cellar.

I dropped into a severe depression. I was certain that I had made a big mistake leaving law and becoming an investor. I could not imagine ever admitting to anyone how much money I had lost. All the years of gains were suddenly a distant memory. To everyone around me I lied, told them that I was fine, that the crash had not been such a big deal. My pride had been ripped open by the crash. I knew now I was not a genius and that I was not superior to other people and that I might have to live on an average income again. Only my three-and-a-half-year-old son really knew. One morning he handed me a toy Medal of Honor telling me he thought I needed it.

After six months or so, I began seriously changing my asset allocation, believing that would prevent anything like this from ever happening again. With gains from the last two months of 1987, I paid off my mortgage so I would not lose my house if the crash continued as in 1930.

I Had to Change Myself

It never once occurred to me that market conditions would always be the same, ups and downs, bull runs and bear crashes, and that if I was going to be happy in the lifestyle I was leading I had to change myself, not the market or my asset allocation.

Several years later, I realized 1987 as a whole had been a down year only because of my excess spending. I was spending to compensate for a busted ego. The pain of financial losses for me was much greater than the joys of all my previous gains. I had to take a look at why these pains were so great.

My financial losses in 1990 were about half those of the second half of 1987. I had changed my asset allocation, but, unfortunately, a small business I had invested in was on the brink of bankruptcy by the end of that year. Although the losses were less than in 1987, my reaction was much worse. Looking back, I realize I never dealt with my feelings about 1987. Instead, I tried to stuff those feelings with fine wine, huge meals, and verbal denial that I had such feelings. My pride had recovered only to be shot down.

In 1990 my despair over again losing a huge sum of money was uncontainable. By the end of October 1990, the thought of suicide was with me occasionally. I never reached the point of making a suicide plan or an attempt. But the thoughts scared me. Intellectually, I knew that I could put everything in treasury bonds, cut down on expenses a bit, and have enough to live on the rest of my life. Emotionally, I would not dream of giving up like that. I had to stick to my guns.

It never occurred to me that my problem was not financial. It never occurred to me that my belief system was leading me toward death and not toward a more meaningful life. It was clear from everything I read and everyone I talked to that the market would come back. But I was not sure I would be alive to see it happen.

On matters of my thoughts and feelings, whether of despair or joy, I had always gone it alone. I read several books that stated flatly that one cannot get out of depression of this type without help. For the first time in my life I made a decision to ask for help from strangers on a nonfinancial issue. I have not had a single drink since, and I have learned to keep my financial life in perspective.

In 1994 my asset allocation resulted in a positive return on my investments but it was less than my family's living expenses. More important, I got divorced. There is an old adage: the best financial advice of all time is, do not get divorced. The divorce has cost me more than four-fifths of my assets. Yet in 1994 I knew exactly what to do and what not to do about my financial situation.

I did not change my asset allocation. I did not deal with my money problems at all because I came to realize that I did not have money problems. I had enough money to pay my bills and my children's bills for the moment. In 1994 I worked on my attitude. The first thing every Monday morning I volunteered in my son's second grade classroom. Every day I did my spiritual practices, sought and got support from others, and exercised. At least every other day I did volunteer work for an hour or more, sometimes for entire days. Once a week I went to therapy. I enrolled my children in therapy and divorce support groups. I worked on my friendships, and I learned to spend time alone but connected to society and nature. As the year went on, my attitude got better and better.

From 1987 to 1990 my attitude went from depressed to suicidal. In 1995 and early 1996 my investments came on strongly and out-performed all the relevant benchmarks. I had recovered long before.

Take Loss Prevention Measures Now

Intentionally taking financial losses to promote your emotional and spiritual growth is not a good idea. The first chapters of this book set out a strategy for producing steady returns. The most important tactic is to establish an asset allocation of three to five noncorrelated asset classes. If I had known about this strategy and implemented it in 1980, my losses in 1981 to 1982, 1987, and 1990 would have been much smaller. If possible, pay off your mortgage. This will eliminate a monthly expense and remove substantial assets from the market.

Within each chapter there are suggestions on reducing taxes, management fees, commissions, and other preventable losses. The real estate chapter suggests using 50% or less leverage to prevent disasters. For foreign and emerging market stocks, it is suggested that you own at least fifty stocks to prevent losses. As soon as possible read, study, and follow as many as you can of these and the other loss prevention strategies.

The Market May Not Recover This Decade

Do not try to time the market. If you have just suffered a big loss, do not wait for recovery to follow these suggestions. Recovery may not follow. Markets can take a long time to come back. In 1973 the Dow Jones Industrial Average hit 1052. It did not get higher than that level again until 1982. After 1929, the stock market did not recover for fifteen years. The prices of office buildings in most major U.S. cities were higher in 1986 than they were in 1996. If you are on a roll with your one or two asset classes, do not wait for that roll to end before you change your asset allocation. Overpriced asset classes have a tendency to correct quickly and dramatically. In 1989 the Japanese market hit 39,000 and everyone thought that the next move was to 50,000 on the way to 100,000. A year later, the market was down 40%. Two years later it was down 60%. In 1999 it was less than 14,000. Gold was over $800 an ounce in 1981. Eighteen years later it was less than $300 an ounce.

Checklist of Actions to Take When Losses Do Occur

Once you have set up your asset allocation and followed the other suggestions in this book, there are no other financial actions to take. Do not try to make back losses quickly by putting everything in emerging market stocks or buying highly leveraged real estate. The trick is to meaningfully do nothing to your investments while you wait for some markets to recover. Meaningfully doing nothing requires other actions that are psychological, spiritual, and physical.

Study Market History

Try to understand the underlying forces at work. It is psychologically helpful to know that markets come back. Read about worse markets than the one that has you down and look for reasons the current situation could be better. The crash of 1929 lasted for three years, and the market lost 90% of its value. The economy crashed with the market. Stocks and real estate both went down because there was no demand in the economy and excess supply. Yet treasury bonds did well. The right asset allocation would have done fine in 1929.

In 1987 the economy was practically unaffected by the crash. Government programs put in place in the 1930s ensured that the demand side of the economy would not collapse in 1987. The growth of pension funds and insurance companies ensured that the demand for stocks would not evaporate in 1987. Stocks represent the ownership of businesses. Business was good in 1987. It was very likely that stock prices would come back. It is helpful to know that if you had bought at the peak in 1987, at the worst possible time, but held on, in less than ten years you would have doubled your asset values and received dividends every year.

Acknowledge the Service You Provide

When losses pile up, you may start thinking investing is just gambling. It is not real work like carpentry or plumbing. Investors take from society without providing any kind of a service. This is the time when it is important to study economics.

One of the first things they did in Poland, Hungary, and Czechoslovakia when they got free from the Soviet Union was to set up stock exchanges. They did not get to work building factories. They already had them and they were not improving the quality of people's lives. What those countries lacked was people like you, investors. They knew instinctively that freely mobile capital would seek out and find the best growth opportunities and lead to more and better-quality jobs and products.

Investors allow companies to start and to grow. Investors vote with their dollars for the businesses they believe will grow. This may sound highly undemocratic. But if the businesses go under, investors, not the general public, lose their dollars. Refusing to buy government bonds when inflation is rising is also a vote, a vote against inflation, by those highly affected by it, people living off their assets.

If you do not think you are providing a valuable service by being an investor, make a list of all the people, businesses, and governments that have prospered from your money and taxes. List people who have found living space and working space in your buildings. Be sure to include all employees of those businesses and governments. List all the individuals you have loaned money to over the years to help them go to school, buy cars, get job training, or just pay living expenses. No bank would give them a dime. Remember that you had a choice to stuff cash under a mattress or to take a chance on a stock, a building, or a loan.

Though the general public and your own conscience may think you are a gambler or running some kind of pyramid scheme, the service you provide is invaluable to society. Thousands have died so that a market system could exist. No market system would work without investors.

Acknowledge the Role Money Plays in Your Life

Acknowledge the role money plays in your life and the role it does not play in your life. The greatest benefit of taking severe losses is that it has required me to examine my value system. When I was sure in 1994 that I would be losing at least three fourths of my assets, I made a list of what was important to me in life. Everyone's list will be different. Here was my list taken from my journal in 1994.

1. Do not take a drink.
2. Actively love someone each day.
3. Work, produce something. Grow investments like a farmer grows corn and harvest them.
4. Socialize with people.
5. Exercise.
6. Laugh.
7. Breathe.
8. Eat healthy, good-tasting food.
9. Be with plants, birds, animals, the sea, trees.
10. Pray.
11. Feel my feelings and emotions.
12. Learn to improve my relationships with other human beings. Set boundaries with love.

When I found this list in my journal as I was drafting this chapter, it surprised me to realize that having a bigger house, a fancier car, or nicer clothes did not appear on the list. I do want those things at some level, but they did not come up when I made my list of my values. The point for me was that losing most of my money had not changed who I was or what I believed in. It had created fear but had not led me back to thoughts of suicide. My fears were that I would be alone and would not be able to work. To realize my values I did not set out to make money but to actively love people through volunteer work and to start a service-oriented business.

Tell Someone How Much You Lost

Tell someone you can trust with your confidence how much money you lost and how you lost it. If you find it hard to tell anyone, start by writing out what you would say if you could. Then spend time figuring out who to tell or who could listen to you read this statement. A therapist, a clergyperson, or a lawyer will keep what you say confidential. The point is, tell someone as soon as possible. Be sure to disclose any risky, shady, or dishonest deals. In 1987 and 1990 I never told anyone. Keeping these deadly secrets led me to thoughts of suicide. It did not matter that from 1980 through 1994 I had made huge net profits. I also kept that a secret. It was the losses that were so painful to keep inside. In 1994 I sat down with a close friend and advisor and went over every aspect of my financial life in detail. Though I had fear going into the meeting, my sense of isolation was broken when I left. It was a tremendous relief.

Find a Support Group

Find a support group where you can talk openly about your financial situation and clarify your values. There is a group called Vanguard Public Foundation run by and for people who have inherited money. It is not connected to the Vanguard Mutual fund group. There are several women's money groups. I have used paid therapy groups and free twelve-step groups. Others have used church groups. I have also started my own free group. Telling my truth and hearing others' truth in a group setting has been very healing for me.

Take Care of Yourself Physically

Take care of yourself physically. Emotional stress can have physical consequences. Heart attacks, cancer, digestive problems, skin problems, and many other physical diseases have been linked to stress. Get a checkup. Exercise every day. Improve your diet. Eliminate poisons like alcohol, drugs, and cigarettes. In 1994 the stress was so great that I had ringing in my ears. I did the right thing. I got a physical and saw an ear specialist, and neither could find anything wrong with me. When the stress let up, the ringing went away.

Laugh

Increase the laughter in your life. Rent funny movies, watch funny TV shows, go to comedy clubs, go to funny movies, call up your funny friends, read funny books. Laughter is always available.

Sex Anyone?

Increase the sex in your life. Do not go to prostitutes or do anything else that will leave you with remorse or an emotional hangover. But if you have a mature sex partner, regular sex can do wonders for your outlook on life.

Volunteer

Volunteer your time to a good cause. Do not give money. There is no point in making your financial situation worse. The benefits of spending time with people in need or working on causes that improve the world are immense. Helping sick people get well, watching children learn, and seeing the environment improve will do wonders for you. Your attitude about yourself and those around you will improve. Hope will pervade your life. Many of the sick will not get well, many of the children will refuse to learn, much of the environment will stay dirty, but by being part of the solution *you* will get emotionally and spiritually healthier.

Healthy Friendships

Renew healthy friendships, pursue new healthy friendships, and let go of unhealthy friends. A walk in a park with an old friend who gives you no advice, who likes you whether you are poor or rich, who can listen to your concerns and trust you with his, is an experience not to be missed. The excitement of finding a new friend at an old age will overcome depression. But avoid those people who tell you how wrong you are and how wrong you will be. If they are family members, do the right thing. Send Christmas presents and birthday cards, but do not spend time with them. Take actions to relieve your guilt, but do not put yourself in a position to be abused by them.

Spiritual Activities

Pursue spiritual activities. Churches, prayer groups, meditation groups, twelve-step groups, retreats, treks, there are endless choices. This will lead you to understand the meaning of your losses, to know that they are not in vain. I have come to believe that one reason I had the losses I had and the life I have had is so I can help others who are going through similar things. I tell others that they are not alone, that I survived it and grew from it, and that they too will survive and grow. It is not necessary to kill yourself.

Get Out of Town

Travel for short periods. I do not recommend leaving town indefinitely. That avoids working on your attitude. But a week at the beach, two weeks in the mountains, a month in Thailand will give you some relief and perspective. You do not have to tough it out. Staying home and working late hours on your investments will not cause the stock market to go up, it will not make the real estate market less overbuilt, and it will not improve your attitude. But a nice vacation can improve your attitude and give you some fresh energy.

Honestly Appraise Your Efforts

Did you put in enough hours investing before the crash? Were you ready for it? Were you honest with yourself and your financial advisors about your financial situation? Did you take on too much risk? Did you investigate thoroughly before you bought, sold, or held? Are you blaming others for your own negligence? Have you been spending beyond your means, using credit, leverage, mortgages to hype your returns and your lifestyle? Have you failed to declare income or declared phantom expenses? Ask these and similar questions. Write out the questions and the answers. Then go around making apologies where necessary. Pay back any money you have borrowed. Clean up your taxes. Start fresh. No debt. No tax liability. No outstanding dishonesty. Life will take on new meaning. You will never need to cross the street to avoid anyone again. You will be lighter and free.

Cry

When you are ready, either alone or with a professional therapist or spiritual advisor, let yourself feel your losses as deeply and as often as you can. Cry, get angry, have a fit, mope, yell, scream, write a letter (and do not send it) telling everybody off, really get into all the feelings. Try not to act in any disrespectful or hurtful way to anyone or any property. But if you do, when you are ready, go back and apologize for that. I beat chairs in my therapist's office and cried on her floor. Unfortunately, I also yelled and screamed at my ex-wife. But I was able to tell her that I was wrong to have done so, and I apologized. Within a few months, I was ready to go on to . . .

Consider a Job

When you are ready, if your losses are permanent, if on working through the formula in Chapter 1 there is no doubt that you do not have enough to live on, start the process of finding a job and cutting down on your expenses. Go slow. When you are still grieving the loss of most of your assets, you are not going to be a good employee, and you are not going to have the energy necessary to start your own business. Use the assets you have left to live on for a while and to get professional help or to further your education. Use a career counselor or any other help you can find. You do not have to do this alone. There is help out there. There are groups for housewives going back to work, groups for anybody changing careers, there are school and job training. Build support for yourself in this process. I started my own career transition group. Tell friends about what you are doing. They will support you, and they may have leads for you as well. It's a tough process.

Contact Me

If I can be of any help, contact me at at my Web site TheRetiredInvestor.com.

index